Ibrahim Ali

USTAD AMIR KHAN

Life and Contribution to Indian Classical Music

LAP LAMBERT Academic Publishing

Impressum/Imprint (nur für Deutschland/ only for Germany)
Bibliografische Information der Deutschen Nationalbibliothek: Die Deutsche Nationalbibliothek verzeichnet diese Publikation in der Deutschen Nationalbibliografie; detaillierte bibliografische Daten sind im Internet über http://dnb.d-nb.de abrufbar.
 Alle in diesem Buch genannten Marken und Produktnamen unterliegen warenzeichen-, marken- oder patentrechtlichem Schutz bzw. sind Warenzeichen oder eingetragene Warenzeichen der jeweiligen Inhaber. Die Wiedergabe von Marken, Produktnamen, Gebrauchsnamen, Handelsnamen, Warenbezeichnungen u.s.w. in diesem Werk berechtigt auch ohne besondere Kennzeichnung nicht zu der Annahme, dass solche Namen im Sinne der Warenzeichen- und Markenschutzgesetzgebung als frei zu betrachten wären und daher von jedermann benutzt werden dürften.

Coverbild: www.ingimage.com

Verlag: LAP LAMBERT Academic Publishing GmbH & Co. KG
Dudweiler Landstr. 99, 66123 Saarbrücken, Deutschland
Telefon +49 681 3720-310, Telefax +49 681 3720-3109
Email: info@lap-publishing.com

Herstellung in Deutschland:
Schaltungsdienst Lange o.H.G., Berlin
Books on Demand GmbH, Norderstedt
Reha GmbH, Saarbrücken
Amazon Distribution GmbH, Leipzig
ISBN: 978-3-8433-8900-6

Imprint (only for USA, GB)
Bibliographic information published by the Deutsche Nationalbibliothek: The Deutsche Nationalbibliothek lists this publication in the Deutsche Nationalbibliografie; detailed bibliographic data are available in the Internet at http://dnb.d-nb.de.
 Any brand names and product names mentioned in this book are subject to trademark, brand or patent protection and are trademarks or registered trademarks of their respective holders. The use of brand names, product names, common names, trade names, product descriptions etc. even without a particular marking in this works is in no way to be construed to mean that such names may be regarded as unrestricted in respect of trademark and brand protection legislation and could thus be used by anyone.

Cover image: www.ingimage.com

Publisher: LAP LAMBERT Academic Publishing GmbH & Co. KG
Dudweiler Landstr. 99, 66123 Saarbrücken, Germany
Phone +49 681 3720-310, Fax +49 681 3720-3109
Email: info@lap-publishing.com

Printed in the U.S.A.
Printed in the U.K. by (see last page)
ISBN: 978-3-8433-8900-6

Copyright © 2011 by the author and LAP LAMBERT Academic Publishing GmbH & Co. KG and licensors
All rights reserved. Saarbrücken 2011

CONTENTS

CONTENTS	PAGE
Foreword	004
Preface	006
Acknowledgement	009
Some Opinions	12
Chapter-I – Initial Period of Life	016
1. Birth and Childhood	017
2. Introduction of Ancestry [Genealogy]	018
3. Family Background	019
Chapter-II – Learning of Music	022
1. Initial Training by Father-Shahmir Khan	023
2. Influence of Other Artists on the Vocal Style	028
3. Study of Karnatak Music System	077
4. Devotion for Khayal Style with Practice and Self Inspiration	084
5. Patronage of State and Migration from Indore	085
Chapter-III – The Vocal Style of Ustad Amir Khan	089
1. Form of Khayal	090
2. Accurate Posture and Gesture [Shuddha Mudra]	095
3. Accurate Voice [Shuddha Vani]	096
4. The Swara Aspect of Gayaki	100
5. Alap, Sargam and Tan	104
6. Laya and Tal Aspect	116
7. Raga Profile	121
8. Sangat [Accompaniment]	127
9. Rasa and Bhava Aspect [Aspect of Aesthetic Expression of Sentiment and Mood]	128
10. Adjustment between Swara, Laya and Lyric	134

CONTENTS	PAGE
11. View about Other Modes of Singing	135
12. Effect of Age on His Vocal Style	137
13. Important Reactions about the Style of Ustad Amir Khan	138
Chapter-IV - Experimentations by Ustad Amir Khan	141
1. Ragas, Tals, Bandishes, Taranas etc-applied by Ustad Amir Khan	141
2. Self-composed Compositions under Pen-name 'Sur Rang'	147
3. Notations of Bandishes	153
Chapter-V - The Place of Indore Gharana in the Tradition of Khayal Singing	170
a) The Gharanas of Khayal Singing	171
b) Introduction of Disciples	184
c) Influence of Ustad Amir Khan's Style on Contemporary and Successive Vocalists and Instrumentalists	196
Chapter-VI - Vocal Performances and Honors Achieved	201
1. Vocal Performances:	202
a) At the Centers of Akashwani [radio] & Doordarshan [TV]	202
b) Vocal Performances at Music Concerts	219
c) Other Vocal Programs in India	233
d) Vocal Program – Abroad	239
2. Interaction with Eminent Musicians	243
3. Audio Records of Vocal Presentations	262
4. Honors and Titles	269
Chapter-VII - Contribution of Ustad Amir Khan in the Field Of Cinema Music	277
Chapter-Viii - Life Style	283
1. Temperament, Life Style and Philosophy of Life	284
2. His Basic Views and Values	287
3. Interesting Reminiscences	292
4. Untimely Demise	296

CONTENTS	PAGE
Chapter-IX - Conclusion	300
Appendix	302
Appendix-I - List of Reference Books	302
Appendix-II – List of Records and Cassettes	305
Appendix-III – List of Helpmates	307

FOREWORD
ACHARYA GOSWAMI GOKULOTSAVJI MAHARAJ

Late Ustad Amir Khan, the founder of *Indore Gharana*, was dynamic person having talent with multiple dimensions. In addition to being a top vocalist, he was a sober man of *Sufi* temperament. His contemplation was so deep rooted that he occupies a unique place in the *gayaki* of every vocalist of today.

It has been the quality of his *gayaki*, that his vocalism was not merely a demonstration but it was real form of philosophy. *Khayal* is a meditation, *Dhyan-yoga*, and imagination generated from it, which is reflected every moment and manifests its existence in his singing. Probably, his inclination towards philosophy brought him near the literature, replete with philosophy of our *Vallabh* sect and *Pushti Marg*. As the nature of water is cool, howsoever hot it may be made, it becomes cool again. Similarly, with inclusion of all aspects, effortlessness is the permanent characteristic of his vocalism. The ease and soberness of his *gayaki* enabled the *khayal* singers with that culture [*Tehzeeb*] again, which should be expected from the form, considered to be classical and traditional. This publication is to bring in light the personality and his contribution, occupying the place of mile stone in the history of Indian Classical Music. This is the best utilization of high quality research work and dissertation.

Not focusing only on the biography of Ustad Amir Khan, the specialty of this book is that it analyses every possible aspect of his vocal style and provides balanced comments to arrive at proper conclusions. It is an able Endeavour to express in words, the specialty of *swara* salient expressive style.

It would be appropriate to mention about author of this book also. Dr. Ibrahim Ali has been receiving *talim* [training] in *khayal gayaki* from me since 1986. The capability he has acquired in practical aspect of music vocal, so we should hope for his bright future. There has been shortage of contribution of creative writing amongst artists themselves in India. Hence, I consider it as a good sign in this direction. If artists themselves write in the subject of music, then it makes possible to communicate authentically both aspects, musical expression and its impression, because along with practical presentation, it is natural for an artist to be a wise listener. Probably it would be the reason for success of this book.

Acharya Goswami Gokulotsavji Maharaj,
Vocalist of Hindustani Classical Music,
Special Top Grade Artist of All India Radio & Doordarshan,
Scholar of Indian Philosophy & Ved-Vedant

PREFACE

Ustad Amir Khan was an internationally acclaimed artist of *khayal gayaki*. Without any controversy, it can be stated that along with being a successful vocalist, he was a thinker, an innovator in the field of music, a setter of new trends, and also having an attractive and handsome personality. He provided to *Khayal* style such a peculiar format, which proved to be very effective and popular.

He achieved big successes in his life. His disciples and fans and experts, who came in his contact, bear witness to his valuable contribution. Though today he is not present amongst us physically, his existence is experienced. The real time of a great man is that, when he survives only by virtue of his work and its impact on coming generations.

In the world of music, Ustad Amir Khan is an ideal for those, who follow him. Who do not follow him; it is difficult for them also to ignore him. Ustad Amir Khan's contribution is acknowledged as a link between the old conventions of classical music and new values. As per his name, he was 'prosperous' [*Amir*] of genius and imagination, based on aesthetic sense. He is considered as an artist of artists.

Even today performances of Khan Saheb are preserved in the form of gramophone records, audio cassettes and CDs, and are available for desiring listeners. It is hoped that it will remain available in distant future also. The present and coming generations can enjoy by listening to it, and intelligent students of music can also take guidance from it in development of their singing style. Nevertheless, no authentic book has been written based on facts, determined after total investigations and research about him, which throws light on his style. Before my research project, the information provided in publications and in individual recollections, scattered here and there, could not fulfill this purpose. Therefore, I made humble attempt to fulfill this void from 1988 to 1993.

The result was that Vikram University, Ujjain [M.P.] conferred on me the degree of Ph.D. Music in 1993. Thereafter, my research work has been published in the form of book, in the year 2000, for the benefit of curious lovers of music. Vikram University had given a grant under the scheme of the University Grant Commission, and it was published in Hindi by Classical Publishing Company, New Delhi. Afterward I could create my website: http://sites.google.com/site/amirkhanikhayal and then a part of my work reached to the readers in English. Fortunately now the time has come, when my work is going to be published in English language in book form on international level.

This book is mainly divided in eight chapters. Ninth chapter contains conclusion wherein a brief description of the achievements of the research has been given.

The technical terms of Indian Classical Music have been italicized in this book. Therefore it would be clear that these are not only the words of Hindi, Urdu or other Indian languages, but are also the terms of Indian Classical Music having some special meaning in the tradition of Indian music. The readers familiar to these terms will understand the analysis easily; those who need description of basic theory and terminology can explore 'Wikipedia, the free encyclopedia' for the italicized terms used in the book. Besides, some glossaries are also available over internet as:
http://www.culturalindia.net/indian-music/index.html,
http://www.itcsra.org/sra_glossary_index.html,
http://www.santoor.com/glossary etc.

Some of the *Bandishes* presented by Ustad Amir Khan have been set in a new modified Notation System, which can be called IMSOC Notation System [Ibrahim's

Microsoft Office compatible Notation System]. The notations of *bandishes* have been given in the end of the 4th chapter.

Dr. Ibrahim Ali, Ph.D.
Asst. Prof. Music
Govt. Kalidas Girls College,
Ujjain
Web: http://sites.google.com/site/alisuchi,
http://sites.google.com/site/amirkhanikhayal

Res. & Postal Address:
20 D.N. Marg, Khara Kuwa,
Ujjain (M.P.)-456006.
Ph: 91-0734-2551949
Mob: 9425093621
Email: ali.suchi@gmail.com

ACKNOWLEDGEMENTS

The author expresses gratitude to all those persons, who have extended their valuable cooperation and made it possible to complete this research dissertation and to present it in the form of book.

The author is disciple of the famous vocalist, Goswami Gokulotsavji Maharaj of Indore since 1986. Goswamiji is influenced by the style of Ustad Amir Khan. Therefore, the author got an opportunity to receive training of *khayal* and *tarana* styles on that pattern. In research work, this training was very much helpful in analyzing that style minutely. Though the words are not capable to express, the author expresses his deepest gratitude to his respected Guru.

The author has been getting continuous inspiration and blessings from his respected mother, Mrs. Amtullah and father, Dr. Qasim Ali, to do some thing in the field of music. The present book is also the result of their encouragement. Author's father was kind enough to spare his valuable time from his busy schedule in helping in typing the English version and to provide his valuable advice. The author is most obliged to his parents.

Mrs. Suchitra Ali, the true life partner, is also a real companion of the author to face the ups and downs coming in the path of music field and academic career. How much her help provides strength, the author can't assess it. If he tries to assess it, definitely he will fail in it. Honestly speaking, the author's success itself is due to her; so she deserves actually to be congratulated for it.

Skillful supervision of the famous musicologist of India, Dr. Pyarelal Shrimal removed difficulties of the research work coming in analyzing the vocal style of the top *khayal* singer, Ustad Amir Khan. Besides it, he made available the collection of issues of monthly journal, 'Sangeet' for the last 35 years, so that important facts concerning the subject could be searched. The author considers his duty to express gratitude to him.

Mr. Jayant K. Dange had been generous enough to permit the author to use his vast collection of LP records, rare 78RPM records and cassettes. Also he provided useful material for research from his vast collection of literature regarding music, published in Hindi, Marathi and English news papers and journals. He also provided help in translation of the material available in Marathi language. Not only this, Mr. Dange provided his valuable time and services as an assistant. The author expresses his deep gratitude to him.

The author is thankful to his young disciple and expert in Hindi/English typing, Mr. Rajesh Kumar Madrosia. Mr. Rajesh discharged his responsibility excellently in rough and fair typing of the dissertation during the time of PhD research.

Mr. R.K. Dixit had spared his valuable time in translating the manuscript in English. It was a challenging task to translate a research work which is highly technical and full of technical terms of Indian classical music. Mr. Dixit has done his job very well. I express my thanks to him for his valuable contribution.

Mr. Ismail Daddu Khan, late Mr. Krishnarao Majumdar and late Mr. Vasant Potdar are prominent persons, with whom the author came in contact personally to obtain information about the subject, as they had been in close contact with Ustad Amir Khan. During the interview, valuable information and recollections could be obtained. Similarly, Mr. Amir Karam Ali, Director of Rhythm House PVT LTD, Bombay, gifted to the author, from his personal collection, the audio recordings of some *ragas* performed by Ustad Amir Khan in *mehfils*. These recordings were very much helpful in understanding the technique of vocal presentation of Khan Saheb particularly in *mehfils*. The names of all those musicians, music lovers and music organizations, who extended their cooperation, have been given in the Appendix.

Even besides the names mentioned in appendix, all those who extended their cooperation directly or indirectly, the author expresses his gratitude to them.

Dr. Ibrahim Ali

SOME OPINIONS

DR. ARUN KUMAR SEN

Former Vice Chancellor Indira Kala Sangeet University, Khairagarh [C.G.]
Director, Bhatkhande Sangeet Sansthan, Raipur [C.G.], India

In the present research, Padmabhushan Ustad Amir Khan's initial training, vocal style and his performances at Akashwani, Doordarshan, music concerts, programs given in and out of the country, have been reviewed; and also there is analytical study of his audio recordings etc.

The researcher has worked out in great detail his genealogy, family status and education of music. His unique singing style and Karnatic Music System have also been studied; and investigating the *gharanas* of *khayal gayaki*, researcher has ascertained the place of Indore Gharana. His *bandishes* composed under the pen name of 'Sur Rang' and composition of new *ragas* are high lighted; and their specialties have been well investigated. This research in itself is a complete work, through which the posterity in music will have complete introduction of Ustad Amir Khan's contribution and his life.

PROF. PREMLATA SHARMA

An Eminent Musicologist
Former Vice Chancellor Indira Kala Sangeet University, Khairagarh [C.G.], India

In this research, there is a good analysis of Ustad Amir Khan's *gayaki*. There is much scarcity of such literature in Hindi, so also the value of this research is enhanced. This publication will be useful as a reference for the students of graduate and post graduate classes.

DR. MRS. ANITA SEN
An Eminent Artist and Musicologist
Raipur [C.G.], India

The personality and work of Ustad Amir Khan in the field of music has been divided in nine chapters by the researcher. While discussing the specialties of Ustad Amir Khan, the researcher has also expressed his own opinions, which appeared to be quite original.

Pandit Ganesh Prasad Sharma
Eminent Composer, *Guru* and Writer in the Field of Indian Classical Music
214, Ajit Nagar, Ambala Cant. [Haryana], India

This book is an encyclopedia on Ustad Amir Khan Saheb, as it deals exhaustively with all the aspects of his *gayaki* which has a monumental place in the history of Hindustani Music. The author has taken great pains to go into minute details of his various renderings, providing examples from Khan Saheb's recordings, which he has collected from different sources. His close association with Ustad's style is clearly noticeable in his delineation of the subject matter of the *gayaki* of Ustad Amir Khan. Almost all the aspects of Khan Saheb's *gayaki* have been dealt meticulously, such as- accuracy of *swara*, refined tonal quality without any dramatic contrasts, brisk and flawless *tans* and avoiding rhythmic variations, which could disturb the serenity and depth of melody.

While explaining the '*sachha sur*' [true *swara*], Khan Saheb once told, "*sur* must be transparent to such extent as in a water pond made of marble, the eye of a needle lying on the surface is clearly visible". My personal association with Khan Saheb reminds me of two incidents out of several such, which are etched in my memory and portray him as a man with great patience and affection. Once he was in my home town, Allahabad, for a concert. I and Shankarlal Mishra, another disciple of my *guru*, had arranged for his stay in a guest house and went to meet him there. Khan Saheb was having toothache; instead he asked me to pick up the Tanpura. He started rendering fast *tans* and paused in between to subdue his pain, saying 'Hai Allah!'; thus finding solace in his music only.

When I shifted to Ambala, I invited him for a concert and he stayed at my home. I requested him to proceed for meals to a hotel but he expressed his desire to eat Puris prepared by my wife, whom he addressed as Bhabiji affectionately.

There is a concise presentation of useful information in this excellent work. The references are thorough and show that the writer has tried to accumulate data from all available sources. It is an outstanding and authentic work on the life and contribution of the Ustad.

TRANSLATOR'S NOTE
MR. R.S. DIXIT

9, Jall Boarding, Ujjain [M.P.], India

When I was called upon to translate Dr. Ibrahim Ali's book on Ustad Amir Khan into English, I felt that the task was challenging because my relation with music had been confined only to listening of film music which is usually broadcast from radio and television. So far as the knowledge of classical music is concerned, it does not go beyond Sargam. Nevertheless, I accepted the job and after about six month's constant labor, the result is before the reader for their appreciation.

I have tried my best to remain verbatim as far as possible, because that is the cardinal rule of translation.

In preparing the final draft, Dr. Ibrahim Ali himself and his father, Dr. Qasim Ali have been generous enough to suggest suitable corrections in the text, for which I feel highly obliged to them.

CHAPTER-I

INITIAL PERIOD OF LIFE

CHAPTER-I

INITIAL PERIOD OF LIFE

[1] BIRTH AND CHILDHOOD: -

Ustad Amir Khan was born in Akola [Maharashtra] in the month of April 1912. He himself has said about his birth: "The birth is in Akola. It is in between 1912-13. Had come to Indore at the age of one and a half year."[1] That his birth place is Akola is proved by his own interview and information provided by his brother Bashir Khan [Sarangi player]. According to Bashir Khan, "Amir Khan was born in Akola in 1912."[2] There lived his maternal uncle, Moti Khan, [Tabla player]. In this context, Prof. Chandrakant Lal Das wrote in his article: "Ustad Amir Khan was born in Akola in 1912."[3] Similarly Mr. Madanlal Vyas wrote about his birth in an article: "The great life which came to end in an accident, had begun in April 1912."[4]

As it is published on LP records and in many books that the birth place of Ustad Amir Khan is Indore; for example it is written in the book 'Hamare Sangeet Ratna': "Amir Khan born in a prosperous family of musicians of Indore."[5] But from the information obtained from various sources, it is established that he was born in Akola.

Amir Khan's father, Ustad Shahmir Khan was well known for his hospitality. Every week a *mehfil* [sitting] was used to be held at his home. Almost all the vocalists and instrumentalists of Indore used to participate in it. In those days, Indore was a center of attraction for musicians. Artists like Babu Khan, Bundu Khan, Maglu Khan [*Bin* player], Wahid Khan, Jahangir Khan [Tabla player], Munnu Khan, Latif Khan etc

---
[1] 'Sangeet'-Nov. 1971, P.24, 'Interview-Ustad Amir Khan', Writer: Shambhunath Mishra.
[2] Maharashtra Times-5 Sept. 1976, 'Amir Khan', Writer: Vasant Potdar.
[3] 'Sangeet'-May 1973, 'Ustad Amir Khan Aur Unki Kala' [Ustad Amir Khan and his Art], Writer: Prof. Chandrakant Lal Das.
[4] 'Sangeet'-Dec. 1976, 'Sangeet Jagat Ke Amir Ustad Amir Khan', Writer: Madanlal Vyas.
[5] 'Hamare Sangeet Ratna'-P.89, 'Amir Khan', Author: Lakshminarayan Garg.

used to gather there. Rajab Ali Khan used to come from Dewas. In such an environment of music, Amir Khan's childhood passed. From the very childhood, he had started visiting Ustad Rajab Ali Khan. That is why he had become his favorite.

In addition to music, Amir Khan was also interested in sports and games. With Ramnath Shrivastav, who subsequently became a Sitar player and owner of India Tea Hotel, he used to play foot ball at Chhatri Bag and chess at home.

[2] INTRODUCTION OF ANCESTRY [GENEALOGY]: -

Among the ancestors of Ustad Amir Khan, there was one Chhange Khan, who was one of the musicians during the reign of the last Mughal emperor, Bahadur Shah Zafar [1849-1857]. Ustad Amir Khan himself says: "My ancestor, Miyan Chhange Khan was among the group of musicians during the reign of last Mughal emperor, Bahadur Shah Zafar."[6] Probably, Ustad Change Khan was the first to embrace Islam amongst his ancestors; as is mentioned in 'Hamare Sangeet Ratna': "During the time of last Mughal emperor, one of his musician ancestors had embraced Islam."[7]

Shahmir Khan-Artist of a Royal Court: -

The name of Ustad Amir Khan's father was Shahmir Khan. Shahmir Khan was son of Chhange Khan. Shahmir Khan was mainly a Sarangi player. He also played *Bin*. According to Mr. Madanlal Vyas: "Grandfather Ustad Chhange Khan was a vocalist and father Shahmir Khan was a Binkar and Sarangi player."[8] Basically Shahmir Khan was a resident of Kalnour [Haryana]. He had obtained training of Sarangi playing from the elders of his family. After death of elders, as nobody was left to guide him, he went to Bombay. The singing style of musicians living in the area of Bhindi Bazar

---

[6] 'Sangeet'-November 1971, P.24, 'Interview with Musicians-Ustad Amir Khan', Interviewer: Shambhunath Mishra.
[7] Book 'Hamare Sangeet Ratna'-P.89, 'Amir Khan', Author: Lakshmi Narayan Garg.
[8] 'Sangeet'-Dec 1976, P.24, 'Sangeet Ke Amir: Ustad Amir Khan', Writer: Madanlal Vyas.

is well known as Bhindi Bazar *gayaki*. In those days, there lived three famous Sarangi players and vocalists-Nazir Khan, Chhajju Khan and Khadim Husain Khan. Nazir Khan was vocalist also. Shahmir Khan received training in singing and Sarangi playing from Nazir Khan and Chhajju Khan. His power of assimilation was good. Ustad Aman Ali Khan, the founder of Bhindi Bazar Gharana and by whom Amir Khan was influenced, was son of the same Chhajju Khan. The detail information about Aman Ali Khan is given in subsequent chapter. Shahmir Khan came to Indore after becoming expert in music. Thereafter he was married.

At Indore, he lived under patronage of Maharaja Tukojirao Holkar. There he gradually cultivated friendship with the main vocalists and instrumentalists of Indore and Dewas. The famous Sarangi player, Alladiya Khan, became his disciple, who was his brother-in-law by relation.

Shahmir Khan had a rich collection of *bandishes* too. Famous musicologist, Pt. Vishnu Narayan Bhatkhande took help of Shahmir Khan, while collecting traditional *bandishes* of Hindustani Classical Music. The information about this fact is obtained from an article written by the musician, Joep Bor as under: -
"- - - the well known and highly knowledgeable Sarangi player Badal Khan of Calcutta, Nazir Khan of Bombay, Shahmir Khan of Indore and Bundu Khan of Delhi helped him [V.N. Bhatkhande] in his endeavor to collect traditional compositions and also supported his movement to revive Hindustani music."[9]

[3] FAMILY BACKGROUND: -

In about 1914, at the age of one and a half year, Amir Khan was brought to Indore by his father, Shahmir Khan. The name of Amir Khan's younger brother was Bashir Khan. Both the brothers were trained by their father in Sarangi playing after they grew up. Later Amir Khan entered in the field of singing and when he used to sing,

---

[9] 'The India Magazine'-Sept. 1990, P.59-60, 'The Sarangi', Writer: Joep Bor.

Bashir Khan accompanied him with Sarangi. Then Bashir Khan became a famous Sarangi player and served Akashwani Indore as a staff artist for a long period.

In 1921, Amir Khan's mother expired and in 1937, his father, Shahmir Khan also passed away. Amir Khan lived in his ancestral house at Bombay Bazar, till his father's death. Since childhood, both brothers had love for each other and it lasted through out their life. Ustad Amir Khan didn't consider the family of Bashir Khan apart from his own family; therefore no partition of their ancestral property took place. Bashir Khan's wife, Munavvar Bi [known as 'Manno Apa' among the circle of musicians] has written an article- 'Amir Khan was not my brother-in-law but was my father'. He wrote in that article: "Amir Khan had no family of his own. His family life remained broken and scattered. He considered Bashir Khan, his wife and their four children as his own real relations. Amir Khan was not my brother-in-law, he was my father. He didn't maintain separately his own house hold, due to which the progress of lives of his brother's children would be impeded. Disputes regarding property would arise."[10]

Munavvar Apa said with great pride: "During the time of brother-in-law, great artists had been guest of this house. After staying for many days, they had learnt and understood some thing. Among some guests were Shamta Prasad [Tabla player], Leela Chitnis [film actress], Gohar Bai, Begum Akhtar, Allarakha Khan, Thirakva Khan, Amjad Ali etc whose names I remember."[11]

The tension and disorientation in the family life of Ustad Amir Khan had affected his performance also. Acharya Brihaspati has written: "The vocalism of late Ustad Amir Khan had some what declined in his last few years due to many worldly reasons."[12]

---

[10] 'Kalavarta'-February/March, 1989, P.35, an article centered on the founder of Indore Gharana.
[11] Same as X.
[12] 'Sangeet'-March, 1974, P.35, 'Do Shraddhanjaliyan' Writer: Acharya Brihaspati.

Ustad Amir Khan had married four times. His first marriage took place at Indore when his father was alive, but after some time his wife died. He married again but the marriage was not successful. After four or five years divorce took place. His divorced wife was Sharifan, who was sister of famous Sitar player, Vilayat Khan. Third time he married Munni Bai of Delhi. She was disciple of Ustad Abdul Wahid Khan of Kirana Gharana. Through this Munni Bai, he had an opportunity to study from close quarters the *gayaki* of Abdul Wahid Khan. He had a son from Munni Bai whose name was Akram. Instead of adopting family profession of music, he studied engineering and settled in Canada. Once, Ustad Amir Khan had visited Canada on his invitation.

His fourth wife is Raisa Begum, from whom his second son, Haider [nickname: Babloo] was born at Indore on 10th March 1966. During life time of Ustad Amir Khan, Haider had been living in a hostel at Nagpur and was studying in a Convent School. He studied up to B.Com. at Nagpur. At present, he is a film actor at Bombay. He didn't adopt ancestral art of classical music.

"In the TV serial, 'Tipu Sultan' the role of Hider Ali was played by the actor, whose real name too is Haider Ali. He is son of Ustad Amir Khan of Indore. In the serial, his name has been changed to Shahbaz Khan. The audience will be surprised to know that Shahbaz Khan is a good player of cricket also. After matriculation from St. Joseph Convent, Nagpur and during his graduation at Hislop College, Nagpur, Shahbaz Khan acted on the stage also. - - - His impressive voice is an important part of his acting. Born at Indore, Shahbaz Khan is also working in film being produced under Indo-Russian collaboration."[13]

Thus in the family of the great musician, Ustad Amir Khan, there was not a single member who could carry forward his tradition of music.

---

[13] 'Nai Duniya'-10th October, 1990, 'Ustad Amir Khan Ka Beta-Haider Ali' [Ustad Amir Khan's son-Haider Ali], Writer: Sanjay Patel.

CHAPTER-II

LEARNING OF MUSIC

CHAPTER-II

LEARNING OF MUSIC

[1] INITIAL TRAINING BY FATHER-SHAHMIR KHAN: -

At the early age of ten, Amir Khan started receiving training from his father, Shahmir Khan. Though Shahmir Khan himself was an established Sarangi player, he wanted to make his son a vocalist. Though Shahmir Khan was professionally a Sarangi and vina player, he had studied art of singing also along with instrumental. His *guru* [teacher], Chhange Khan, was a vocalist, who was his father. From very childhood, Amir Khan's grasping power was adequately developed. Whatever he had opportunity to listen, vocal or instrumental, and whatever *swara* phrases taught by his father, he had wonderful capability to reproduce it instantly.

During this period of initial training, Shahmir Khan started to make him practice of *paltas* [permutations] based on *meru khand* system, which is very hard and complex method. Thus, it was but natural that at that early age, such practice seemed to be boring to Amir Khan. Except the training given by father, to hear or sing anything else was prohibited. In this context, a recollection narrated by his younger brother, Bashir Khan, is worth mentioning.

"Father started giving training to brother, Amir Khan. From the very first day, he persisted for preparation of *meru khand*. To sing anything else was not allowed. In total, 5040 *tans* were taught and were got crammed. Brother used to get annoyed very much. A drama company had come to Indore. Whole of the city was crooning its songs. But brother was to keep away from every thing except *khand meru*. When father went for Namaz [prayer of Muslims], brother used to croon songs of Marathi dramas. Once he was caught and was beaten severely."[14]

On attainment of adolescence, the physical process of breaking of voice began. The voice was not fit for singing in such condition. Then Amir Khan thought that botheration of practice to sing was now over. As is generally seen, at this stage, practice of singing is halted for one or two years. But Shahmir Khan took advantage of this period by handing over Sarangi to Amir Khan, as per rich tradition of Sarangi playing in his family. Being a genius, he began playing Sarangi skillfully in a very short time. He wanted to take down on Sarangi, every *swara* phrase which he had learnt during his training of vocalism. According to Bashir Khan, Amir Khan was a good Sarangi player, this fact is known to very few people. He was not satisfied himself by this progress achieved in Sarangi playing. Because of being ambitious, it seemed to him that to become a vocalist would be a right aim for him. The reasons which were in the back ground of his mentality are worth noting.

During training of Sarangi playing by father, Shahmir Khan, Amir Khan had bitter experience of father's short temperament. Such behavior of his father was just in conformity with the behavior of *Ustads* of those times. Amir Khan's close friend and Sitar player, Mr. Ramnath Shrivastava, who himself was also learning Sarangi playing along with Amir Khan from Shahmir Khan, have expressed his recollection: -

"In childhood, we both learned together Sarangi from Shahmir Khan. Once, on incorrect playing, his father [Shahmir Khan] struck forcefully on his neck with a box. Then Amir Khan proceeded towards vocalism leaving Sarangi."[15]

By this event, Amir Khan was so much affected that he decided to become a vocalist. For this, he got support of his younger brother. In beginning, he started practice of

---
[14] Maharashtra Times-5th September 1976, 'Amir Khan' part 2, Writer: Vasant potdar.
[15] Kalavarta-February/March 1989, P.34, 'Jab Amir Khan Saheb Gate-Gate Ro Pade' [When Amir Khan Saheb started weeping while singing], Writer: Ramnath Shrivastava.

vocal in secret, in which Bashir Khan gave him accompaniment on Sarangi. During training of Sarangi playing from his father, he used to learn *gayaki ang* [instrumental technique similar to vocalism] and specialties of *ragas*. This knowledge helped him in practice of vocal.

In another context, Amir Khan had to face an insult for being son of a Sarangi player, which made firm his determination to become a vocalist. Giving account of this event, a famous harmonium player of Indore, Mr. Bapurao Agnihotri has written: "Once in Indore, at a street called Gafoor Ki Bajariya, a music program was held. At the time of Maharaja Tukojirao Holkar [3rd], Ustad Nasiruddin Khan Dagar was his court musician. It is said that at the place of music program n Bajariya, there Amir Khan Saheb saw a book, named *meru khand*, and he took it and started reading; but Nasiruddin snatched the book from him saying that it was of no use for a child like him. Amir Khan was deeply hurt by these insulting words and then and there he decided that in any way he would become a vocalist of high standard. So what was to do then! He asked his friend Ramnath to bring that book from anywhere and Mr. Ramnathji Shrivastava [of India Hotel], who was his close friend, copied the book within few days by his own hand and gave it to Amir Khan."[16]

Acharya Brihaspati has also narrated an incident of similar type in this way: "Amir Khan was a child at that time. At that time, a very eminent *dhrupad* singer lived at Indore. One day, he was teaching *paltas* [permutations] of *khand meru* to students of his family. Amir Khan reached there coincidently and the subject was changed. How could practice of *khand meru* be carried on in the presence of son of a Sarangi player? Amir Khan, even though a child, could understand actual thing and was deeply hurt."[17]

---

[16] Kalavarta-February/March 1989, P.19, 'Gambhir Vyaktitva Kay Sath Prakriti Ka Gayan', Writer: Bapurao Agnihotri.
[17] 'Sangeet'-March 1974, P.9, 'Aik Darun Aghat, Aik Aur Patra', Writer: Acharya Brihaspati.

By this event, Amir Khan evidently realized that depending upon 'Sarangi', an instrument associated with infamous persons and considered suitable only for accompaniment; no honorable place could be achieved in the society and among artists. He saw that his predecessors, two great artists of Kirana Gharana, Ustad Abdul Karim Khan and Ustad Abdul Wahid Khan, though originally trained as Sarangi players, proceeded in the field of vocalism and earned name as founders of a *gharana* of vocal music that is Kirana Gharana. Accordingly, Amir Khan left Sarangi playing and started his endeavor to become a vocalist and subsequently became famous as a founder of Indore Gharana.

Alap, behlava, meed, gamak, tans, khatka etc elements which are applied for embellishment of a *raga* have almost similar form, both in Sarangi playing and in vocalism. Hence, it was not difficult for Amir Khan to enter into one field leaving the other. The first aim before him was to culture the voice suitable to the desired style. Besides, there is tremendous scope for expression of sentiments in vocal, in comparison to any instrument. Probably that is why, in the three modes of music [vocal, instrumental and dance], vocal is ranked as first.

In early age [ten years], when Amir Khan's initial training started, at that time he was made to practice of singing for a very short duration; but as he started entering adulthood, the duration of his practice started increasing. In an interview, he himself says: -

"My training started at the age of ten from my father. I was young; he made me sing for half or one hour. He made me sing for an hour each in morning, in afternoon and in evening for years together. Afterwards I came to understand. I questioned him one day, why you ask me to sing for an hour only? He said: 'it is not right to sing more at present. The mind will not be able to respond for the purity of the *swaras* by practicing more; hence, sing less now'. This process continued till 1937, that is, till the death of father."[18]

During the period of initial training, along with all the parts of *khayal gayaki*, father Shahmir Khan made him practice very hard *paltas* of *meru khand*.

Pt. Amarnath wrote: "Shahmir Khan became a disciple of Bhindi Bazar musicians to understand the Merukhand system, Amir Khan received this Merukhand Taaaleem [teaching] through his father."[19]

This *riyaz* [practice] of *meru khand paltas* subsequently became helpful in the development of peculiar vocal style of Ustad Amir Khan. This process of training under 'the teacher and the taught tradition' [*guru-shishya parampara*], continued uninterrupted until his father's death; thereafter he never became ceremonial disciple of any established contemporary vocalist by accepting anyone's tutelage.

He had not availed any formal school education. Mohan Nadkarni mentions in an article: "Although he had no formal education, he was well versed in Urdu, Persian and Hindi. He had basic knowledge of Sanskrit. He had studied works of many Indian mystical saints also. It is amazing but fact that because of this combination, he tended to execute difficult research in various styles of North Indian music."[20]

After studying his whole life, we find that this lack of formal education didn't hinder the development of his personality and his carrier in music.

---

[18] 'Sangeet'-November 1971, P.26, 'Sangeet Sadhakon See Bhent: Ustad Amir Khan', Interviewer: Shambhunath Mishra.
[19] 'Living Idioms in Hindustani Music: A Dictionary of Terms and Terminology'-P.55, 'Indore Gharana', Author: Pt. Amarnath.
[20] 'Madhyavarti'-P.35, 'Amirkhani Shaili', Author: Mohan Nadkarni.

[2] INFLUENCE OF OTHER ARTISTS ON THE VOCAL STYLE: -

Amir Khan received training in music from his father, Shahmir Khan, for a long period of fifteen years. After completion of that training and death of his father, he didn't confine his vocal style to the training received from his father. He listened to the great maestros of all the *gharanas* of his time very attentively. Among them were included top artists of all modes of classical music, that is, vocalists of *dhrupad-dhamar*, vocalists of *khayal* and instrumentalists. During this period of his practice [*sadhana*], those founder senior artists of different *gharanas,* whom he had heard, in them the names of top most artists like Ustad Abdul Karim Khan and Ustad Fayyaz Khan are worth mentioning.

In an article, based on research about the *gharanas* of music, under the direction of Pt. Amarnath, Ms. Bindu Chawla writes: -
"Ustad Amir Khan Saheb had a great love for *quawaalee* and was influenced by masters of more than two *gharanas.*"[21]

This quotation shows that Khan Saheb had love for *quavvali* personally but it wouldn't be proper to conclude that this style had any influence on his *khayal* style, directly or indirectly.

In the words of Acharya Brihaspati: "He had listened to his predecessor experts; he appreciated their virtues and prepared a new bouquet of his own *gayaki*."[22] Making it more clear, Ustad Moinuddin Khan, Sarangi player of Indore, said: "Khan Saheb listened very attentively to Ustad Rajab Ali Khan [Dewas], Ustad Aman Ali Khan [Bhindi Bazar] and Fayyaz Khan etc, all the top artists, and molded the best aspects of their *gayaki* in his *gayaki* in a distinct manner."[23] He also considered the *gayaki* of

---

[21] Hindustan Times-30 Oct. 1988, 'The Leading Schools', Writer: Bindu Chawla.
[22] 'Sangeet'-March 1974, P.10, Writer: Acharya Brihaspati.
[23] Kalavarta-February/March 1989, P.22, 'Shagird Ka Hak Shagird Ko, Writer: Moinuddin Khan.

Ustad Abdul Karim Khan. In this context, he himself says: "I also saw to it what did Abdul Karim Khan do."[24]

Music being his family profession and Indore being the center of great artists in those days, Amir Khan had the opportunity to listen to all top vocalists and instrumentalists and to have personal contact with them. As previously mentioned, on every Friday, after the afternoon prayer, there used to be a gathering at his house, where Wahid Khan, Rajab Ali Khan, Allah Bande Khan [*dhrupad* singer], Bundu Khan [Sarangi player], Murad Khan [*Binkar*], Nasiruddin Khan Dagar, Bashir Khan, Krishna Rao Apte [*dhrupad* singer], Ustad Alladiya Khan [Sarangi player], Ustad Dhulji Khan [Tabla player], Ustad Jahangir Khan [Tabla player] etc great artists used to come. He also remained in close contact of Babu Khan [a famous Sitar player], a disciple of Murad Khan [*binkar*]. Babu Khan and Amir Khan used to have a sitting regularly at the place of Goswami Krishnaraiji Maharaj. There Nasiruddin Khan [*dhrupad* singer] also used to come. Goswami Krishnaraiji Maharaj had so much interest in music that any vocalist who visited the court of Maharaja Tukoji Rao Holkar, was called by him several times to perform at his place. Here it is to be noted that Goswami Gokulotsavji Maharaj, famous vocalist of the style of Indore Gharana at present, is grandson of the said Goswami Krishnaraiji Maharaj and this information too was received from him. The author is *gandaband shagird* [disciple] of Goswami Gokulotsavji Maharaj since 1986.

Ustad Amir Khan received fine knowledge of *tal* and *laya* from his maternal uncle, Ustad Rehman Khan, during the course of his guidance in Tabla playing. This fact was confirmed by famous Tabla player, Ustad Ismail Daddu Khan, resident of Indore in those days, in an interview given to the author on 22-05-1988. Besides being a relative of Ustad Amir Khan, Mr. Daddu Khan remained in his contact for a long time as a Tabla accompanist. He considered Ustad Amir Khan's knowledge of Tabla playing and *tal* of high standard. In this context Prof. Chandrakant Lal Das informs:

---

[24] 'Sangeet'-January/February 1980, P.19, 'Meri Gayaki Meri Avaz Hay', Writer: Ravindra Visht.

"It is necessary to say about Khan Saheb's knowledge of music that his maternal uncle, Ustad Rehman Khan had been a great Tabla player. Because of his grasping power, Amir Khan has acquired complete knowledge of Tabla in his company. Consequently some of top Tabla players of the country receive embellished Tabla-compositions from him."[25]

As has been mentioned previously, Ustad Amir Khan came in contact with many senior musicians but he was mostly and directly influenced by representative vocalists of the three different styles were Ustad Rajab Ali Khan, Ustad Aman Ali Khan and Ustad Abdul Wahid Khan.

The follower of vocal style of Ustad Amir Khan, Mr. Gajendra Bakshi, who has practiced vocalism sufficiently, remaining in his contact, writes in an article about Ustad Amir Khan's contact with these three great vocalists: "In his youth, he found opportunity to listen Ustad Wahid Khan Saheb, Rajab Ali Khan Saheb and Ustad Aman Ali Khan Saheb from close quarters. Amir Khan Saheb had great respect for these artists. Remaining in their contact, Amir Khan Saheb had opportunity to hear them."[26]

In the above statement of Mr. Gajendra Bakshi, the sequence of these three names is not correct chronologically. Actually, Amir Khan Saheb first came in contact with Ustad Rajab Ali Khan, then with Ustad Aman Ali Khan and lastly with Ustad Abdul Wahid Khan. The influence of these three vocalists exercised on the vocal style of Ustad Amir Khan, is mentioned as under.

1- Ustad Rajab Ali Khan [Dewas] and his Influence: -
Ustad Rajab Ali was born in Narsinghgarh [Madhya Pradesh] in 1874 AD. He received training in music from his father, Mughal Khan, who was an artist in the

---
[25] 'Sangeet'-May 1973, 'Ustad Amir Khan Aur Unki Kala' [Ustad Amir Khan and his art], Writer: Chandrakant Lal Das.
[26] Kalavarta-February/March 1989, P.17, 'Gayaki Kee Amiri', Writer: Gajendra Bakshi.

court of Dewas of that time. Thereafter, in 1890, he became a ceremonial disciple of Bin player, Ustad Bande Ali Khan and was trained in Bin playing. After death of Bande Ali Khan, both father and son went to Kolhapur where they lived for a long time. There he came in contact with Ustad Alladiya Khan, famous singer of Jaipur-Atrauli Gharana. There he received generous patronage from the ruler of Kolhapur, Chhatrapati Sahu Maharaj. There he received the title of 'Dakshin Ka Sher' [The Lion of South]. He was influenced by *gayaki* of Jaipur Gharana through Haider Baksh [Sarangi accompanist of Alladiya Khan]. In 1908, he came to Dewas from Kolhapur and became the court singer of Maharaja Malhar Rao Pawar, the ruler of Dewas Junior. Afterward he joined the court of Dewas Senior. When attached with Dewas court, he presented many vocal programs organized in India and Nepal.

There was close friendship between Shamir Khan [father of Amir Khan] and Ustad Rajab Ali Khan. That is why, Amir Khan used to go to the residence of Ustad Rajab Ali Khan at Dewas, since his childhood. Rajab Ali Khan also used to visit his home at Indore. Those days, Ustad Rajab Ali Khan was supposed to be an expert in winning the *mehfil* [concert]. Also Shahmir Khan wanted that Amir Khan should listen to the *gayaki* of Ustad Rajab Ali Khan attentively and should try to understand his complex and difficult style. Hence being inspired by his father, it was natural to increase the interest of Amir Khan in the vocal style of Ustad Rajab Ali Khan. Thus the first influence on *meru khand* based style given by his father, was that of Ustad Rajab Ali Khan. Amir Khan paid respect to him like a *guru*. He used to offer money as a mark of respect and used to put some money under his bed stealthily, so that he should not feel offended.

Ustad Rajab Ali Khan also had listened singing of Amir Khan since his childhood and was optimistic for his progress in music. Therefore he used to guide him from time to time and encouraged him to establish himself as a professional singer.

The specialty of *gayaki* of Ustad Rajab Ali Khan was his *tans*. He reached the peak of popularity due to *tans*. Late Amique Hanafi, who had been producer at Akashwani Indore, used to meet Ustad Amir Khan from time to time, has narrated an event in these words: -

"In the room for *riyaz* in the new house of Amir Khan Saheb, there was only the picture of Khan Saheb [Rajab Ali Khan] facing to the place of sitting. I said, Khan Saheb! What is this? He replied 'Oh! There is no equivalent to the practice of *drut* and *tanaiti* of uncle Rajab Ali Khan. I pray Almighty that if only a part of *tanaiti* of Bade Miyan would come into my voice, I would be enriched. I sing keeping him in front me."[27]

Ustad Rajab Ali Khan had an expertise for application of straight and *chhoot ki tan* in mixed and complex *ragas* in easy and natural manner. Ustad Amir Khan adopted this quality excellently keeping in mind the quality of his own voice and the nature of style. Before coming to *madhya shadja* [keynote] after finishing a *tan*, that is while making descending part of the *tan*, where Amir Khan applied *chhoot* and descending straight *tan* in *ragas* having mixed and complex *swara* application, such as *shuddha kalyan, nand kalyan* and *bhatiyar*; there the influence of Ustad Rajab Ali Khan can be clearly discerned.

Pt. Amarnath has explained the meaning of *chhoot tan* as follows: -
"Fast, straight *tan* of shooting nature, essentially skipping some notes of the scale."[28]

Saral, firat, ragang, alankarik etc the types of *tans* have been applied traditionally in *khayal gayaki*. Not depending on these prescribed *tan* patterns, usage of various complex *swara* applied *tans* was an important feature of Ustad Rajab Ali Khan's style.[29] This feature too was excellently adopted by Amir Khan, because he had

---

[27] 'Ustad Rajab Ali Khan'-P.66, Author: Amique Hanafi.
[28] 'Living Idioms in Hindustani Music: A Dictionary of Terms and Terminology'-P.34, Author: Pt. Amarnath.
[29] On the basis of LP record issued by HMV containing *raga jaunpuri*.

become mature in the practice of *merukhand*. Thus he was capable to apply difficult *swara* phrases easily. Prolonging the sound of *akar, Ikar* etc vowels, and extending pronunciation of the words of *bandish*, whatever difficult and untraditional *tans* Amir Khan presented; it was the influence of the flight of imagination of Ustad Rajab Ali Khan. Both the vocalists didn't applied *alankars* in *tans* in even sequence, as – *ni re ga, re ga ma', ga ma' pa* etc. On the contrary, they produced variety by mixed application of different phrases of *alankars* and produced peculiarity by giving stress beyond imagination. For example – **n** r g, r g m̲, **n** m̲ r g, m̲ d p.[30]

Before Amir Khan reached Bombay, his style had been influenced by the *tans* of Ustad Rajab Ali Khan. There he lived in company of Amanat Khan, nephew and favorite disciple of Ustad Rajab Ali Khan. Whatever direct influence of Rajab Ali Khan had been on Amir Khan, was fortified through Amanat Khan.

Amanat Khan was son of Jamal Khan, brother of Rajab Ali Khan and was elder to Amir Khan by eleven years. From the very childhood, Amanat lived in close contact of Rajab Ali Khan, learnt his *gayaki* by heart and represented his style. Rajab Ali Khan also considered Amanat to be true representative of his style and used to say: "Amanat is the lamp of mine, he would illuminate my name."[31]

Amanat Khan had very melodious voice. He was skillful in *firat* and *tayari* [rapidity] and even in *drut laya*, he sustains *dana* [grain] and clarity in his *tans*, like Rajab Ali Khan. The relation between Amanat Khan and Amir Khan were friendly. In Bombay, they lived in the same room for many years and practiced together. According to late Mr. Krishnarao Majumdar, one of the main disciples of Ustad Rajab Ali Khan, Ustad Amir Khan prepared *drut tans* of *khayal* with the help of Amanat Khan, which were the prominent part of Rajab Ali Khan's *gayaki*. These two friends used to come to

---

[30] The introduction of IMSOC Notation System is available in chapter IV/[3].
[31] 'Ustad Rajab Ali Khan'-P.68, Author: Amique Hanafi.

Dewas together from time to time and took advantage of the valuable advice of Rajab Ali Khan regarding music.

According to late Mr. Krishnarao Majumdar "Amanat, nephew of Rajab Ali. There will be no vocalist like him again. His speed was like lightening. Amir took up that fast speed also. *Tan* and *drut*, that is 2/3rd part of vocalism. Remaining is *vilambit*."[32]

From the above statement, it seems that 2/3rd part of the vocal style of Ustad Amir Khan was the result of influence of Ustad Rajab Ali Khan. But this ratio exceeds too much from the reality, *drut tans* and *drut khayal* are employed only for 1/3rd of time in the presentation of *khayal gayaki*. Besides it, Amir Khan gave much importance to the *vilambit khayal* and the gradual movement of *raga* falling under it, in comparison to Ustad Rajab Ali Khan. On the basis of available audio recorded *gayaki* of Ustad Amir Khan, it can be said that the statement of Mr. Krishnarao Majumdar about consisting 2/3rd part of total *gayaki* of Ustad Amir Khan by *tans* and *drut gayaki*, is far from reality.

After attaining maturity in age and in vocalism, Ustad Amir Khan reduced application of *tans* of fast speed and adopted grave *vilambit gayaki*. As there is not much scope for fast speed and *atidrut tans* in *shant rasa* salient *vilambit gayaki*. Hence it is clear that the influence of *drut laya* of Rajab Ali Khan in his youth, appears rarely in his matured vocalism. This change in *tans* was related to speed; the form of *tans* technically remained almost the same.

According to his nature, he found himself more befitting for grave *gayaki*, instead of the style of fast *tans* in *drut laya*. Besides, he felt that in the contemporary field of music, it would much better for him to make progress by the *gayaki* based on *rasa* [sentiment], instead of demonstration of miracles and strength. In this context, his own ideas are worth mentioning: "Uncle Rajab Ali Khan rides on lightening. It is not

---

[32] 'Nal'-P.137, 'Abhijat Surrang-Khan Saheb Amir Khan', Author: Vasant Potdar.

possible for every one to ride on such a horse and again there is no more field to run such a horse."[33]

Amir Khan used to have conversations with Rajab Ali Khan Saheb regarding prevalent and non prevalent *bandishes* of *khayal* and used to be benefited from his treasure of knowledge of *bandishes*. His curiosity about those *bandishes* can be gauged from the recollection of Pt. Amarnath: "Once, after staying at my residence in Delhi for eight to ten days, he was to proceed for Bombay, perhaps to participate in some program. I had just told to my disciple to bring a ticket. He called him back to say that he would go first to Indore and Dewas. I said, why to make such a round? Why don't go to Bombay directly? He said: 'Son! Rajab Ali Khan is ill at Dewas. He has a *sthayee* of *raga shankara*, whose refrain is in lower octave. I have to take it. Bombay can be visited later. Programs are held often.'"[34]

In an interview given to the author on 9th April 1989, Mr. Krishnarao Majumdar told about the said *bandish* of *raga shankara* as follows: "*kaisee been bajai sanvaro, been bajai mana har leeno - - -*".

Similarly, Rajab Ali Khan Saheb's favorite *bandish* of *raga miyan kee malhar* '*barsan lagee ree badariya savan kee*' was also used to sing by Ustad Amir Khan with great interest. This *bandish*, sung by Ustad Amir Khan, is audio recorded in HMV Cassette No.STC04B-7373, on side b.

In spite of said similarities and influences, difference between *gayaki* of the two vocalists can be clearly discerned. In other words, there were many elements in the *gayaki* of Ustad Rajab Ali Khan which were not adopted by Ustad Amir Khan at all. For example, the *khayal* rendering of Ustad Rajab Ali Khan starts from *madhya laya* and reaches *madhya, drut* and *atidrut*. On the contrary, Amir Khan starts presentation

---

[33] Weekly Dinman-3rd March 1974, 'Tumhare Sharan Ab Kiyo Vishram', Writer: Amique Hanafi.
[34] Kalavarta-February/March 1989, P.10, 'Aisay Thay Meray Satguru', Writer: Pt. Amarnath.

of any *raga* with *ativilambit laya* [less than 1/4th of ordinary *vilambit*] and after devoting a long time for *vilambit khayal*, he sings *chhota khayal* or *tarana* in *madhya laya*, whose *laya* is somewhat speeded up afterwards.

After the *bandishes* of *madhya laya*, by various mutual combination of *swara, laya* and words of *bandish*, and by demonstration of variety of *behlavas, bolbat* and *boltan* etc in the *raga*, Ustad Rajab Ali Khan comes to *tans*. Whereas Ustad Amir Khan improvises the *raga* by detailed grave *alap* after the *sthayee* and after a long time, he applies *tans* etc, the elements of fast movement.

Layakari had a special role in the *gayaki* of Ustad Rajab Ali Khan. Along with every beat of *tal*, the connection between *tal* and *swara* was maintained by stress on *swara*. He used abundantly difficult *layakaris* full of peculiarity; and applying *layakaris* of *aad-kuad* [3/2 & 5/4] in *adachautal* [a *tal* supposed to be difficult] to make the audience fascinated, was an ordinary thing for him. But the vocalism of Ustad Amir Khan was centered on *swaras*. He didn't try to make the audience spellbound by applying the application of complex *layakaris*. He brought stability to *swaras* to increase sobriety. So to lay stress on *swara* with every beat was not appropriate to his style. Ustad Rajab Ali Khan came to *sama*, by taking refrain full of variety from an unimaginable place, by taking full refrain in very narrow space before *sama* and by applying *tihayee*. These applications prove his command on *tal* and *laya*. Ustad Amir Khan's refrain [*mukhda*] used to be of natural manner only. Under *layakaris*, Ustad Rajab Ali Khan applied *bolbat* in various *layas* profusely. '*Bolbat*' means performing the lyric of *bandish* by dividing it into different *laya* sections, in which extempore improvisation is applied on the place of basic notation of *bandish*. This part is considered to be an influence of *dhrupad* on *khayal gayaki*. Such *bolbat* was skillfully applied by Ustad Rajab Ali Khan in *tayar* [fast but clear] *laya*. But Ustad Amir Khan didn't give a role to *bolbat* in his *gayaki*, nor did he consider it proper to use lyric for that purpose. At such places, he thought it proper to use *sargam* [sol-fa], instead of verse [words of *bandish*].

Thus, Amir Khan Saheb was specially inspired by Ustad Rajab Ali Khan in order to develop his own style, but at many places he adopted different view point. Close relations remained between the two artists till the death of Ustad Rajab Ali Khan. After the death of his nephew and beloved disciple, Amanat Ali Khan, Ustad Rajab Ali Khan considered Amir Khan in the place of his nephew. Ustad Amir Khan too called him uncle. Ustad Amir Khan always tried for the well being and social dignity of Ustad Rajab Ali Khan. He used to organize his programs and also remained himself present there.

The last big program of Ustad Rajab Ali Khan was held at Bombay on 2nd April 1957, organized by Sursingar Sansad, where Ustad Amir Khan was also present along with great artists like Ustad Bade Ghulam Ali Khan and dancer Sitara Devi. Before it, Ustad Amir Khan had organized a program of Ustad Rajab Ali Khan in the library of Akashwani Indore, on 27th March 1956, where the Tabla accompanist was Mr. Ahmad Jan Thirakwa.

Without having any ceremonial relationship of *ganda bandhan*, the relations between Ustad Rajab Ali Khan and Amir Khan were like a *guru* and *shishya* [the teacher and the taught]. "Once Amir Khan Saheb invited Ustad Rajab Ali Khan on dinner at his residence. Ustad Rajab Ali Khan came with Mama Krishnarao Majumdar. Other Musicians were also present in the dinner. After dinner, Ustad Rajab Ali Khan said: 'Amir Khan! As you have hosted a feast, now you will have to sing also. '*Mehfil*' was held and Amir Khan Saheb started singing. While singing, he again and again looked towards Ustad Rajab Ali Khan and then on the picture of his father, late Shahmir Khan, Sarangi player, hanging on the wall above him. Suddenly Amir Khan Saheb became very emotional, a gush of tears started flowing from his eyes and his voice was choked. Amir Khan Saheb enjoyed the great delight of vocalism which he had learned from his father; because while singing, he was applauded by the dancing eyes of Ustad Rajab Ali Khan blessing him as '*marhaba-marhaba*' [congratulations].

Then Ustad Rajab Ali Khan said: 'I feel proud today that you have achieved expertise and fame of an *Ustad* in *gayaki*.' Though Amir Khan Saheb had not been tied *ganda*, yet he had a sense of respect for Ustad Rajab Ali Khan like a *guru*. He said to Ustad: 'all this is due to you.'"[35]

In the said *mehfil*, famous Tabla player Ismail Daddu Khan, Sarangi player Alladiya Khan and Tabla player Jahangir Khan were present. Ismail Daddu Khan had given Tabla accompaniment in the singing of Ustad Amir Khan. In the interview taken by the author on 22-05-1988, Mr. Ismail Daddu Khan told: "At that time being very happy, Ustad Rajab Ali Khan said affectionately: 'Amir Khan! Having heard your singing today, I am so happy that even I die, I shall not be sad for the reason that a good vocalist will be there after me.'"

After a very short period of the said program, Ustad Rajab Ali Khan died on 8th January 1959 at Dewas, at the age of 85.

Thus the first influence on the *gayaki* of Ustad Amir Khan, inherited from his father, was of Ustad Rajab Ali Khan.

2- Ustad Aman Ali Khan of Bhindi Bazar and his influence: -

Ustad Aman Ali Khan was born in 1884 at Bijnore [Dist. Muradabad, Uttar Pradesh]. His grand father, Dilawar Husain Khan lived at Muradabad. Afterwards his family migrated to Bombay and resided in Bhindi Bazar area; that is why they were called Bhindi Bazar Walas. Dilawar Husain had four sons- 1. Chhajju Khan, 2. Nazir Khan, 3. Haji Vilayat Husain Khan and 4. Khadim Husain Khan. Aman Ali Khan was the son of Chhajju Khan. Chhajju Khan was also known by the name of Amarsha Saheb. Shahmir Khan, father of Ustad Amir Khan lived in the same area of Bombay and had received training from the same Nazir Khan and Chhajju Khan.

---

[35] Kalavarta-February/March 1989, P.34, 'Jab Amir Khan Saheb Gate-Gate Ro Pade', Writer: Ramnath Shrivastava.

Aman Ali Khan had no interest in music in childhood but he was attracted to it later on and started having training from his father Chhajju Khan. Afterwards he was also guided by his two uncles, Nazir Husain and Khadim Husain. He was well known for application of *sargam* based on *merukhand* and became famous as *nayak* [composer] because of *bandishes* composed by him. He had composed about five hundred *bandishes* in different *ragas* under the pen name 'Amar'. He died in 1953.

Ustad Amir Khan had ample opportunity to listen to Aman Ali Khan and to understand his style, during his residence at Bombay, in his youth. He had received training of the same style from his father as inheritance, in the form of basic education; so it was natural to be attracted towards similar musical elements. Ustad Amir Khan got refinement and maturity in his ancestral vocal style, because of this contact with Aman Ali Khan.

The specialty of Aman Ali Khan's *gayaki* was his method of presentation of *sargam* in *khayal gayaki*. The general meaning of *sargam* is to present the notes of music by pronouncing their brief names. In the training of music and for its practice, the tradition of use of *sargam* is old; and for the preparation of *tans*, *paltas* of *sargam* are practiced. But subsequently, *sargam* got place for itself as an element of *khayal gayaki*, which can be seen especially in the *khayal* style of Kirana, Bhindi Bazar and Indore Gharana.

On the presentation style of *sargam* of Ustad Abdul Karim Khan of Kirana Gharana and Aman Ali Khan of Bhindi Bazar, there was more of less influence of Karnatak Music; but *sargam* of Aman Ali Khan was more complex and he allotted comparatively more time to *sargam* in his *gayaki*.

How *sargam* found a place in *khayal gayaki* with the inspiration of Karnatak Music, Dr. Prabha Atre, an eminent vocalist and a researcher on '*sargam*', writes in her

Marathi book: "In addition to instrumental style, influence of Karnatak Music can also be seen in the presentation of *sargam*. The *andolan* and stress on *swara*, and the pronunciation of *swara* name also appear to be inclined towards Karnatak Music."[36]

Ustad Amir Khan treated the style of Aman Ali Khan as an ideal, in the presentation of *sargam*. The purpose of giving importance to *sargam* in Bhindi Bazar style was to present the qualities of *layakaris* in the *khayal*, without doing any harm to the beauty of lyric. In this context, Pt. Ramesh Nadkarni, a disciple of Aman Ali Khan, says in an interview: "The application of *sargam* is not only the exercise of *palta*. It is applied to show the beauty of *laya*. It is used there, where the words of lyric are likely to be broken; so that the beauty of lyric could be maintained and beauty of *swara* combination could be emphasized."[37]

In *khayal* singing, Ustad Amir Khan gave much importance to pronunciation of words, their accuracy and the aesthetics based on *swara* and lyric, generated by it; therefore he was influenced by the style of Aman Ali Khan. The traditional link between *alap* and *tan*, that is *bolbat*, was not accorded a place in the style of Ustad Amir Khan and instead he adopted the method of presentation of *sargam*, here the same principle is seemed to have been applied.

In spite of absence of lyric; *meed, khatka, gamak* etc embellishing elements are applied in *sargam* also to make it manifest. After applying one *swara* with *khatka* reaching immediately to another *swara* and then to stabilize voice, to join two *swaras* with *meed* in ascending or descending order and to pronounce *tans* of *gamak* in the form of *sargam* etc, are the stylistic qualities of Ustad Amir Khan, which are supposed to have been influenced by Aman Ali Khan.

---

[36] 'Swarmayee'-P.67, 'Sargamanch Rag-Sangeetatit Sthan', Author: Dr. Prabha Atre.
[37] 'Sangeet'-October 1985, P.47-48, 'Sangeet Shastragya Evam Guni Gayak: Pt. Ramesh Nadkarni', Writer: Madanlal Vyas.

In the *gayaki* of Ustad Amir Khan, there was rationality in application of '*sargam*'. He didn't allow this element to be all pervading in his whole *khayal* style, contrary to Aman Ali Khan. The application of *sargam* by Ustad Amir Khan in *chhota khayal* and *tarana* is seem to be similar to that of Aman Ali Khan, but in *bada khayal*, wherever he applied *sargam*, that was his own specialty. It is fact that Ustad Amir Khan has expressed the connection between *tal* and *swara* by *sargam* with *laya* even in *bada khayal* of *ativilambit laya*; it again appears to be nearer the principle of presenting the *laya* by *sargam* as enunciated by Bhindi Bazar Walas.

Aman Ali Khan accorded much importance to *merukhand* system in his *gayaki*, which was not so prevalent in North Indian music in those days. After Bhindi Bazar *gayaki*, similarly singing style of Ustad Amir Khan is based on *merukhand* system of movement, whose principle source is 'Sangeet Ratnakar', written by Pt. Sharangdeo, in 13th century.[38] This information is given in an English article, written by Ms. Bindu Chavla, which is based on a research conducted by Pt. Amarnath, that is as follows: - "The Style [of Amir Khan], after the Bhindi Bazar Gharana, is based on the *merukhand* system of improvisation that appears in the thirteenth century Sangeet Ratnakar of Sharangdeo"[39]

Shahmir Khan, father of Ustad Amir Khan, became disciple of Ustad Chhajju Khan [father of Aman Ali Khan] and Ustad Nazir Khan of Bhindi Bazar Gharana for the purpose of imbibing the *merukhand* system. Hence, Ustad Amir Khan was attracted towards Ustad Aman Ali Khan of the same Bhindi Bazar Gharana in order to base his *gayaki* on *merukhand* system.

Changing the order of *swaras* in any *swara* phrase is called *merukhand, khandmeru* or *swara prastar* [spreading of *swara* by permutation]. While presenting a *raga*, this is generally done in three, four or five *swaras*. Bhindi Bazar Gharana adopted the

---

[38] Detail description of Sangeet Ratnakar is given afterward, in same chapter.
[39] Hindustan Times-Oct. 30, 1986, 'the Journey of the Gharana', Writer: Bindu Chavla.

merukhand system to get various and maximum number of *swara* phrases on mathematical basis by application of *swaras* in a definite number. By changing the order of *swaras*, maximum how many *swara* phrases can be obtained, the *merukhand* system provides guidance in this regard. On the other hand, the grammar of *raga*, that is the principle of prohibited or allowed *swaras* in ascending or descending, rareness or prevalence of a note, saving from the *ragas* of same nature etc are the reasons which limit application of maximum *swara* phrases. So Ustad Amir Khan got benefited from the experience of Aman Ali Khan to acquire skill of selecting *swara* phrases suitable to *raga*. The maximum forms of *swara prastars* [permutations] have been used by Ustad Amir Khan in *ragas-malkauns, megha, abhogi, kaunsikanada* etc which are of *audav jati* [pentatonic class] or of *audav sampurna jati* [pentatonic-heptatonic] or the *ragas* where there is more scope for independent improvisation. Ustad Amir Khan has been cautious in presentation of various *swara* phrases in the *ragas* which are of serious nature and provide limited independence, like *darbari kanada*. Hence the *gayaki* of Ustad Amir Khan can not be blamed for those accusations which have been leveled against the predecessor maestros of Bhindi Bazar Gharana, that by their system of *swara prastar*, the *raga* is damaged.

Aman Ali Khan gave much importance to *madhya laya* in his style, which concluded on reaching the *drut laya*. All of his self composed *bandishes* are set in *madhya laya*, that is why link between verse, *laya* and *swara* is always maintained. His *bada khayal* too used to start from *madhya vilambit laya*. There was no role for *ativilambit laya* in his style. Because of *madhya vilambit laya*, link between *swara* and *laya* could be maintained even in *bada khayal*.

Where Ustad Amir Khan has vocalized compositions of Aman Ali Khan in the form of *bada khayal*, he has maintained Aman Ali Khan's *madhya vilambit laya*. For example, *bandish* of *raga-hansadhvani* set in *ektal*, composed by Aman Ali Khan '*jai mate vilamb tajde*' and the *bandish* of *raga basant mukhari* set in *jhaptal* '*Prabhu data vidhata*'. As far as Ustad Amir Khan's own style of *bada khayal* is concerned, he applies *ativilambit laya* in *jhumra tal*. In available audio recordings of his vocalism, there are few examples where he has sung *bandishes* of *bada khayal* in *madhya vilambit trital* [like the *tal* applied with *masitkhani gat*], whom he used to sing in *ativilambit jhumra* often. For example, the *bandish* of *raga-malkauns* in *ativilambit jhumra* presented in HMV LP No.IASD1357, '*jinkay mana ram biraje*', he sang it in *madhya vilambit trital* in the program of Akashwani Indore. In the background of such experiments, influence of Aman Ali Khan's style of singing *bada khayal* in *madhya vilambit laya*, might be the reason indirectly. This aspect is about the presentation of *bandish*. Ustad Amir Khan didn't make unnatural efforts to demonstrate the link between *tal* and *swara* in his *gayaki*. He had not adopted Aman Ali Khan's *layakari* in extempore improvisation of *bolbat*.

There is not as much space available for imagination based *raga* improvisation in *madhya vilambit laya* as is available in *ativilambit laya*. The reason for this is that the rotations of *tal* are completed comparatively in short time because of speedy *laya*. Besides, the strokes of *tal* beat coming speedily, the stability of *swaras* and *shant rasa* can not be produced. And if *shant rasa* is tried to be produced intentionally in such *laya*, there being no adjustment with such rhythmic environment, it will appear to be artificial. Hence, the style of Ustad Amir Khan was different from that of Ustad Aman Ali Khan, because he made *bada khayal* a medium of expressing *shant* and *karun rasas*.

There was no distortion of posture and gesture in vocal presentation of Aman Ali Khan. Ustad Amir Khan too was very cautious in keeping his expression natural in his vocalism. In this matter, Ustad Aman Ali Khan might have been an ideal for Ustad Amir Khan, besides other great vocalists.

Special emphasis is laid on *layakari* in Bhindi Bazar Gharana and Aman Ali Khan presented its refined form. His presentation of *drut khayal* full of *laya* is considered equivalent to the steps of dance. As vocal style of Ustad Amir Khan produced *shant rasa*, therefore there was no excitement in his vocalism generated by *layakari*. The stability of *swara* is related to the stability of mind, whereas the result of *layakari* is mobility. Hence the *layakari* is more suitable for *shringar rasa*, *veer rasa* etc. Therefore where the lyrics in which such expressions are found, there the stepping of dance can be discerned also in the presentation of Ustad Amir Khan because of miraculous *laya* parts. Mr. V. H. Deshpande in this way: "In his *madhya laya*, inclining towards *drut laya*, again he makes feel in his *gayaki* the dance like *gayaki* of Bhindi Bazar."[40] But Ustad Amir Khan's *laya* fullness is not due to *bolbat*, speedy word pronunciation or *layakari* with *tihayees*; instead its peculiarity of *laya* lies in stress on particular places in *tans*. He has increasingly applied *tan* salient *swara* phrases even in the basic *swara* compositions of such *bandishes*.

This effect can be seen in his *gayaki* in following *drut bandishes*: -
1. *raga-bilaskhani todi, trital-* 'Bajay Neekay ghungaariya'
2. *Raga-malkauns, trital –* 'Aaj moray ghar aaila balma'
3. *Raga-bihag, trital –* 'Aali ree Albeli'
4. *Raga-hansadhvani, trital –* 'Lagi lagan pati sati sang'.

3- Ustad Abdul wahid Khan and his influence: -

Respectively third main influence on the *gayaki* of Ustad Amir Khan was that of Ustad Abdul Wahid Khan, the famous maestro of Kirana Gharana. Ustad Abdul Wahid Khan was a main representative of Kirana Gharana. His hearing capacity being impaired, he was known as Behre [deaf] Wahid Khan. The eminent Sarangi player of Kolharapur, Khan Saheb Haidar Khan was his *guru* and by relation he was his uncle. He lived with him from his very childhood and received training in music from him. Thus, Abdul Wahid Khan obtained all those *gharanedar* [of *gharana*] music compositions through Haidar Khan, which Haidar Khan had received from the contemporary *binkar*, Bande Ali Khan of Kirana.

---

[40] 'Gharanedar Gayaki'-P.93, 'Indore Aur Amir Khan', Writer: V. H. Deshpande.

After leaving Kolhapur, Wahid Khan lived first in Bombay and thereafter at Lahore and Delhi respectively.

Improvisation of *raga* by *alap*, with gradual movement of *swaras*, is considered to be the specialty of his *gayaki*.[41] His *tans* used to be complex and peculiar. He used to sing prevalent *ragas* such as *malkauns, multani, lalit, darbari kanhada, miyamalhar* etc. He died in 1949, at the age of 78, in Kirana [near Dist. Saharanpur, U.P.].

Having been influenced by Ustad Rajab Ali Khan and Aman Ali Khan, the style developed by Ustad Amir Khan himself was highly influenced by the *gayaki* and the principles of Kirana Gharana; the medium was Ustad Abdul Wahid Khan. While living in Siddique Building [from 1944 to 1951] situated at the crossing of G.B. Road and Ajmeri Gate, old Delhi, Ustad Amir Khan came in contact with Ustad Abdul Wahid Khan. In those days, Ustad Abdul Wahid Khan Usually lived in Delhi and Used to visit this area. This area was the center of many important artists in those days.

Ustad Amir Khan liked the *gayaki* of Ustad Abdul Wahid Khan very much. He was eager to listen to him as much as possible. A vocalist, Ms. Munni Bai, resident of Delhi, was disciple of Abdul Wahid Khan. After being acquainted with Munni Bai, in order to understand Abdul Wahid Khan, Amir Khan adopted the method that he used to be present while Munni Bai took lessons from Abdul Wahid Khan and listened to him. Subsequently, Amir Khan married the same Munni Bai. He always tried to maintain contact and closeness with Ustad Abdul Wahid Khan. He wanted to become host of Abdul Wahid Khan, so that enough opportunity could be availed for mutual discussion about music. Being influenced by his eagerness, curiosity and perseverance, Ustad Abdul Wahid Khan also accepted to become his guest many times and provided him opportunity to understand important factors of his style and thus increased the knowledge and experience of Ustad Amir Khan.

---

[41] On the basis of LP record issued by HMV, containing *raga multani, patdeep* and *darbari*.

Though Ustad Amir Khan got benefited by the *gayaki* and experience of Ustad Abdul Wahid Khan, he didn't give much importance to ceremonial formality of '*ganda bandhan*', nor did Abdul Wahid Khan expect it from him. Despite it, illusion prevails that Amir Khan formally had become disciple of Abdul Wahid Khan. As Ms. Chhaya Bhatnagar wrote in an article: "Afterwards he practiced art becoming disciple of the great musician, Ustad Abdul Wahid Khan Saheb of Kirana Gharana for some time due to which he got new elegance in his *gayaki*."[42]

Two main instances are available which prove wrongness of above statement, which are as follows: -
In an interview given to Ravindra Visht by Ustad Amir Khan, this part is worth paying attention: "I [Ravindra Visht] asked- have you learnt from Abdul Wahid Khan of Kirana Wala? Some people say so. Khan Saheb got a bit angry, when I have listened to him? Once or twice face to face, and from radio. I have adopted method of improvisation from him. The rest of *gayaki* is my own."[43]

The second reference is from an article of Mr. Amique Hanafi. He writes: "the mutual relation of respect and love between Amir Khan Saheb and Wahid Khan Saheb was that of heart and spirit. The ceremonial custom of basic formality of *ganda bandhan* had nothing to do with it. Though Ustad Amir Khan was a man of open heart and mind and was receptive to virtue, available from anywhere; nevertheless due to his individualistic tendency and emphasis on his own style, he was not willing to accept tutelage of any one, other than his father, Ustad Shahmir Khan."[44]

Although Abdul Wahid Khan and Amir Khan didn't give importance to the formality of the *guru* and *shishya* relationship between them, some of the devotees of Abdul

---

[42] 'Sangeet'-March 1985, P.24, 'Sangeet Madhurya Kay Samrat Ustad Amir Khan', Writer: Chhaya Bhatnagar.
[43] 'Sangeet'-January/February 1980, P.18, 'Meri Gayaki Meri Avaz Hay', Writer: Ravindra Visht.
[44] Weekly Dinman-3rd March, 1974, 'Ustad Amir Khan: Tumharay Sharan Ab Kiyo Vishram', Writer: Amique Hanafi.

Wahid Khan wanted that Amir Khan should become his disciple ceremonially. But because of the reasons mentioned above, Amir Khan didn't succumb to their pressure. This information was provided to the author by Mr. Potdar in an interview on 9th April, 1989.

Amir Khan's style of presentation of *vilambit khayal* and the method of *raga* improvisation by *shabdalap* [*alap* with words] was particularly influenced by the vocal style of Ustad Abdul Wahid Khan. In this context, Mr. Krishnarao Majumdar, who was well acquainted with Ustad Amir Khan and also had heard Ustad Abdul Wahid Khan in music concerts, told the author in an interview on 9th April, 1989: "Abdul Wahid Khan had an extraordinary command over *vilambit khayal*. Simply by listening to him, Amir Khan imbibed the *vilambit* style. Also in application of *ativilambit laya* in *bada khayal*, Amir Khan was inspired by Abdul Wahid Khan."

The gradual *raga* improvisation in *vilambit khayal*, which is by movement [*badhat*], is supposed to be main characteristic of vocal style of Kirana Gharana. Abdul Wahid Khan became famous due to being authority on this part. '*badhat*' means presentation of a *raga* by gradual addition of each applied *swara* one by one, showing the role and importance of each *swara* according to the grammar of *raga*. Through this *badhat*, he used to sing a *raga* for long time. Ustad Amir Khan endeavored to imbibe this quality of Abdul Wahid Khan to the maximum, and he was successful in it to a great extent.

The influence of Abdul Wahid Khan on *vilambit khayal* style of Amir Khan brought very significant changes in his style. "The deep impression of *alap-bazee* [the game of *alap*] of Abdul Wahid Khan is found so much on Amir Khan that in his *vilambit khayal*, one can remember Wahid Khan and here he [Amir Khan] completely forgets the danceful *gayaki* inherited from Bhindi Bazar and its *layakari* too [whether it is of *madhya laya*] is not given any opportunity."[45]

---

[45] 'Gharanedar Gayaki'-P.92, 'Indore Aur Amir Khan', Author: V.H. Deshpande.

Alap becomes effective due to *badhat* style and besides it unnecessary repetition is avoided. In the words of Mr. Chetan Karnani: "Amir Khan believed in a simple principle of architectonics known as *badhat*. This is a Kirana Device that he borrowed from Wahid Khan, whereby the musical edifice is built up note by note in observance of the principles of Gestalt Psychology-namely, when you touch the next higher note, an entirely new configuration is formed in relation to the earlier notes. The observance of this principle can be seen in his rendering of *darbari* where in he elaborates the *raga* for about ten minutes using the notes only below the *gandhar* of the middle octave."[46]

As there being a system of *raga* improvisation by *badhat* in Kirana Gharana, its vocal style is *alap* salient. The detailed *alap* is done before *bandish* in *dhrupad gayaki* and *binkari*. Almost similar *alap* is done in Kirana *khayal gayaki* with *tal* after the *sthayee*, including application of words of *bandish*; the reason is that the origin of this style is from the style of *bin* players like Bande Ali Khan. In midst of other factors, the ratio of *alap* was considerably increased in the vocal style of Ustad Amir Khan due to influence of *alap* presentation technique of Ustad Abdul Wahid Khan. The *ragas* where there is more scope for presentation of various *alaps*, were favorite *ragas* of Abdul Wahid Khan and also of Amir Khan, such as: *shuddha kalyan, darbari, malkauns, bhimpalasi, multani, todi, asavari, lalit, miyamalhar, yaman kalyan* etc. While being absorbed in presenting *alap* in such *ragas*, to pass a period of half an hour or more in grave *alap* in complete bass octave and *purvang* of middle octave, is an ordinary thing. The recording of Khan Saheb's *yaman kalyan* preserved with the archive of Akashwani Indore and *shuddha kalyan* rendered in a concert at Bombay, are excellent examples of it.

Being influenced by the Kirana style, Amir Khan adopted many of its *bandishes* also, as for example: *chhota khayal* of *raga darbari*- '*Jhanjhanakwa bajay bichhua*', The *bandish* in *jhaptal madhya laya* of *raga abhogi*- '*Charan ghar aye*', *chhota khayal* in

---

[46] 'Listening to Hindustani Music'-P.86, 'The Lonely Tower: Ustad Amir Khan', Author: Chetan Karnani.

raga shuddha kalyan- 'Mandar bajo', *vilambit khayal* of *raga miyamalhar-* 'Karim naam tero'.

The tradition of tuning the first string of Tanpura with *shuddha nishad* along with singing, instead of *pancham swara*, has started with Kirana Gharana. The followers of this *gharana* opine that the clear sound of *nishad swara* available on Tanpura, creates a peculiar environment full of *swaras*, which helps the vocalists to reach the stage of *samadhi* by means of *swaras*. Ustad Amir Khan also adopted this system. He got prepared a special Tanpura having five strings, which he used in his singing; so that one additional string could be tuned with *shuddha nishad*.

Ustad Abdul Wahid Khan used to sing most of *bada khayals* in *vilambit jhumra tal*, whereas in practice, application of this ancient *tal* was declining. Even as application of *jhumra tal* not being encouraged by the contemporary vocalists, Ustad Amir Khan was not discouraged and by adopting application of *jhumra tal*, he made it alive.

After considering all these influences, although Amir Khan could not receive any systematic and direct training from Ustad Abdul Wahid Khan by becoming his disciple; still by listening only and adding this experience to his thinking, he shaped his style in such a form, wherein qualities of Abdul Wahid Khan were incorporated to a great extent. After listening to Amir Khan from radio, he was very pleased and blessed him in such terms which could be treated no less than a certificate or degree. He said: "I believe that after me, my *gayaki* will remain alive only because of you."[47]

Influence of Hazrat Amir Khusro and his Literature: -
Amir Khusro was born in 1253 A.D. at Patiali, a small town of Etah District of Uttar Pradesh. His father, Amir Mohammed Saisuddin came to India from Khurasan [a city of Iran] and settled in Etah. He was Turkish Muslim and his wife was Hindu.

---

[47] 'Sangeet Kalavihar' [Monthly]-December 1956.

Amir Khusro was a lover of arts and had interest in poetry. In books of history, the name of Amir Khusro is mentioned as Abul Hassan and Hazrat Amir Khusro Rehmatullah Aleh.

After his father's death, Amir Khusro came to Delhi, where he found patronage of Ghayusuddin Balban of Ghulam dynasty. Here he came in contact with artists and literary persons and so his talent got advanced more and more. He also found patronage of Alauddin Khilji [1295-1316 A.D.]. From the decline of Ghulam dynasty to the rise of Tughalak dynasty, he had seen 11 rulers.

Amir Khusro was disciple of famous Sufi saint, Hazarat Nizamuddin Auliya. That is why a clear influence of Sufi philosophy can be seen in his thoughts and literature. He was a man of versatile genius. He expressed his views on the subjects regarding religion, philosophy, grammar, mathematics, science, music etc. Besides being a poet and Sufi saint, his achievements in the field of music are considerable. Thus, his name became permanent in the history. *quol, tarana, quavvali* and *khayal* style are considered his creations. Similarly for instruments, he is considered to be inventor of Sitar and Tabla. He is credited also to have composed certain *ragas* and *tals*. Some of the *ragas* invented by him were born out of the fusion of Iranian music and Indian *ragas*. An Urdu book regarding music, 'Risal-e-Amir Khusro' was written by him, which available with Mohammed Karam Imam, the author of 'Madan-ul-Mousiqui'. For the first time, Amir Khusro applied Iranian '*Usoole-Makam*' [principle of scale] to Indian music, resulting in *mail* or *thaat* system in place of ancient *murchhana* system.

During the reign of Kaikobad and his permission, Amir Khusro wrote 'Kiram Ussaden Masnavi' [ovation of the ruler]. Besides it, he wrote some other books also, such as 'Nuhsipahar', 'Khajainul Futuh', 'Divalrani Khizrakhan' etc. He had also written 'Khalakbari', a collection of poetic creations, wherein synonymous poems of Arabic, Persian and Hindi have been given. He had good knowledge of Persian,

Arabic and prevalent Brij Bhasha. Hence he wrote poems in all those languages. Brij Bhasha was his mother tongue. In addition he had sufficient knowledge of Sanskrit also. His books in prose and verse have been given high place in Persian literature. He had an equal command on Indian and Persian music.

In 1324 A.D., his Ustad [guide], Nizamuddin Auliya passed away. Depressed by his death, Amir Khusro became a recluse and after a year, in 1325 A.D. he left his mortal body. His grave lies beside the grave of Nizamuddin Auliya in Delhi, where Urs [death anniversary of a saint] is celebrated every year.

An all pervading influence of his literary creations on the culture and arts in India can be seen today, even after many centuries of his death. The various classes of society, who were influenced by him knowingly or unknowingly, are mainly poets, thinkers, historians, learned men of Hindi literature, musicians and *quavvals*. In this context, while delivering lecture at Raza College, Rampur [U.P.] in 1966, Acharya Brihaspati says: "Whether may be a poet or critic, whether a thinker paying attention to important aspects of civilization and culture or a ordinary *quavval*, whether an Indian or Pakistani professor writing history of Urdu language or a *pandit* writing glossary of Hindi literature, whether an old lady telling stories and riddles or an expert of music, is not devoid of the influence of Hazrat Amir Khusro, knowingly or unknowingly."[48]

Self made *ragas*, *tals*, singing modes and language style, all these factors collectively have been identified as 'Ilme Khusro' by contemporary Muslims; and subsequently by Hindus as 'Indraprasth Mat'. Looking to such an all pervading influence of Amir Khusro, it was but natural for a person like Amir Khan, a musician and lover of literature to be attracted towards Amir Khusro's ideology, literature and philosophy and to prosecute his studies towards it.

---

[48] 'Sangeet'-February 1966, P.5, 'Amir Khusro'-an article read by Acharya Brihaspati at Raza College, Rampur.

Amir Khan Saheb was fond of poetry and was very much interested in Urdu and Persian literature. A poet, Mr. Bismil Sayeedi was his friend at Delhi. And at Calcutta, Mr. N. Rashid Khan who was well versed in Hindi, Urdu, Persian, Bangla and English languages, was in close contact with him. Exchange of ideas on various aspects of Urdu and Persian literature used to continue with these literate persons. The role of Khusro in music and his works were the main subjects of discussion under this exchange of ideas.

Ustad Amir Khan often used to say: "Music becomes more expressive if words are sung with feeling. The poetic aspect of *khayal* is as much important as its *raga* aspect. If an artist wants to become a good musician, it is necessary for him to have poetic imagination."[49]

The above view expressed by Ustad Amir Khan shows the influence of Amir Khusro on him, because in the Indian history Khusro is such a two fold individual in the Indian history, who played very important role in the fields, poetry and music.

Ustad Amir Khan had opinion that the *khayal* of today and its *bandishes* have deviated from its original form. In this context, he used to present references from the history, about the origin of *khayal* and other vocal styles by Amir Khusro, their purpose and form. Whatever study he made about Amir Khusro, he derived following conclusion about him:
"Khusro invented *quol, kalbana, naksh, gul, tarana* and *khayal*; out of these the first four remained confined to tombs, only *tarana* and *khayal* could come out."[50]

---

[49] Nai Dunia-29 March 1989, 'Unhone Lokranjan Kee Sharton Se Samjhota Nahin Kiya' [He didn't compromise with the conditions for public entertainment], Writer: Mohan Nadkarni.
[50] 'Sangeet'-November 1971, P.25 & 34, 'Sangeet Sadhakon Se Bhent: Ustad Amir Khan', Writer: Shambhunath Mishra.

In another statement, he said: "Amir Khusro made the *drut* part of *khayal* and Sultan Husain made *vilambit*."[51]

From the above statement of Amir Khan saheb, it becomes clear that along with other vocal styles [which subsequently extinct from Hindustani music], he considered Amir Khusro the inventor of *khayal* and *tarana* styles. About the origin of above vocal styles, Acharya Brihaspati expresses his view, referring to the Urdu book 'Maodanul Mousiquee', written by Hakim Mohammed Karam Imam,: "Karam Imam himself has said that Amir Khusro had made prevalent *khayal, quol, kalbana, naksh, gul* and *tarana* in place of Hindustani *dhrupad, doha, matha, chhand, prabandh* and *kavitta*."[52]

Mr. Haldhar Prasad Singh 'Indu', in an article about Khusro, has credited him with the origin of *khayal* and *tarana*. The quotation in this reference is as follows: "Among his [Amir Khusro's] vocal styles *ghazal, quavvali, tarana, khayal* etc are very much in vogue."[53]

About the creation of *khayal* and *tarana* by Khusro, the ideas of Ustad Amir Khan and the prevalent views are almost same.

Ustad Amir Khan didn't consider *khayal* style simply a means of entertainment; therefore he didn't like *bandishes* of *khayal* replete with obscene and amorous poetry. If he himself composed any *bandishes*, all were of *bhakti rasa* [devotional sentiments]; otherwise he sang poetry of Sufi saints giving them the form of *khayal bandish*. For example, see the first two lines of a *rubayee* of Sufi poet, Sarmad Shahid, which were sung by Ustad Amir Khan in *raga priya kalyan*:

"*Sarmad! gham-e ishque bul-hawas ra na dihand.*

---

[51] 'Sangeet'-December 1976, P.26, 'Sangeet Jagat Kay Amir: Ustad Amir Khan', Writer: Madanlal Vyas.
[52] 'Sangeet'-February 1966, P.12, 'Amir Khusro'-an article read by Acharya Brihaspati at Raza College, Rampur.
[53] 'Sangeet'-April 1962, P.53, 'Kavi-Sangeetagya Khusro', Writer: Haldhar Prasad Singh 'Indu'.

Soz-e-dil-e-parwana magas ra na dihand."

The sense of this is- "Sarmad! The grief of love can not be imparted to every one, as the compassion of a lamp insect can not be imparted to a fly."

Similarly Ustad Amir Khan presented Persian *rubayees* also in other *ragas* in the form of *bada khayal*, such as written by Hafiz: '*Salahbar kuja va*' in *raga purvi* and '*Shahaje karam*' of Hafiz in *raga yaman*.

Ustad Amir Khan has mostly applied *jhumra tal* in *vilambit khayal*. There are total 14 beats in this *tal*, which are divided in four parts of 3-4-3-4. As has already been mentioned that Amir Khan sang his *vilambit khayals* set in *jhumra tal*, like Ustad Abdul Wahid Khan of Kirana Gharana. Besides, this fact is also worth considering that Ustad Amir Khan had tendency to make efforts for revival of the modes invented by Khusro. It is believed that Khusro had invented 17 *tals*, which include *jhumra* and *soolfakhta*, which were vanishing from vogue.

The information given by Acharya Brihaspati, about 17 *tals* of Khusro, is as follows: "According to Karam Imam, Hazarat Amir Khusro invented 17 *tals* on the basis of Persian *behars* [meters], the names of which are *pashto, jobhar, quavvali, soolfakhta [usool fakhta], jat, jalad, tritala, savari, aadachautala, jhumra, zananisavari [jamani savari], dastan, khams, farodast, kaid, pehalvan, pat* and *champak*."[54]

The basic form of *tal jhumra* is given below: -

Tal jhumra-

dhin	'-dha'	'tirakita'	dhin	dhin	'dhagay'	'tirakita'
X			2			
tin	'-ta'	'tirakita'	dhin	dhin	'dhagay'	'tirakita'
0			3			

---

[54] 'Sangeet'-February 1966, P.12, 'Amir Khusro'-an article read by Acharya Brihaspati at Raza College, Rampur.

Ustad Amir Khan applied *jhumra* in *bada khayal* of *ativilambit laya*. Hence some times in the place of additional pause of half beat, coming after the first and the eighth beat, all the beats were allotted equal duration, so that the Tabla accompanist should not feel inconvenience.

It is believed that Amir Khusro created many *ragas* by fusing the Iranian and the Indian music systems. Among the *ragas* performed by Ustad Amir Khan, in them *sarparda, yaman [iman], puriya, todi, purvi, suha, shahana [bashit shahana]* and *sugharayee* are such *ragas* which are believed to have been invented by Amir khusro. The information available regarding *ragas* invented by Amir Khusro is as follows: -
1- *jeelaf,* 2- *rajgiri,* 3- *sarparda,* 4- *yaman,* 5- *rat ki purya,* 6- *barari,* 7- *todi,* 8- *purvi,* 9- *suha,* 10- *hua,* 11- *bashit shahana,* 12- *sughrai,* 13- *usyak,* 14- *bakharja,* 15- *munam,* 16- *nigar.*

The most influence of philosophy and literature of Khusro was on the *tarana* style of Ustad Amir Khan. Ustad Amir Khan believed that *tarana* was invented by Amir Khusro. In this context, he had been curious and inquisitive for long for the purpose of bringing out clear and authentic facts and for research about *tarana* and in-depth meaning of its words. He kept under consideration the prevalent various opinions and historical facts also regarding *tarana*. Thus he became the first modern vocalist who tended to make a research about *tarana*, keeping a different point of view. In this context, one of his own recollections is worth mentioning: -

"I often heard from persons that *tarana* had no meaning. I thought that I should search for every thing about *tarana*. There was a poet friend, Bismil Sayeedi at Delhi. One day he made me hear a *sawayee* [a type of poetry] written by Khusro. It is said amongst us that when an effigy of Adam was created, the soul was ordered to enter it. But the soul was not ready to enter in to that place. Then Hazarat Daud recited a *lehan* [melody] to the soul. Then the soul became so rapt that it entered in to the effigy. On this he told a *rubayee*:
'*Anroz ke ruhe-pak ke Adam babadan,*

Har chand daranami sudastar sabadan,

Khanand palayka balhane-Daud,

Das-das dartan darad dartan-dartan'

I felt that *tarana* began from here. '*Na dir dani to dani*' is a sort of *jap* [devotional words], which were repeated by Sufis during the state of 'Haal' [deep meditation]. I continued to think and to search."[55]

The findings on *tarana* presented by him became a topic of discussion among musicians, musicologists and critics. In this regard, the opinion of music reviewer, Chandrakantlal Das is as follows: "After research, the findings about *tarana* presented by Ustad Amir Khan are logical and reliable."[56]

Ustad Amir Khan was not ready to accept that *tarana* should be considered a type of singing of meaningless words, the application of which could be made for the word pronunciation to demonstrate tongue skill in fast *laya* and to show various acrobatics of voice in the *laya* increasing continuously. He believed that the *tarana* invented by Khusro, was full of spiritualism in its original form. The meaningful words of Arabic and Persian were applied in repetition, like the words of '*jap*'. This method of *jap* is called '*virad*' in the terminology of Sufis. Besides, the Persian poetry was placed as *antara*. That is, *tarana* was a medium for a devotee to identify himself with God. later on the vocalists who had no knowledge of Arabic and Persian languages, changed the form of this vocal style and filled the sounds of Tabla and pakhavaj in place of Persian poetry occurring in *antara* and made the words of *tarana* meaningless. Amique Hanafi illustrates the link between devotion of Sufis to God and *tarana* as follows: "His [Amir Khan's] view was that the form of *tarana* was established by '*zikra*' [illustration], the specific devotion of Sufis. As Sufis recite the name of God repeatedly in '*zikra*', in the same way also in *tarana* there is repetition

---

[55] 'Sangeet'-November 1971, P.25, 'Sangeet Sadhakon Say Bhent-Ustad Amir Khan', Interviewer: Shambhunath Mishra.
[56] 'Sangeet'-May 1973, 'Ustad Amir Khan Aur Unki Kala', Writer: Prof. Chandrakantlal Das.

of words. Amir Khan Saheb thought that the words of *tarana* were mystical forms of Arabic and Persian words."[57]

In order to prove that the prevalent words of *tarana* are distorted form of Arabic and Persian words, by his research Ustad Amir Khan presented Arabic and Persian words having similarity with the words of *tarana*. The list of such words along with their meanings, is as follows: -

Dar tan aa	Enter into the body
Nadir dani	You know the most
Tan dar dani	Who knows all of inner
Dara	Come inside
Tanandara	Enter into the body
Tom	I belong to you
Odani	He [God] knows
Tudani	You know
E-la-layee	Aye! Ali
Yalalla	Oh! God
Yalalli	Oh! Ali

Besides the above list, *ala, alhila, lilla, alalum* etc are words indicative of God; the original word of which is '*Allah*' [God].

The eminent vocalist and researcher of music, Dr. Prabha Atre's conception of *tarana* is sufficiently similar to that of Ustad Amir Khan, which is confirmed from a part of her article: -

"There had been a great musician named Amir Khusro, in 13th century, who gifted five types of vocal modes of devotional sentiment, namely *quol, kalbana, nakshe-gul,*

---

[57] Weekly Dinman-3rd March, 1974, P.36, 'Ustad Amir Khan-Tumharay Sharan Ab Kiyo Vishram', Writer: Amique Hanafi.

tarana to the world of music. Subsequently all became extinct, except the *tarana*, and the form of *tarana* has also changed. The origin of *tarana* was from meaningful words, such as '*dar aa tanam*' means 'you come into my body' and '*yo allah*' whose form was changed to '*yalali-yalali*'. Later on the artists, who were unable to understand meaning of these words, pronounced them wrongly and made it the vocal style of meaningless words."[58]

In the context of basic form of *tarana* vocal style created by Khusro, opinion of Ustad Amir Khan is how much near to the fact, it would be proper to consider the *bandishes* composed by Khusro and are traditionally presented by *quavvals*.

On the basis of a statement in Hadis of Arabic language, Khusro composed a *bandish* giving it the form of Hindustani music, which is sung by *quavvals* even today. The *quavvals* of modern age like Shankar-Shambhu of India and Sabari brothers of Pakistan have sung it.

"*man kunto molah fa Ali molah*
Dir tum na na na-na na na na-
Le ala li aala li allilalah
Ya lalal lali alali ya lale.
man kunto molah fa Ali molah"[59]

In the first line of above *bandish*, describing the greatness of Hazrat Ali [son-in-law Prophet Mohammed and a caliph of Muslims], Prophet himself says: 'Of whose Molah I am, Ali is his Molah'. Rest of the words of lines of *bandish* are the same kind, whom Ustad Amir Khan says to be similar to the '*jap*' of Sufis.

There seems to be some similarity between the words of *tarana* and *bols* of *gat* of Sitar. Hence, it is also said that the influence of Sitar playing style might have been

---
[58] 'Sangeet'-November 1967, P.29, 'Bhartiya Sangeet Kee Do Shailiyan', Writer: Dr. Prabha Atre.
[59] Urdu monthly-'Aajkal'-August 956, article 'Quavvali', Writer: Maikash Akbarabadi.

on *tarana* presentation. When Ustad Amir Khan's opinion was sought about it, he opined that since the Sitar and *tarana*, both were created by Amir Khusro, it is but natural that a similarity can be seen between the two. According to his opinion, the technique of Sitar playing developed by Amir Khusro is the result of the same words, on the basis of which *tarana* came into existence.

Ustad Amir Khan thinks that Amir Khusro might have composed many *bandishes* of *tarana* also, as he was a top poet of Persian language and he played an important role as a composer of music. Here it is also to be noticed that Pt. Vishnu Narayan Bhatkhande's 'Kramik Pustak Malika' contains such traditional *bandishes* of *tarana*, in whose *antaras* the *rubayees* of Khusro are present. For example, an *antara* of a *tarana* in *raga-kafi* is present, whose words are as follows: -
"*Khalke main goyad ke khusro*
Butparasti main kunad
Aare aare main kunadwa
Khalke mara karnestan"[60]

The style of *tarana* may be prevalent at the time of Amir Khusro, considering it as basic form of *tarana* and to revive the tradition of Khusro, Ustad Amir Khan himself started creating *bandishes* of *tarana*.

There is a *bandish* of Khusro, called '*kalbana*', which is sung by vocalists of Sufi tradition. Ustad Amir Khan introduced it again in the classical music. '*Kalbana*' is a form of Sufi poetry, which is concerned with soul and God and is presented in the form of *quavvali*. Pt. Amarnath gave following definition of *kalbana*: -
"Qalbaanaa: Qalab is the word for soul in Urdu. Qalbaanaa, the Sufi verse relating specifically to the soul, is sung in Quwaalee style."[61]

---
[60] 'Kramik Pustak Malika'-Vol-2, P.337, *raga-kafi*, Author: Vishnu Narayan Bhatkhande.
[61] 'Living Idioms in Hindustani Music: A Dictionary of Terms and Terminology'-P.89, Author: Pt. Amarnath.

Ustad Amir Khan has sung the above *bandish* in *madhya laya ektal* setting it in *raga-darbari*, which is as follows: -

Sthayee: -
Yare-man biya biya
Dartan tadeem tananana deem tom tananana
Antara: -
Balabam rasida janam
Tubiya ke zindamanam
Pas azan ke man na manam
Bachekar khwahi aamad.

Translation: -
Sthayee: -
My friend! Come come,
Come into my body.
Antara: -
My life has come to the lips
You come so that I may live
If I will not survive,
What will be the use
Of your coming afterwards.

Here Khusro, giving the simile of lover and beloved between the soul and God, has given compassionate expression of separation. In the *tarana* of *raga-jog* composed by Ustad Amir Khan, a *rubayee* of Khusro has been applied. Its words are as follows: -

"*Basast keemate Khusro ke goyee*
Ghulame rai-e-gani e mane ab"

For the purpose to give practical shape to the ideas had by Ustad Amir Khan about meaningfulness of words of *tarana*, in addition to Khusro, he also applied poetry of other Persian poets in *bandishes* of his *tarana* and paid special attention to select poems suitable to the sentiment of the *raga*. For example, following *rubayee* of famous Persian poet, Hafiz, was sung in the *tarana* of *raga-megha*: -
"*Abre tar, sehne chaman,*
Bulbulo gul, fasle bahar,
Saki o mutaribo main,
Yar bashane gulzar."

In addition to above mentioned *taranas*, he sang *rubayeedar taranas* in other *ragas*; such as-*hansadhwani, shuddhakalyan, malkauns, chandrakauns, suha* etc. Explaining the meaning of '*rubayeedar tarana*', Pt. Amarnath writes: "*rubaaee* is a complete expression of poetic thought, in one or two couplets; and the *taraanaas* in which *rubaaees* are sung are known as *rubaaeedaar taraanaas*."[62]

On the basis of his distinct opinion about *tarana* described above, Ustad Amir Khan had also written an article in the magazine, 'Music-East and West', published by Indian Council for Cultural Relations. In order to give shape to his ideas practically, whatever efforts he made, resulted in influencing the frame of *bandish* of *tarana* and other elements of improvisation [*alap, sargam, tan* etc], and a distinct style of *tarana gayaki* came into being. Like *khayal*, meanings of words and sentiments were also given importance in it. So much so that some times *tarana* became an alternative to *drut khayal* in his vocalism. Considering this distinct style of *tarana*, Dr. Prabha Atre throws light on the *tarana* vocal style as follows: -
"At present generally we get to hear two types of *tarana*. There is one concept of *tarana* of its own, which means to increase the *laya* and to improvise it with *Sitar ang*

---

[62] 'Living Idioms in Hindustani Music: a Dictionary of Terms and Terminology'-P.89, Author: Pt. Amarnath.

[Sitar pattern]. The second is to present *tarana* like *drut khayal*. In it, *alap-tan ang* is more."[63]

It can be concluded that the specialties which are found in the *tarana gayaki* of Ustad Amir Khan, deviating from the contemporary form, were made possible due to influence of Khusro on his thinking. He had high regard for Khusro. He used to listen to *quavvali* with interest and considered it a musical mode invented by Khusro. He used to go to the tomb of Amir Khusro to pay his homage.

Merukhand System Mentioned by Sharangdev in 'Sangeet Ratnakar': -

The life span of Sharangdev is said to be from 1175 AD to 1247 AD. His grand father, Bhaskar, left Kashmir and went towards /South India in search of patronage. Father of Sharangdev, Shodhal, found patronage from the first ruler of Yadav dynasty, Bhillama, at Dolatabad. Sharangdev himself was working on the post of Auditor General during the reign of Yadav Ruler, Sinhdev [1212 AD to 1247 AD]. He was musicologist, expert in Ayurveda and scholar of Vedanta. He wrote a book on music in Sanskrit, named 'Sangeet Ratnakar'. This book contains abstract of findings of the contemporary scholars and description of prevalent music during the period of Sharangdev. Among the ancient books of Sanskrit, this is the last such book which has been accorded equal importance in both classical music systems of the south and the north. Commentaries on this profound book were written in Sanskrit by Sinh Bhoopal [14th century] and by Kallinath [15th century], and in Telgu by Vitthal.

This book is divided into seven chapters, in which *swara, raga, prakirnata* [dispersion], *prabandh* [composition], *tal,* instruments and dance have been discussed. Applying the mathematical principle of permutation on the *swaras* of music, Ustad Amir Khan used the system of *merukhand* in *raga* improvisation and *tan* creation, the theoretical original source of which is the same book, 'Sangeet Ratnakar'.

---

[63] 'Sangeet'-November 1967, P.28, 'Bhartiya Sangeet Kee Do Shailiyan*', Writer: Dr. Prabha Atre.*

Written originally in Sanskrit, Hindi translation of this book was published in 1968 in two volumes. In the fourth chapter of first volume of this Hindi translation, '*Gram, murchhana* Kram, *Tan* prakaran', I have concentrated on *tan, prastar* [spread], principle of *prastar*, *khandmeru*, the form of *khandmeru*, finding of *tan* by *khandmeru*, types of *tan* etc; because *khandmeru* system of Ustad Amir Khan is related to this. The following important points can be discerned from this chapter of the book, whereby the theoretical aspect of Amir Khan's *merukhand* system can be made clear.

1- *koottan*: - By making permutation in the order of *swaras*, the obtained variations of *tan* are called '*koottan*'. By this permutation or changing of order, the form of *tan* becomes complex. Hence, a complex *tan* is generally called *koottan* ['*koot*' means 'complex']. Dr. Ashok D. Ranade, in his book, tells about *koottan* of Sharangdev as follows: -

"*Tan*, as it was understood in the early and medieval phase of musical development was in fact a *murchhana* characterized by a predetermined omission of a note or two. The resulting pattern was, according to Bharata, a *murchhana-tan*. In the event the sequence of notes in a *murchhana* was after a special type of *tan* called *kut-tan* resulted."[64]

Keeping stable the quality of his voice, by means of this change of order in *swaras*, Ustad Amir Khan made the basis of producing variety in *tan* and *sargam*, however he did not used the word '*koottan*' for his *tans*.

2- 5040 *Koottans* and their Method of Spreading: - 5040 *Koottans* are produced out of seven *swaras*. The mathematical method to find out the total number of permutations of the articles of certain number is to gradually multiply numbers from one to that certain number, such as for seven *swaras*: 1x2x3x4x5x6x7=5040.

---

[64] 'Maharashtra Art Music'-P.25, 'The Musico-literary Scene: The Yadavas', Writer: Dr. Ashok D. Ranade.

This mathematical method of *koot tan* has been called *swara prastar*. In the words of Pt. Omkarnath Thakur: "One, two, three, four, five, six or seven *swaras*, which can be placed in different orders, they all fall under *swara prastar*. The basis of *swara prastar* is the rule of mathematics, called permutation and combination."[65]

By means of different number of *swaras*, following *swara prastars* are obtained: -

Number of *Swaras*	Number of *Swara Prastars*
Archik [one *swara*] *swara prastar*	1 x 1 = 1
Gathik [two *swaras*] *swara prastar*	1 x 2 = 2
Samik [three *swaras*] *swara prastars*	2 x 3 = 6
Swarantar [four *swaras*] *swara prastars*	6 x 4 = 24
Audhav [five *swaras*] *swara prastars*	24 x 5 = 120
Shadhav [six *swaras*[*swara prastars*	120 x 6 = 720
Sampurn [seven *swaras*] *swara prastars*	720 x 7 = 5040

The *swara prastars* of different number of *swaras* are formed as under. While making permutations, it is necessary to keep in mind that none of the *prastars* should be repeated, nor any left out. Hence, one should go ahead by adopting a certain order.

In a *swara prastar* of one *swara*, as there is only one *swara*, there will be only one *swara prastar*; because there is no possibility of changing the order. Two *swaras* will form two *prastars*. For the first time, both the *swaras* will be placed in ascending order and next time in descending order. For example: *sa re – re sa*.

While making six *prastars* by three *swaras*, from basic *swara* phrase *sa re ga, ga, re* and *sa* placing at the end, and placing remaining two *swaras* first in ascending and then in descending order, six *swara prastars* will be formed as: 1. *sa re ga*, 2. *re sa*

---

[65] 'Sangeetanjali'-Vol.V, P.117, 'Varna, Alankar, Tan, Swara Prastar', Author: Pt. Omkarnath Thakur.

ga, 3. *sa ga re*, 4. *ga sa re*, 5. *re ga sa*, 6. *ga re sa*. The first two *prastars* of these six *prastars*, the last *swara* of the basic *swara* phrase *sa re ga*, or the *swara* of right hand side, *ga* will be kept stable at the end and thus two *prastars* will be formed. Afterwards the second of the *swaras* from right hand side, *re* is kept stable at the end and two *prastars* are formed. In the last, the third and last of the *swaras* from the right hand side, *sa* is kept at the end and thus last two *prastars* are formed.

By changing the order of four *swaras*, twenty four *prastars* are formed. In the first six *prastars*, the last *swara* of basic *swara* phrase, *sa re ga ma*, will stay at the end and six *prastars* of the three *swaras*, *sa re ga*, will be added before it. Then keeping the *swara*, *ga*, at the end, the six *prastars* of three *swaras*, *sa re ma*, will be added before it and will form next six *prastars* of four *swaras*. Similarly keeping *re* at the end, six *prastars* will be made of *sa ga ma,* by changing their order and the last six *prastars* will be created by keeping *sa* at the end and changing the order of *re ga ma*. Twenty four *prastars* of four *swaras* are as follows: -

01	sa re ga ma	13	sa ga ma re
02	re sa ga ma	14	ga sa ma re
03	sa ga re ma	15	sa ma ga re
04	ga sa re ma	16	ma sa ga re
05	re ga sa ma	17	ga ma sa re
06	ga re sa ma	18	ma ga sa re
07	sa re ma ga	19	re ga ma sa
08	re sa ma ga	20	ga re ma sa
09	re ma sa ga	21	re ma ga sa
10	ma sa re ga	22	ma re ga sa
11	re ma sa ga	23	ga ma re sa
12	ma re sa ga	24	ma ga re sa

While making 120 *prastars* of the five *swaras, sa re ga ma pa*, the same method will be adopted, that is from the original order, one *swara* will be taken from the right side and will be kept stable at the end of the *prastar*; before it, twenty four *prastars* of four *swara* will be added. The twenty four *prastars* formed out of the remaining four *swaras*, the order will be same, that is from the right side of the original order, every *swara* [before the last *swara* in five *swara*], will be kept stable at the end six times. To sum up, every *swara* will be kept stable at the end or at the right side of the *prastar*, twenty four times, at the second place from right side six times and at the third place two times. The 120 *prastars* of the five *swaras* are formed in that order as on next page.

120 *Prastars* of five *Swaras*

	Prastars ending with *pa*		*Prastars* ending with *ma*		*Prastars* ending with *ga*
001	sa re ga ma pa	025	sa re ga pa ma	049	sa re ma pa ga
002	re sa ga ma pa	026	re sa ga pa ma	050	re sa ma pa ga
003	sa ga re ma pa	027	sa ga re pa ma	051	sa ma re pa ga
004	ga sa re ma pa	028	ga sa re pa ma	052	ma sa re pa ga
005	re ga sa ma pa	029	re ga sa pa ma	053	re ma sa pa ga
006	ga re sa ma pa	030	ga re sa pa ma	054	ma re sa pa ga
007	sa re ma ga pa	031	sa re pa ga ma	055	sa re pa ma ga
008	re sa ma ga pa	032	re sa pa ga ma	056	re sa pa ma ga
009	sa ma re ga pa	033	sa pa re ga ma	057	sa pa re ma ga
010	ma sa re ga pa	034	pa sa re ga ma	058	pa sa re ma ga
011	re ma sa ga pa	035	re pa sa ga ma	059	re pa sa ma ga
012	ma re sa ga pa	036	pa re sa ga ma	060	pa re sa ma ga
013	sa ga ma re pa	037	sa ga pa re ma	061	sa ma pa re ga
014	ga sa ma re pa	038	ga sa pa re ma	062	ma sa pa re ga
015	sa ma ga re pa	039	sa pa ga re ma	063	sa pa ma re ga
016	ma sa ga re pa	040	pa sa ga re ma	064	pa sa ma re ga
017	ga ma sa re pa	041	ga pa sa re ma	065	ma pa sa re ga
018	ma ga sa re pa	042	pa ga sa re ma	066	pa ma sa re ga
019	re ga ma sa pa	043	re ga pa sa ma	067	re ma pa sa ga
020	ga re ma sa pa	044	ga re pa sa ma	068	ma re pa sa ga
021	re ma ga sa pa	045	re pa ga sa ma	069	re pa ma sa ga
022	ma re ga sa pa	046	pa re ga sa ma	070	pa re ma sa ga
023	ga ma re sa pa	047	ga pa re sa ma	071	ma pa re sa ga
024	ma ga re sa pa	048	pa ga re sa ma	072	pa ma re sa ga

	Prastars* ending with *re		***Prastars* ending with *sa***
073	*sa ga ma pa re*	097	*re ga ma pa sa*
074	*ga sa ma pa re*	098	*ga re ma pa sa*
075	*sa ma ga pa re*	099	*re ma ga pa sa*
076	*ma sa ga pa re*	100	*ma re ga pa sa*
077	*ga ma sa pa re*	101	*ga ma re pa sa*
078	*ma ga sa pa re*	102	*ma ga re pa sa*
079	*sa ga pa ma re*	103	*re ga pa ma sa*
080	*ga sa pa ma re*	104	*ga re pa ma sa*
081	*sa pa ga ma re*	105	*re pa ga ma sa*
082	*pa sa ga ma re*	106	*pa re ga ma sa*
083	*ga pa sa ma re*	107	*ga pa re ma sa*
084	*pa ga sa ma re*	108	*pa ga re ma sa*
085	*sa ma pa ga re*	109	*re ma pa ga sa*
086	*ma sa pa ga re*	110	*ma re pa ga sa*
087	*sa pa ma ga re*	111	*re pa ma ga sa*
088	*pa sa ma ga re*	112	*pa re ma ga sa*
089	*ma pa sa ga re*	113	*ma pa re ga sa*
090	*pa ma sa ga re*	114	*pa ma re ga sa*
091	*ga ma pa sa re*	115	*ga ma pa re sa*
092	*ma ga pa sa re*	116	*ma ga pa re sa*
093	*ga pa ma sa re*	117	*ga pa ma re sa*
094	*pa ga ma sa re*	118	*pa ga ma re sa*
095	*ma pa ga sa re*	119	*ma pa ga re sa*
096	*pa ma ga sa re*	120	*pa ma ga re sa*

To form 720 *prastars* of six *swaras*, from right side of the original order, each *swara* is kept stable one by one at the end and 120 *prastars* of remaining five *swaras* are added before it. The *prastar* method of five *swaras* has been explained previously. In the *prastars* of six *swaras*, *dha* will be placed at the end of first 120, *pa* will be placed at the end in next 120 and then *ma, ga, re* and *sa swara* will be placed at the end respectively; thus 20 x 6 = 720 *prastars* will be formed by six *swaras*. Exactly the same method will be applied for the *prastars* of seven *swaras*, that is, *ni, dha, pa, ma, ga, re* and *sa* will be kept stable at the end respectively and every time 720 *prastars* of remaining six *swaras* will be added before it. Thus, 720 x 7 = 5040 *sampurna prastars* of seven *swaras* will be formed.

After understanding the method of permutation by change of order in phrases of different number of *swara*, an important thing comes to light that maximum part of the original of *swara* phrase is kept stable as much as possible and change in order is started in rest of it and gradually the entire order starts changing. The maximum part of *swara* phrase from right side is kept stable and the change of order starts from two initial *swaras* of left side, because the ascending order must precede the descending order. We can demonstrate this by making some *prastars* of seven *swaras*: -

1) *sa re ga ma pa dha ni*
2) *re sa ga ma pa dha ni*
3) *sa ga re ma pa dha ni*
4) *ga sa re ma pa dha ni*
5) *re ga sa ma pa dha ni*
6) *ga re sa ma pa dha ni*
7) *sa re ma ga pa dha ni*
8) *re sa ma ga pa dha ni*
9) *sa ma re ga pa dha ni*

It is clear from above permutations that in first two permutations, except the initial two *swara*, other five *swaras* [*ga ma pa dha ni*] remain in their original order. Thereafter, from third to sixth *prastar*, *ma pa dha ni* remained stable in the end. In seventh and eighth *prastar*, *ma* was included in process of change of order and only *pa dha ni* remained stable in original order. In this way, the process of change of order begins from left and reaches gradually to the right and ends at 5040th permutation *ni dha pa ma ga re sa*. Thus a straight descending order is obtained. No *swara* can be used more than once in any permutation.

In 'Sangeet Ratnakar', a table of *khandmeru* has been shown based on numbers, which is used in the process of '*Nashta*' and '*Uddishta*'. The meaning of *nashta* and *Uddishta* is given in 'Sangeet Ratnakar' as follows: -

"*Khandmeru* is helpful to find out following *tans*: -
1. *Uddishta tan-* to find out order of a given *tan* in the *swara prastar*.
2. *Nashta tan-* to find out the form of a *tan* of a particular serial number in *swara prastars*."[66]

Here it is not required to explain in detail the above procedure of *nashta* and *uddishta* because the change in order of *swaras*, applied in the vocal style of Ustad Amir Khan, is specifically related to permutation method only and not to the serial numbers of permutations. Now a days, the same method of permutation is known by the name of *merukhand, meerkhand, merkhand, sumerkhand, khandmeru, swara prastar* etc. It has gained importance in the field of applied music because on the basis of mathematics, the maximum number of *swara* phrases and *swara* combinations, which can be obtained from a certain number of *swaras* suitable to *raga*, could be taken into consideration. Pt. Amarnath has defined the *merukhand* system as follows: -

---

[66] 'Sangeet Ratnakar'-Vol.I, P.50, Chapter 4, 'Gram, Murchhana Kram, Tan Prakaran', Author: Acharya Sharangdev, Translator: Lakshmi Narayan Garg.

Merukhand- "Meru means spine; Khand means portion. The *merukhand* system discussed in the Sangeeta Ratnaakara by Sharangadeva is a mathematical ordering of notes through which 5040 taans are possible in seven notes."[67]

The extent to which Ustad Amir Khan has accepted influence of *khandmeru* of 'Sangeet Ratnakar' on his *gayaki*, is explained by Mr. Mohan Nadkarni in his book as follows: -

"Ustad himself claimed that he represented the *merukhand* style of vocalism, mentioned in 'Sangeet Ratnakar', a classical Sanskrit treatise of the famous Sharangdev of fourteenth century."[68]

Here it is to be noted that in above statement, the period of Sharangdev has been mentioned as of fourteenth century, which is not correct, actually it is thirteenth century. Whereas in the fourteenth century and afterward, some commentaries were written on this book.

Ustads of Bhindi Bazar Gharana used to study the classical music of the South and they adopted some of its elements for their style. They obtained this *merukhand* system too from the South. Thus this system of 'Sangeet Ratnakar' reached to Ustad Amir Khan indirectly.

In the context of training of *merukhand* received by inheritance and refinements done as per his own judgment, Ustad Amir Khan says: "For the knowledge of *swara* and for *riyaz*, practice of *aroha-avaroha* [ascending-descending] is the first step. In our system, there are 360 *alankars* and 5040 *paltas* of *merukhand*. To remember all of them orally is very difficult, if not impossible. Therefore I have prepared 168 *swara mailas*. The constant practice of them provides base to a great extent."[69]

---

[67] 'Living Idioms in Hindustani Music: a Dictionary of Terms and Terminology'-P.74, Author: Pt. Amarnath.
[68] 'Madhyavarti'-P.36, 'Amirkhani Shaili', Author: Mohan Nadkarni.
[69] 'Sangeet'-December 1976, P.115, 'Sangeet Jagat Kay Amir: Ustad Amir Khan', Writer: Madanlal Vyas.

Here it is to be noted that in the above quotation, the word *'maila'* is synonymous with the word 'combination'. It is not related to the *thaats* of seven notes having *shuddha-vikrit* forms.

The above mentioned 168 *swara* combinations are formed by combining four-four *swaras* as under: -

There will be 24 permutations with four *swaras*, *sa re ga ma*, which has been described previously under '5040 *Koottans* and their Method of Spreading'.

The second *swara* phrase will be *re ga ma pa* and its 24 permutations will also be formed as under:

01	re ga ma pa	13	re ma pa ga
02	ga re ma pa	14	ma re pa ga
03	re ma ga pa	15	re pa ma ga
04	ma re ga pa	16	pa re ma ga
05	ga ma re pa	17	ma pa re ga
06	ma ga re pa	18	pa ma re ga
07	re ga pa ma	19	ga ma pa re
08	ga re pa ma	20	ma ga pa re
09	re pa ga ma	21	ga pa ma re
10	pa re ga ma	22	pa ga ma re
11	ga pa re ma	23	ma pa ga re
12	pa ga re ma	24	pa ma ga re

Thereafter carrying forward the same procedure, 24 permutations of *ga ma pa dha*, 24 permutations of *ma pa dha ni*, 24 permutations of *pa dha ni Sa*, 24 permutations of *dha ni Sa Re* and in the 24 permutations of *ni Sa Re Ga* will be formed.

By mixed application of these permutations, Ustad Amir Khan created a treasure of *badhat*, *raga* improvisation and *sargam*.

By including the *shuddha-vikrit swaras* according to the *raga*, Ustad Amir Khan prepared *audhav* permutations of five *swaras*, and by practicing it, made the base of his *gayaki*. Mathematically, only 120 permutations can be formed of five *swaras*, which automatically include 24 permutations of four *swaras* and six permutations of three *swaras*. But when Amir Khan made them suitable to *raga*, they constituted an indefinite number. Because of change in the *shuddha* or *vikrit* forms of *swaras* and due to exclusion of two *swaras* out of seven *swaras* in different manner, Many variations are formed. It does not mean that any permutation can be used at any time, because to present permutations is not a goal in itself; but it is acceptable as a useful mean for *raga* improvisation. Hence, when Ustad Amir Khan, Besides The *riyaz*, applied *merukhand* in *khayal gayaki* and *raga* presentation, the grammar of a particular *raga* restricted the number of admissible permutations naturally. The rules of *raga* that restrict the number of admissible permutations are mainly- the rule of exclusion and non exclusion in *aroha* and *avaroha*, rareness or prevalence of a note, prescribed *shuddha-vikrit* form of a note etc. For example, in *raga darbari*, making four *swara's* permutations, *sa re ga ma*, on the basis of *prastar* method, if *raga* improvisation or *badhat* is made; keeping in view the vocal style of Ustad Amir Khan, division of admissible and inadmissible will be as under: -

s r g m, m s r g, g m s r, r g m s, g m r s – these will be admissible. Whereas s g r m, g s r m, r g s m, r m s g, s m g r, m g s r, g r m s, m g r s etc will not be admissible keeping in view the form of *raga darbari kanhada*, because due to *kanhada ang*, *gandhar* is kept *andolit* and in *avaroha*, it is applied in curved manner; then only it will be convenient to restore the form of *raga*. It is not sufficient to keep in view only the grammar and the form of *raga*, but also a mature aesthetic sense is required as to at what place and which *swara* phrase will be melodious and worth listening. In this context, personal opinions of Ustad Amir Khan were in effect.

Importance of imagination is very much in improvisation of *raga* of *audhav* type, and in addition to prescribed *swara* combinations and *swara* phrases, different *swara* combinations and permutations are admissible. In addition, the form of *aroh* and *avaroh* used to be simple and straight and because of being only five *swaras*, all of them have prevalence. To sum up, in the *ragas* of *audhav* type, despite application of various permutations, identity of the *raga* remains intact. On account of these reasons, Ustad Amir Khan used to sing *audhav* or *audhav-sampurna ragas* specially and there in applied *swara* phrases based on *merukhand* frequently.

Ustad Amir Khan's *sargam* based on *merukhand* is considered to be complex. The reason is that he applied various permutations in a mixed manner in *sargam* and in *tans* also. This admixture used to be so peculiar that after one *swara* phrase what would be the next, was not possible to anticipate. This is the practical aspect of the application of *merukhand*. Hence, there is no prohibition of repetition of *swaras*; whereas in view of *shastra* [theory], every *swara* can be used only once in a permutation. For example, see a *tan* in *raga malkauns*, wherein admixture of above permutations, peculiarity and repetition of *swaras*, which make it a special form: -
s d̲ g̲ m n̲ d̲, m d̲ n̲ S d̲ S n̲ m n̲ m d̲, s g m d̲ g m g s **n** s.

Support is being taken from *swara* phrases obtained from permutation method for making *alankarik tans* [figurative *tans*]. *Alankarik tan* is the application of *swaras* in orderly movement. Any particular permutation can also be made the basis of said orderly movement. For example, if the permutation 's g d̲ m' is made the basis of *tan* in *raga malkauns*, the *alankarik tan* 's g̲ d̲ m, g m n̲ d̲, m d̲ S n̲, d̲ n̲ G S' can be formed. Generally in these figurative *tans*, certain type of *laya*, movement and stress is extended in a uniform pattern. Peculiarity of *tan* and *sargam* of Ustad Amir Khan depends on application of stress beyond imagination, for which he devised his own method of combining various permutations, wherein different types of laya khand and bal [stress] emerge automatically. He does not sing *tans* by applying *alankar* in a definite order.

The influence of *merukhand* on the *tans* and *sargam* of Ustad Amir Khan is already known; the influence of *merukhand* was sufficient also in developing the required power of imagination for the improvisation of *raga* and *alap*. *Badhat* provides a disciplined form to the system of *raga* improvisation, as improvisation begins with some *swaras* of bass and middle octave and gradually next *swaras* are included in it. Patience is required in this system and the next *swara* is included when the *raga* improvisation has been effected by previous *swaras* as much as possible. It is the same that when all the permutations of two *swaras* have been accomplished, then the next permutations of three *swaras* begin. When permutations of three *swaras* are accomplished, then next *swara* is included and permutations of four *swaras* are started. Thus, to proceed ahead, paying attention to all possible *swara* phrases, is the common element in *badhat* and *swara prastar* both. The influence of *merukhand* is known mostly on *sargam* and *tans* of Ustad Amir Khan, because his *alap* being very sentimental, its technical aspect is almost concealed. His disciple, Pt. Amarnath also accepts influence of *merukhand* on *badhat* of Ustad Amir Khan, which is made clear by his following statement about establishment of 'Indore Gharana' by Ustad Amir Khan: -

"The stylistic features of this gharaanaa are: detail barhat [aalaap] with bol in vilambit laya based on Merukhand thinking - - -"[70]

In order to maintain importance of *nyas swaras* [final notes] of a *raga* during *alap*, Ustad Amir Khan considered only those permutations admissible in particular *raga*, in which no harm was done to the *raga*, if pause was laid on the final note. For example, Ustad Amir Khan has applied *pancham swara* sufficiently both in *aroha* and *avaroha* in *raga-bageshri* but didn't pause on that *swara* as a final note. Similarly, maintaining importance of *komal rishabh* in *raga-ahir bhairav*, while improvising with the *swaras* 's r g m' in application of permutations, 's g m r, s m g

---

[70] 'Living Idioms in Hindustani Music: A Dictionary of Terms and Terminology'-P.55, Author: Pt. Amarnath.

r̲, s r̲ g m, s g r̲ m, g m r̲ s' etc *swara* phrases were applied very emotionally during *alap*.

Generally, with some of the *swaras* of an octave, all variations which can be obtained by changing order of those *swaras*, they find a place in permutation method and they are used in singing at appropriate places. In addition to change of order of *swaras*, Ustad Amir Khan has produced a variety by various divisions of permutations in different octaves. For example, in *raga-hansadhwani,* keeping the *swaras* 's r g p', in the same order and adding other *swara* phrases to it, the *tan* will be formed in the style of Ustad Amir Khan in following manner:

1- s r g p S n p g r
2- s r g P P G R S n p –
3- s r g **p** g g r n n p g r s

Thus, besides permutations of *swaras*, to produce variety by change of octave, was the specialty of Ustad Amir Khan's own. In presenting such *swara* phrases with ease, his voice used to remain so natural that it was not detected how all of sudden, the octave was changed and by application of distant *swaras* [long interval], how peculiar *swara* combinations emerged.

Repeated usage of *raga* identifying *swara* phrases and *swara* combinations in the *gayaki* and application of ascending-descending etc *varnas* in improvisation of *raga* is available in *gayaki* of Ustad Amir Khan too. Nevertheless his vocalism does not remain restricted only to the formality to demonstrate the form of *raga*. Here and there, he used to apply such *swara* usage, which on the basis of traditional *raga* form, neither can be considered *raga* identifying nor distorting the *raga*. Here his expression of sentiments based on aesthetics and his power of imagination cultured by *merukhand,* seem to provide him guidance.

In *raga megha* [*vilambit khayal*], sung by Ustad Amir Khan, recorded on side a of LP record No.EASD-1331 of HMV, following *swara* phrases can be listened: -

Alap – p n̲ s r m s, n̲ m r s, r m n̲ m r.

Bol alap – 'n̲ s' r m p s
          'ba -' - ra - kha

Sargam – p n̲ s m s r m p, 'rm' 'pn̲' 'rn̲' p m r n̲ s.
         'rm' 'n̲p' 'mr', 'mp' 'Sn̲' p 'mn̲' 'rn̲' p.

Tan of *sargam* – s r R S n̲ p m M R S n̲ p n̲ R r m R S
         n̲ p n̲ m p m r s.

Though being his application of *merukhand* so complex and peculiar in *sargam*, instead to keep emergence of emotion and stimulus of *raga* as usual [like in improvisation and *behlava*], he does not leave his voice culture of *meed, ghaseet* and *gamak*.

[3] STUDY OF KARNATAK MUSIC SYSTEM: -

Ustad Amir Khan attentively heard and understood all the modes, styles and artists of North Indian Classical Music. But his curiosity was not restricted to it and he took enough interest in the music system of South [which is known as Karnataka Music System] and whenever he got opportunity to understand important elements of Karnataka Music, he took advantage of it. In an interview given to Mr. N. Rashid, main disciple of Ustad Amir Khan, Pt. Amarnath says about Amir Khan's knowledge of Karnataka Music: "Telling about the *bandish* of *raga-charukeshi*, Amarnath said, Rashid! Khan Saheb has composed this *bandish* in Karnataka style. He had deep knowledge of the music of South.

A detailed description of the influence of Bhindi Bazar *gayaki* has already been given previously. Here it is to be noted that Bhindi Bazar *gayaki* establishes Amir Khan's link with the music system of South, as the Ustads of Bhindi Bazar were particularly inspired by Karnataka Music regarding the *sargam* as a link between *alap* and *tan*. In both, the Amir Khani style and the Bhindi Bazar *gayaki*, *khandmeru* system is accepted as the basis to produce variety in *sargam*. And South is the main source of this *khandmeru*. Karnataka system was adopted not only as a form of permutation in *swaras* of *sargam*, but even in the discharge of *sargam* there was influence of refined elements like *khatka* etc, as the representative vocalist of Bhindi Bazar, Ustad Aman Ali Khan was very much influenced by hearing the *gayaki* of some artists of South. In fact, placing *sargam* as a part of *khayal gayaki* itself is a result of the influence of Karnataka Music. If previous history is searched it is found that before Aman Ali Khan, Ustad Abdul Karim Khan, the founder of Kirana Gharana, on hearing the music of South, adopted the method of presenting some *swara* phrases in the form of *sargam* at appropriate places during *alap*, which was new thing for prevalent North Indian Music.

Abdul Karim Khan adopted southern musical elements from Devdasi, Veena Dhannamal, who was a Veena player of South Indian Music. Ustad Amir Khan used to discuss about the two systems of Indian music with the eminent dancer, Ms. Bal Saraswati, who was the daughter of above mentioned Veena Dhannamal.

Keeping a liberal view, Ustad Abdul Karim Khan began trend of adopting fine technique of the South Indian Music system with discretion. Later musicians continued this trend and according to the statement of Ustad Amir Khan, he heard it, understood its importance and accepted it.

While studying *tarana*, Ustad Amir Khan kept in view '*tillana*', a mode of southern classical music, whose form is considered to be equivalent to *tarana*. *Tillana* is presented independently in singing and also in dance. Ustad Amir Khan discussed with the dancer, Ms. Bal Saraswati to elicit information about the origin and history of *tillana*. Bal Saraswati opined that whatever influence of Khusro and thereafter the music of North had on the music of South, *tillana* was the result of it. The information regarding above conversation is available in a recorded interview of Ustad Amir Khan at Bhopal.

During his music tours, Ustad Amir Khan's vocal programs were held in South also and due to this the artists and audience of South had great respect for him. The famous Tabla player, Ismail Daddu Khan recollected about the tours of Ustad Amir Khan to South India in an interview given to the author on 22nd May, 1988: - "I had an opportunity to go to Madras [now Chennai] with Amir Khan Saheb in 1962. Luckily we had an opportunity to stay at the residence of the dancer, Bal Saraswati. There whatever opinion Bal Saraswati expressed, would always be remembered. She said- 'I had believed that after Ustad Abdul Karim Khan Saheb, nobody else of North knew about the music of South India. But listening to your [Amir Khan's] programs on Akashwani, I realized that still in North India, Ustad Amir Khan is such an authority who had influenced the music lovers of South so much that he would be remembered for long time to come.'"

Ustad Amir Khan had a South Indian friend, Mr. K.J. Natrajan By profession he was general manager in State Bank at Madras. He had good knowledge of both [North and South] systems of music and was associated with Times of India as a reviewer of music. Although he had knowledge of South Indian culture and music particularly, yet after hearing Ustad Amir Khan for the first time, how much he was influenced and what was his feeling, he has expressed in following words: -
"When I first heard him, I told myself, what a gross fool you are! This is music, this is music! An out side force kicked me and told me of my total ignorance. - - -
Here was music of infinite contemplation, of introspection, and other worldliness. - -
- - -

Amir Khan has been one of the most central influences in my musical thinking. He has given shades to meaning [that] never existed. A musical experience can not be easily verbetised, as a mystical experience can not. There was about Amir, both wistfulness and mysticism and it was this that placed him as tall he was, taller than the others."[71]

Ustad Amir Khan presented many *ragas* of Karnataka system and also composed *bandishes* in them. He also gave new names to some of these *ragas*.

A recollection narrated by Mr. K.J. Natrajan of a music concert held at Bombay is worth mentioning: -
"Once Khan Saheb was to perform at Bombay. I [K.J. Natrajan] reached there some what late. Wishing me from the stage itself, he started singing. As soon as I heard initial *swaras*, I was surprised. He was singing *raga-manohari*, a Karnataka *Raga*. Very brilliantly he had dressed it up with Hindustani [North Indian] *swaras*. During interval he embraced me and said: 'I have adopted this *raga* to dedicate to the famous dancer Bal Saraswati and to you.' I was over joyed and asked 'what name have you given to it?' He said, '*priya kalyan*'. After interval, he again presented a Karnataka *raga*. Addressing the audience, he said: 'Its Karnataka name is *malayamarutam*. I have named it *jansammohini*.'"[72]

While giving the name of *priyakalyan* to the *raga-manohari*, the *raga* sung by Ustad Amir Khan contains *komal rishabh* and *nishad*, while *madhyam* is *tivra* and *gandhar* and *dhaivat* are *shuddha*. The first tetra chord [*purvang*] of this *raga*, even from *madhya shadja* [keynote] to *dhaivat*, has sufficient similarity with *puryakalyan*. In other words, the *kalyan ang* is included in this *raga* in the pattern of *puryakalyan*. Probably on this account it was named as *priyakalyan*. Ustad Amir Khan himself

---

[71] 'Nal'-P.143, 'Abhijat Surrang', Author: Vasant Potdar.
[72] 'Nal'-P.142, 'Abhijat Surrang', Author: Vasant Potdar.

composed the *bandish* of *vilambit khayal*, applying the Persian *rubayee* of Sarmad '*sarmad ghame-ishque...*'.

The form in which Ustad Amir Khan sang *raga malaya marutam* in the name of *jansammohini* for northern system, the *swaras* applied by him are *shuddha rishabh, shuddha gandhar, pancham, shuddha dhaivat* and *komal nishad*. The *madhyam swara* is omitted [*varjit*]. The ascending form of this *raga* is very much similar to that of *kalavati*. In the *avaroha*, *rishabh* is sufficiently strong; therefore the impact of this *raga* becomes different from that of *raga kalavati*. In this *raga*, the refrain of the *bandish* composed by Ustad Amir Khan is '*kaun jatan soun piya ko manaun*'. Other North Indian musicians subsequently performed this *raga* in the same name; such as Sitar player Pt. Ravishankar, vocalist Mrs. Lakshmi Shankar and Goswami Gokulotsavji Maharaj etc.

The *raga-charukeshi* sung by Ustad Amir Khan is also a *raga* of southern system. Although it is quite prevalent in North India now a days, yet in those days it was placed in the category of non prevalent *ragas*. The *swaras* applied in this *raga* are *shadj, shuddha rishabh, shuddha gandhar, shuddha madhyam, pancham, komal dhaivat* and *komal nishad*. The *bandish* of *madhya laya trital* in *charukeshi* sung by him was also his self composed; its refrain is '*laj rakho tum mori gusaiya*'. Ustad Amir Khan was well acquainted with Vallabh Sampradaya sect and had very close contact with them. That is why the above mentioned *bandish* of *charukeshi* of Ustad Amir Khan was dedicated to son of Vallabhacharya, famous by the name of Gusaiji. One recording of a *mehfil* in which Ustad Amir Khan has sung this *bandish*, is available. The same recording is available in the cassette issued by HMV No.S.T.C.-04B-7371, side a.

Out of 72 *melas* [type of scale] in the theoretical system of South Indian music, one is '*vachaspati*'; wherein *madhyam swara* is *tivra* [sharp] and *nishad* is *komal* [flat].

Ustad Amir Khan composed a *raga* on the basis of this *vachaspati mela*. In the *aroha* and Avaroha of the *swaras* of *vachaspati*, *rishabh* and *dhaivat* were omitted. Its class became *audhav-audhav* type. He did not give any name to this *raga*. That is why it is known as self composed and untitled *raga* of Ustad Amir Khan. The *swaras* of ascending and descending in this *raga* are as follows: -

Aroha [ascending] – s g m̲ p n̲ S
Avaroha [descending] – S n̲ p m̲ g s

In opinion of Ustad Amir Khan, this *raga* can be placed in the category of the *ragas* of *kalyan that* in North Indian music system. The refrain of the *bandish* sung by him in this *raga* set in *madhya laya trital* is '*Par karo gun nahi mome*'. This *raga* is available in Enreko LP No.241-0001 side 1, which is probably the last available recording of his life.

Basically the *raga* of southern system, *hansadhvani* was among the most favorite *ragas* of Ustad Amir Khan. The audience and persons having knowledge of music liked to hear this *raga* from Ustad Amir Khan. There is no exaggeration to say that the credit goes to Ustad Amir Khan to make popular *raga-hansadhvani* in the Hindustani vocal style from Karnataka music, which was less prevalent in North India.

Ustad Amir Khan used to sing two *bandishes* in *raga-hansadhvani*, which were composed by Ustad Aman Ali Khan. The wordings of the composition set in *ektal madhya laya* are '*jay mat vilamb tajde*' and the *drut bandish* is '*Lagi lagan pati sati san*' set in *trital*. In the context of this *bandish* having link with Karnataka music, Pt. Ravishankar writes in his book 'Raga Anuraga' –

Translated from original Bangla – "Like Abdul Karim Khan, he [Aman Ali Khan of Bhindi Bazar Wala] two was very much influenced by Karnataka Music of the South. He composed many beautiful *bandishes* and also presented *sargam* in Karnataka style. His most popular *bandish* is in *raga-hansadhvani*, '*Lagi lagan pati sati san*'; identical to the prevalent composition of the South, '*Vatapi ganpatim bhaje*'"[73]

Ustad Amir Khan composed a *rubayeedar tarana* based on the notations of above mentioned *drut khayal* [*Lagi lagan*], composed by Ustad Aman Ali Khan. In LP No.EASD-1357 side 1, it has been presented after *vilambit khayal* as substitute of *drut khayal*. The nature of *hansadhvani* of the South is enough exciting. Ustad Amir Khan too presented it in increased *laya* in comparison to other *ragas*. He didn't apply his favorite *jhumra tal* of *ativilambit laya* for *vilambit khayal* of *hansadhvani*.

Ustad Amir Khan also performed *raga-abhogi* of Karnataka music. Although this *raga* had already been adopted in Kirana Gharana and Ustad Amir Khan sang the *bandish* of Kirana Gharana '*Charan ghar aaye*' in *madhya laya jhaptal*. After this *bandish*, he used to sing *drut khayal*, the wordings of which are '*Laaj rakhlijyo mori*'. It is his self composition. One remarkable specialty in *raga-abhogi* sung by Ustad Amir Khan is found that some *swara* phrases have been presented with *gamak* of Karnataka style in the bass octave and middle octave in midst of *raga* improvisation; by which it appears that he wanted to make us feel that the *raga* is of Karnataka system. The similar application was made by Pt. Bhimsen Joshi while singing the same *bandish*; who himself was influenced by the *gayaki* of Ustad Amir Khan. The above mentioned application of *gamak* by Amir Khan Saheb is available in HMV LP No.ECLP2765, side 2, *raga-abhogi* [*charan ghar aaye*]. HMV obtained this recording from central archive of Akashwani. Separately the *drut bandish* of same *raga* '*laaj rakhlijyo mori*' is preserved with the archive of Akashwani Indore. He had also composed a *tarana* in this *raga*.

---

[73] 'Raga Anuraga'-P.63-69, Author: Pt. Ravi Shankar.

[4] DEVOTION FOR *KHAYAL STYLE* WITH PRACTICE AND SELF INSPIRATION: -

Keeping in view all the influences, the ultimate form of Ustad Amir Khan's *gayaki* was the result of his own genius and devotion, suitable to his thinking. That is why he can be called a rationalist in the field of modern classical music.

About the practice of music by Ustad Amir Khan, Mr. Krishnarao Majumdar, a friend and contemporary of him and resident of Indore, said in an interview given to the author:
"It is not a game to imbibe the *gayaki* of three top vocalists. During whole of his youth he worked hard and practiced and I am surprised looking to his achievements. His talent and receptivity was wonderful. He realized what was suitable to the nature of his voice. He was also aware of the limitations and horizons of other vocalists."

In above statement of Mr. Krishnarao Majumdar, the subject of nature of voice is of much importance, because the quality of voice played a prominent role in development of Amir Khan's vocal style. He gave much importance to voice culture.

Specific quality of his voice gives a different color to his *gayaki*, despite the influences of aforesaid *ustads*. Though being inspired by the *badhat* of Ustad Abdul Wahid Khan, he didn't sing in a high pitched voice making his voice thin like him. Similarly he kept comparatively less the exciting and quickening *tans* of Rajab Ali Khan in his *gayaki*.

Ustad Amir Khan says about importance of his voice culture in his practice of music:
"People say that singing is done by throat, but the throat is only a means. The voice comes out from the navel or the chest. My *gayaki* is not *ga pa ga ni, re ni ga pa* [that is, *sargam* of *chhoot* or *tan* etc]. My *gayaki* is my voice. If you apply the same vocal

activity, its effect will be one thing, whereas I apply the same, it will be another thing."[74]

Thus we find that the *gayaki* of Ustad Amir Khan was not merely a mixture of styles of his Guru like senior Ustads. He himself was a thinker and relied on his own conjecture for his *riyaz*. Ustad Amir Khan didn't accept any previous or contemporary vocalist or vocal style as his perfect ideal during the period of practice of music; nor did he try to be representative or replica of anyone. The form of his peculiar style found shape only by his imagination and constant experimentation.

[5] PATRONAGE OF STATE AND MIGRATION FROM INDORE: -

After completion of his training in music, Ustad Amir Khan started to sing in music concerts and his fame began spreading. Ustad Amir Khan went to Nathadwara from Indore. His father was also with him. He had already contacts with Vallabh Sect. Nathadwara is main center of Vallabh Sect. There he stayed for some days. He was paid Rs.35/- for singing in a program, entry of which is available in the books of account there. A copy of the same is preserved with Goswami Gokulotsavji Maharaj, Chief of Vallabh Sect.

From Nathadwara he went to Kankrauli for few days and from Kankrauli to the court of Maharaja of Kishangarh, who was follower of Vallabh Sect. From there he went to Raipur and then to Kanpur.

Near about 1936, with permission of his father, Amir Khan went to Raigarh [Chattisgarh] and there he became a singer in the court of Maharaja Chakradhar Singh, for salary of Rs.300/- per month. About his stay at Raigarh, following published record is available: -
"Mr. Amir Khan has live in the court of Raigarh for the period of one year"[75]

---
[74]'Sangeet'-January/February 1980, P.18, 'Meri Gayaki Meri Avaz Hai', Writer: Ravindra Visht.

He came back to Indore from Raigarh. He expressed his desire to his father for going to Bombay. With his permission, he reached Islamic Club at Arab Gali, Bombay, where his maternal uncle, Mohammed Khan and Amanat Ali Khan, a nephew of Rajab Ali Khan lived. For livelihood, There Amir Khan started giving tuitions. While he was staying at Bombay, his father Shahmir Khan passed away.

In 1941, Ustad Amir Khan went to Calcutta from Bombay. There he lived at the residence of Sitar maestro, Vilayat Khan. Vilayat Khan's sister, Sharifan was the second wife of Ustad Amir Khan.

There he could not get desired success in the programs of music, though with help of harmonium player, Gyan Prakash Ghose, he got opportunity to demonstrate his art in some good music concerts. Also he could get job of training some students. The livelihood could be carried on by tuitions and programs of Akashwani.

Later on he lived in Calcutta in a separate house. But in 1944, during the last phase of second world war, he decided to leave Calcutta and go to Delhi, as there was probability of bombardment on Calcutta.

In those days, Akashwani Calcutta paid only Rs. 30/- as remuneration. Akashwani Delhi offered remuneration of Rs. 600/- which he accepted and reached Delhi.

In Delhi, besides giving his programs at Akashwani, he also performed in music concerts. His singing was used to be accompanied on Sarangi by Ustad Bundu Khan.

---

[75] 'Madhya Pradesh Ke Sangeetagya'-P.19, 'Khayal Gayak Padmabhushan Amir Khan', Author: Dr. Pyarelal Shrimal.

Ustad Amir Khan lived in Siddique Building in Old Delhi at cross roads of GB Road and Ajmeri Gate for six to seven years. In those days famous artists lived in Delhi, most important among them was Abdul Wahid Khan.

At the time of partition between India and Pakistan, communal riots started in Delhi. Therefore he returned to Calcutta again. After living there for two to three years, he went to Bombay in 1950. He lived in Bombay for a long period, almost for 21 years.

In beginning, he had to teach music to prostitutes for earning his livelihood. He lived in the second floor of the building named Noor Mohammed, situated near area of prostitutes. This house was located at Girgaon, near Kennedy Bridge, opposite Congress House. The recording executive officer of HMV of those days, Mr. G.N. Joshi writes: -
"The area in Bombay where Khan Saheb lived, going there not only during the night but even in day, was considered socially wrong for a reputed person of noble family."[76]

In the neighboring building of a lady singer lived the famous vocalist, Bade Ghulam Ali Khan and Tabla player, Ahmed Jan Thirakwa. Thereafter, Ustad Amir Khan built his own house 'Basant' at Peder Road and started living there. While living at Bombay, he went to Kabul [Afghanistan] in 1968 and to America in 1969, for a music tour of one year.

Near about 1971, he again went to Calcutta. He had fully assimilated himself with the cultural and musical environment of Calcutta. Besides the artists of field of music, he had acquaintance with Bangali intellectuals; main among them were Sunil Gangopadhyay [Bangla poet], N. Rashid Khan [Urdu writer], and Sagarmay Ghose [Editor 'Desh']. Other main friends were Marketing Director of the Tata, Farhad

---

[76] 'Swara Gangechya Tiri'-P.121, 'Ustad Amir Khan', Author: G.N. Joshi.

Sayeed Khan, Bobby Sethi [residence-Alipur], Mrs. Anita Gosh, Surender Mohan [industrialist] and Rathin Bhattacharya.

During his stay at Calcutta, Sitar player, Jaya Bose, her husband Sanad Vishvas, violin player V.G. Jog, vocalist Purvi Mukharjee, vocalist Ravi Kichlu etc had constant contact with him. They were so much influenced by Ustad Amir Khan that they prepared a series of articles based on interviews with Ustad Amir Khan, which were published in the Bangla Weekly 'Desh'.

After living his last days of life in Calcutta, he left his earthly body on 13th February, 1974.

CHAPTER –III

THE VOCAL STYLE OF USTAD AMIR KHAN

CHAPTER –III

THE VOCAL STYLE OF USTAD AMIR KHAN

AN ANALYSIS BASED ON THE ELEMENTS OF MUSIC

In evaluation of vocal style of Ustad Amir Khan, we get great help from live audio recordings of his stage performances, gramophone records, reviews published in news papers and magazines, and comments expressed by different musicians. Since Ustad Amir Khan had made *khayal gayaki* his goal, so to evaluate his *gayaki*, it is important to understand generally accepted forms and elements of *khayal* prevalent at that time.

1- Form of *Khayal*: - The very word, *khayal*, indicates that it is a style of singing, based on the power of imagination of the singer. That is why, "It has tremendous scope and the capacity to absorb various features of musical expression, such as- *alap, sargam, bol, boltan, behlava, badhat, gamak, khatka, murki, phanda, asthai, antara* and so on."[77]

Along with these, the special application of vocal sound, as *gamak, lahak, khatka, murki, kan, meed [soot], jamjama [kampan], gitkari, andolan* etc are its fine decorations.

Most of above mentioned elements and decorations are found in the *gayaki* of Ustad Amir Khan in various proportions. He did not include *bolbat* with *layakari* in his style and also *tihai* was scarcely used. He was sparing in application of *murki*, but on the other hand, he increased the use of *bol alap* and *sargam* by means of *merukhand* in *raga* improvisation, in comparison to its usage in that period.

---

[77] 'Living Idioms in Hindustani Music'-P.65, 'Khayal', Author: Pt. Amarnath.

"There are two types of *khayal*- *khayal* of *vilambit laya* [slow tempo] and *khayal* of *Madhya laya* [middle tempo], which are known as *bada khayal* and *chhota khayal* respectively. After these, singers also generally sing *tarana* in *drut laya* [fast tempo]. That is, middle tempo after slow tempo, and fast tempo after middle tempo, is used in *khayal* style, which is in conformity with natural activity of our daily life. In the morning, when we go for a walk, we walk slowly with our lazy body. After some time, we feel that our laziness has gone and agility increases. Our pace is quickened. As we walk on, our agility increased further and a situation comes when we want to run for some time and we enjoy running. During this process of walking, the sequence of our movement is the same-*vilambit, Madhya* and *drut,* as has been mentioned above in *khayal* style. Not only in walking, but in all activities of our life, generally the natural order of tempo is the same. That is why rendering first *bada khayal,* then *chhota khayal* and in the end *tarana, this sequence* in *khayal* style is fully psychological. Because of being psychological, the ultimate impact of the *khayal* style is stability, concentration and absorption."[78]

In *khayal* style, there is ample scope for *swara* usage favorable to *ragdari,* nevertheless the discipline of consecutive order based on psychology, provides it a peculiar and classical form. The different elements included in vocal style of Ustad Amir Khan, are elaborated as follows: -

[a] *Bada Khayal* or *Vilambit Khayal*: - As per tradition, Amir Khan Saheb also used to present *alapchari* before *vilambit khayal*, but he used to start *bandish* of *bada khayal* after a quite brief *alap*. His *alap* used to be of one to one and a half minute duration. He did not present detail *alap* of *nom-tom*, as is done in Agra and Gwalior Gharanas.

---

[78] Quoted from the talk by Dr. Pyarelal Shrimal, broadcast in program 'Sangeet Sarita' of Vividh Bharati, dated 1-2-1981.

Usually he presented *sthayee* [refrain] twice in the beginning, which was having some variation. But he has performed *sthayee* only once in the recordings of LPs, as it has a time limitation of about twenty minutes. After the *sthayee* of *bandish*, he used to start *raga* improvisation. He never presented *antara* [second part] of *bandish*, just after *sthayee* of *vilambit khayal*.

Only after stabilizing *tar shadja* in the *alap* of *sthayee*, he presented whole *antara* in a single flow and then again came to the *sthayee*. He did not improvise the *raga* by means of *alap, bol alap, bahlava* etc in the *antara*, as is done by other artists. Only on rare occasions, he presented *antara* of *bandish* of *vilambit khayal*. Many of his recordings are without *antara* in *vilambit khayal*. In the LP recordings having *vilambit khayal*, he has presented *antara* only in *marwa, darbari* and *hansadhwani ragas*.

In the context of *vilambit gayaki* of Amir Khan Saheb, it must be noted that his improvisation goes upward from *mandra saptak* and the sequence of different elements come in such a way that activity of *swaras* gets rapidity increasingly, but the *laya* of *ativilambit jhumra tal* remains constant from the beginning to the end. Generally other *khayal* singers get the *laya* of *tal* increased by Tabla accompanist, along with the part of *bol bat*.

[b] *Chhota Khayal*: - Observing the tradition of presenting *chhota khayal* after *bada khayal*, Amir Khan Saheb also presented *chhota khayal* after *bada khayal*. Exceptionally, he has also concluded some *ragas* just after *vilambit khayal*, for example, *raga bhatiyar* presented at Akashvani, Indore [*Barani Na Jaya*], and *raga jayajayavanti* preserved at the National Archives of Akashvani [*Ay Mai Sajan Nahi Aye*]. In these *ragas*, he did not present *chhota khayal*. Even if *antara* is not presented in *bada khayal* by Khan Saheb, whenever he presented *chhota khayal*, he presented it with *sthyee* and *antara* in the beginning. He used to present *gayaki* of *bol alap* and *bahlavas* and after increasing his *laya*, he splattered his *sargam* and *tans*. Some times he concluded his *raga* with *tihayee*, and some times without *tihayee*.

Amir Khan Saheb had two ways of performing *chhota khayal*. If he sang *chhota khayal* after *bada khayal,* in the same *raga*, he did not emphasize on any sequence of *alap*, *sargam* and *tan*. He blended all these elements very often. In LP records No.EASD-1357 Stereo, EASD-1331 Stereo, and EALP-1253, presented *chhota khayals* in *Raga malkauns, lalit, marva* and *darbari* after *vilambit*, fall in this category. If he presented any *raga* with *chhota khayal* only, then he started it with comparatively slower *laya* [in *Madhya laya*] and improvised it gradually with *chaindari* [patience] and then used to increase the *laya* of *bandish* in conformity with *drut ang,* as per requirement. That is, in *chhota khayal*, presented independently, without *vilambit khayal*, all the qualities of orderliness are found, which are generally seen in his *vilambit khayal*, whether it may be there in a three minutes gramophone record of 78 rpm, as presentation of *raga shahana* [*Sundar Angana Baithee*]. In addition to this, *Raga abhogi [Laj Rakh Lijo Mori]* and *raga ramdasi malhar [Chhaye Badra Kare Kare]* performed at Akashvani Indore and among the audio recordings of concerts, *raga charukeshi* [*Laj Rakho Tum Mori*] etc, are such examples.

[c] *Tarana*: - In the vocal style of Ustad Amir Khan, *tarana* has the same place as that of *chhota khayal*. Hence it is not necessary to keep separate his *khayal gayaki* and presentation of *tarana*, from the point of view of musical elements. The reason is that, as he used to present *chhota khayal* in *madhya* and *drut laya*, in the same *raga*, after *vilambit khayal*, in the same way, he presented *tarana* after *vilambit khayal*, as an alternative to *chhota khayal*. That is why, on 29th June 1974, in All India Program of Akashvani, Acharya Brihaspati said about Ustad Amir Khan's style of *tarana* "Khan Saheb used to sing *tarana* of *khayal ang* [like *khayal* style]."

For his different style of *bandish* and presentation of *tarana* from others, his way of thinking was mainly responsible. In this reference, the influence of Amir Khusro has been described in Chapter two.

Traditionally *tarana* is considered to be the medium of work of *drut laya* [fast tempo] and expression of dexterousness of pronunciation. Therein, *bandish* in *atidrut laya* [ultra fast] is presented along with *atidrut tans*. In the end, along with variety of *laya khand* [rhythmic phrases], *dir, dir, tana, nana, tom* etc syllables are presented with *upaj ang*, in the same *atidrut laya*. These syllables are like *jhala*, which comes at the end of *razakhani gat*, in *tantrakari* [instrumental pattern]. Hence, naturally there is more scope for *laya* in comparison to *swara* and words, because words are meaningless and *laya* dominates the *swara*. That is why, *tarana* is considered to be without song [*nirgeet*]. But, different from all these, Ustad Amir Khan made *swara* the medium of expression in *tarana*, like the *khayal*, and meaningful lyric assisted it.

In the improvisation, coming after the *bandish* of *tarana*, it was specialty of *alapchari*, that he did not make simple *akar* etc the medium, but he used the words of refrain by way of *bol alap*. In these *bol alaps*, the usage of words and application of *swaras* has become as emotional as was in the *chhota khayal*. His view about the words of *tarana* being meaningful appears to be fulfilled here. In *tarana*, he used *sargam* [solfa] and *boltan*, as in *chhota khayal*. Different from *chhota khayal*, there was a specialty in his *tarana* presentation, that he used to conclude the *rubayee*, coming in the *antara*, with a special *atidrut tan* [including three or four *swaras* in one *matra*], which began from the middle of *Madhya saptak* and reached the *tar saptak*, and with the *avaroha* of same speed, joined the refrain of *sthayee*. The usage of such *tans* is available in 78 rpm gramophone record: *raga chandrakauns*, in LP record: *raga megha*, in the program of Akashvani Delhi: in the *taranas* of *raga jog* and *raga shuddhakalyan*[79]. Some of his *taranas* were without *rubayee* in *antara*. But there he did not include *bols* [syllables] of Tabla and Pakhavaj, for example the *taranas* of

---

[79] See The musical notation of *tarana* of *raga megha* in chapter IV/[3].

abhogi and *bageshri*. Even in the *tarana* of *bageshri*, available in LP No. ECLP-41546, he did not perform *antara*. The two styles of presenting *chhota khayal*, 1-after *bada khayal*, and 2-presenting independently, is applied to *tarana* also. The *tarana* of *raga puriyakalyan* is an example. Its audio recordings in two different programs are available with the author: 1-in the form of *drut* composition after *vilambit khayal*, 2-independent presentation.

It has been mentioned before that the *khayal style* is based on psychological reasoning, and its basic purpose is to render a *raga* in such a way that it takes the concentration of mind to its climax. In creating such condition, *laya* also assists *swara*. That is the reason that the order of *laya*, *madhya* after *vilambit*, and *drut* after *vilambit*, is established in the form of *bada Khayal, chhota khayal* and *tarana gayaki*. This sequence provides perfection to the *khayal* style. It was his own view that Ustad Amir Khan adopted *chhota khayal* after *bada khayal* and presented *tarana* in place of *chhota khayal*.

2- Accurate Posture and Gesture [*Shuddha Mudra*]: - The dimensions of *shuddha mudra*, like a serene expression on the face, erect and stable sitting posture as in '*padmasana*' and avoidance of unwanted movement of limbs, were included in his mannerism. While performing, one of hand moved slightly, but it was never raised above shoulder. Pt. Ravishankar, Prabha Atre, G. N. Joshi, C. L. Das, Vasant Poddar, Mohan Nadkarni etc eye witnesses, have admired the *shuddha mudra* and effective view of his concerts.

"A mehfil [concert] of Amir Khan's was always a pleasant experience. He had a very impressive and magnetic personality. At his concerts, he would always sit in the posture of a yogi doing his tapasya [meditation], with closed eyes and deep meditation. He maintained the same position till the end of his concert. His smiling countenance, a total lack of gesticulation or facial distortion, his absolute concentration on the song, and the slow, gradual build-up of a raga picture, invariably kept his audience completely engrossed. He had, for accompaniment, two Tanpuras tuned to perfection, a subdued harmonium and a Tabla with a straight, simple but steady *laya*. An atmosphere of solemnity and tranquility pervaded his concerts, in striking contrast with the noisy and sometimes un musical gymnastic bouts, some singers have with the Tabla player that entertain listeners with acrobatic, rather than providing them with aesthetic delight."[80]

"There had been no singer [like Amir Khan] having such posture and gesture. While performing, there was no facial distortion, neither moving the hands, nor throwing them here and there."[81]

3-Accurate Voice [*Shuddha Vani*]: - To get success in any mode of singing, it is necessary that the devotee should understand qualities of his voice and should keep in mind its limitations. The qualities of voice, after being refined, make the *gayaki* more expressive. Ustad Amir Khan also kept this fact in mind, while deciding about his style. After hearing many singers and having passed from different stages of experiments, he took up that style of vocalism, which most favored to his voice culture [*kanth sanskar*]. As mentioned in Chapter Two, even though being influenced by performers, who were like his *gurus*, he never tried to emulate the voice of any particular performer, but he molded those influences of *gayaki* to suit his voice. His devoted practice of *merukhand* also helped to increase the flexibility of his voice.

Despite of many qualities, there were certain limitations to his voice. It is necessary to consider the effect of these limitations in the context of his style. His voice was particularly embellished in bass octave with *javari* [resonance] and depth. So he applied this quality fully in improvisation. The secret of tranquility in his *gayaki* is that, he succeeded in creating background of *raga* in bass octave excellently. In treble octave, he felt difficulty in stabilizing *swaras* to their accurate pitch [*shruti*] and there

---

[80] 'Down Melody Lane'-P.92, 'Ustad Amir Khan', Author: G.N. Joshi.
[81] Book 'Raga Anuraga'-P.63-69, Author: Pt. Ravishankar.

was risk of committing mistake. Therefore, in *alap*, he never raised his voice to any *swara*, above *tar gandhar*. Looking to the gravity of his style, no necessity is felt for such a deed. Nevertheless, the *tans* used to move among the three octaves. The rapidity of his *tans*, made his voice competent to reach *atitar shadj* [eighth note of treble octave].

In later years, because of inconvenience in maintaining continuity of longer *tans*, he used to sing by dividing it in parts and by reposing on the main *swaras* in between, like *alap*. For example, see the *tan* performed by Khan Saheb in *raga bhatiyar*: -
R̲ R̲ n d d n d p m g m d -, n R̲ n d d n d p m d d p m g p -, m -, p -, g -, p p g r̲ s.[82]

Similarly, his *tan* of *sargam* is also impeded some times, and he joins the *swara* phrases ahead of it very artistically and peculiarly. For example in LP No.EASD-1357, while presenting *raga malkauns*, taking ascending sargam in middle octave from *dhaivat* to *tar gandhar*, he is impeded at *dhaivat*, and again starts next *swara* phrase of *sargam* from the same *swara*. The continuity of his breath remains constant, while singing *bandish* and *alap* in *ativilambit laya*. And because of this stamina, he could stabilize *swaras* and applied *meend*, in a refined manner, unto the last.

From the point of view of pitch, the voice of Ustad Amir Khan was of middle level, that is, it neither low and broad like that of Fayyaz Khan, nor conical like that of Abdul Karim Khan and Abdul Karim Khan. As per recorded collection available with the author, it appears that on an average, the *shadja swara* [keynote] of Ustad Amir Khan was equivalent to first black key *[kali aik]* of the harmonium.

At time of performance, he used the range of his voice culture, from *mandra* [bass] to *tar* [treble], to the extent that it was easy to maintain its natural characteristic. Although he had a complete hold over bass octave and he was competent enough to

---

[82] The introduction of IMSOC Notation System is available in chapter IV/[3].

execute *swaras* of bass octave at every speed, still he never exhibited the resonance and javari of his voice by stabilizing on kharaj [*shadja* in bass octave]. In *alap*, his lower limit was confined to *mandra rishabh* [if confirming to the *raga*]. For example, in LP records, *alap* up to *mandra rishabh* is available in *raga megha* and *marva*. Simply a touch of *mandra shadj* can be heard some where in audio records. Similarly, while applying the *tans* up to *atitar shadj*, he did not show the acrobatics of stabilizing his voice on its climax [*atitar shadj*].

The way whereby he used his voice in bass octave, the bass effect of his voice got specially embellished through microphone and amplifier. He applied open and lofty voice between *Madhya pancham* and *tar shadj*, and application of *swaras* on the basis of pitch only, without increasing the magnitude of voice above *tar shadj*, was his own quality of voice culture.

Khan Saheb maintained continuity of voice and mutual linkage of *swaras* through *kan, meend* and *gamak*, due to which experts have compared his vocal cords with *Sarangi*. For example, Acharya Brihaspati has called him a 'speaking instrument' [according to the information obtained from an article written by Mr. Madanlal Vyas].

About voice culture, the opinion of Khan Saheb himself and that of Dr. Prabha Atre is given below. Mr. Ravindra Visht writes: -
"Khan Saheb gave great emphasis on the quality of voice. One day, he said, 'my *gayaki* is not *ga pa ga ni, re ni ga pa* [i.e. *sargam* of *chhoot, tan* etc], my *gayaki* is my voice. If you apply a vocal activity, it will be another thing, and if I apply the same, it will be different.' Khan Saheb used to tell sarcastically, 'people say that I knew the technique of singing on mike.' People also say that his voice was naturally good. Both the comments are wrong. Actually, the fact is that, the voice of Khan Saheb was made by his hard work."[83]

---

[83] 'Sangeet'-January/February 1980, P.18, 'Meri Gayaki, Meri Avaz Hai', Writer: Ravindra Visht.

Dr. Prabha Atre writes in a book: -

"Comparatively the *gayaki* of Kirana Gharana is of middle [*Madhya*] and treble [*tar*] octaves, whereas the *gayaki* of Khan Saheb is that of bass octave [*kharaj*]. On the whole, the part of *kharaj* is raw and rough, but Khan Saheb had made this *kharaj* soft like greenery, as much as that one would not like to come out of it. Therefore his *gayaki* had obtained three dimensional structure. In spite of adopting fine musical embellishment of this era, his *gayaki* does not appear to be of substandard due to *kharaj*. Serious, traditional, respected, grave, self rectifying, inward looking etc are many adjectives, which can be used for his *gayaki*. In fact, the voice of Khan Saheb was the reason for that. In it [voice], there was a touch of mysticism, and it had a resonance. Besides these natural qualities, he had ideas of his own."[84]

Among the qualities [*guna*] of singers described in the *Shastras*, *shuddha vani* [accurate voice] and *shuddha mudra* [accurate posture and gesture] have been considered very important. Among the modern singers, very few can be considered to be ideal in this respect. Among them, especially the performance of Ustad Amir Khan has been considered praiseworthy. If the accuracy of Amir Khan's voice is tested on the basis of physiology, it had a peculiarity that all kinds of *swara* application were based on movements of vocal chords, with controlled breath. He did not produce voice seem to be artificial, with the help of organs, which could affect voice, like jaws, tongue, nose etc. For example, pronunciation of *swara* names in *sargam*, the natural position of lips and jaws in *akar* and keeping pronunciation of words quite similar to usual conversation in singing etc aesthetic elements were fine and inseparable parts of his vocalism. In *gamak* application, he never used *jabade ki tans* [*tans* with movements of jaws]. Similarly, he never produced distortions, by changing the form of nasals in words, from *rang, dhang, sang* to *raung, dhaung, saung* respectively.

---

[84] Book 'Swarmayee'-P.29, 'Ustad Amir Khan Saheb', Author: Dr. Prabha Atre.

4-The *Swara* Aspect of *Gayaki*: - Ustad Amir Khan gave utmost importance to refinement of *swaras,* in his vocal style. This refinement was based on his practice and his judgment about the timbre [quality of sound], interval [pitch difference between notes], and *shruti* [microtone], the sound between *swaras*. That is why his *gayaki* is considered to be *swara* salient, i.e. in the mutual proportion of *swara, laya* and lyric, the *swara* is given top most place in musical expression.

In his view, the basis of melodiousness of *swara* phrases was in the combination of two perceptions, *merukhand* and gradual improvisation. This perception provided form to the structure of his *swara* aspect and he decorated it with fine embellishment, based on his sense of aesthetics.

Keeping himself away from miracles of *layakari* [rhythmic variations], Khan Saheb firmly believed on the effect of *swara* and he considered satisfactory the success achieved by it only. Because of *swara* dominance in his *gayaki*, it had the effect making the audience fascinated, tranquil, grave and inward looking.

In the vocal style of Khan Saheb, along with the mood generated by the *raga,* attractiveness of the *swara* depended on the fine use of *kan swaras* linked with *swaras*. These *kans* are present in *bandish, alap, sargam* and even in *tans* also. The first *swara* of each *alap* has the touch of another *swara* [generally of the lower *swaras*]. Mostly he has applied *kan swara* for decoration of *swaras* comparing to *murki, gitkari, jamjama* etc, because it was more suitable for his tranquil and compassionate mood of his *gayaki*. The purpose of application of *kan swara* was to make *swara* phrases more expressive. Besides it, *kan swaras* were helpful in presenting *nyas swara* in different ways, so as to provide variety, despite repetition. It is well known that *shruti* of a Swara is changed by application of *kan swara*, and the effect generated by it is also changed. In a program of Akashvani Indore, while paying homage to Khan Saheb, what Thakur Jaidev Singh said in appreciation of application of *swara* in his vocal style, is quoted as follows: -

"The most important peculiarity is embellishment of *swaras*. He never applied *swaras* in flat manner in his life, and I think that this is the inadequacy in today's *gayaki* that we disgrace the *swaras*. The swaras are applied by totally stripping them; that is why they have no effect. Because the art of music is such that it differs in many ways from other forms of art. But mainly it differs from other arts in technique. In that technique there is no aesthetics. When by admixture of technique, a painting is created, or a poem is created, then it gets beauty. It is the peculiarity of music that there is beauty in its technique also. Sing only *swaras* without words, it has also beauty. That is, it is as beautiful in its technique, as in its presentation. This is the specialty of music. Hence, his technique had such mood and such expression that one would remain hearing only, but has no words for its applause."

Khan Saheb had especially acknowledged the importance of fine quality and expression in application of *swaras*. In this context, following quotation gives expression to his belief: -

"In music, his [Ustad Amir Khan's] first belief is that more delightfully the *swaras* are applied, more effective becomes the *raga*. If a child is called with affection, he goes to any unknown person and thinks him to be his own. Similar is the case with creating effect in music. Because of this belief, Khan Saheb shows dominance of delicate feelings in his music. Because of this basic concept of music, he maintains his *gayaki* and he is very cautious about the art of *khayal gayaki*. He considers the whole *gayaki* as an impression. After listening to his music, it seems that he does not believe in uncontrolled demonstration of musical embellishments."[85]

In the very beginning of his *raga* presentation, application of *swaras* is soothing. The reason is that, in the melodious atmosphere created by sound of Tanpuras, tuned minutely, when Khan Saheb started *raga* introducing *alap* before *bandish*, then the action of reaching *shadj* for the first time, was very artistic. From there, the form of *raga* also started taking shape.

---

[85] 'Sangeet'-May 1973, Article: 'Ustad Amir Khan Aur Unkee Kala', writer: Prof. Chandrakantlal Das.

Whatever action was there to create the state of surprise and excitement was found in the vocal style of Khan Saheb, even it was based on *swara* aspect instead of *laya*. He did not surprised the audience by application of *ateet, anagat* or *tihai* [three tier method], but with the stability of *swaras*, he created peculiarity by usage of *shrutis* with *meed* and *andolan*, creation of *swara* combination beyond imagination and by application of *swara* phrases composed joining the *swaras* of different octaves. In the context of refinement in microtonal interval, *komal gandhar* produced in *Raga darbari* and *abhogi*, and *komal nishad* of bass octave in *raga ramdasimalhar*, are worth considering. Similarly, he stabilizes *komal rishabh* in such a fine manner in *raga marva* that while attention is centered on it, the effect of *shadj* of Tanpura is obliterated. In the *ragas* [*chandra kauns* etc], where he has stabilized *shuddha nishad*, the same effect is generated. It is to be remembered that *komal rishabh* and *shuddha nishad*, being nearest to the *shadj*, if one accomplishes them with caution, it is possible to produce such an effect.

Of course there is tranquility in his *gayaki*, because of his deep voice and the act of joining the *swaras* with *meend*, in addition, prolonged stabilization on *swaras* in *alapchari*, is also one of the reasons. As he improvised *raga* by keeping discipline of gradual progression, it was not sufficient for him to accept the *vadi* [dominant] and *samvadi* [subdominant] as the only place of stay. While maintaining the entire form of a *raga*, in addition to *vadi-samvadi*, he dwelt on some other *swaras*, for example, *dhaivat* in *raga abhogi*, and *gandhar* in *raga ahir bhairav* etc.

Though he could present fine vocal activities, such as *khatka, murki, gitkari* etc, very effectively, but despite being much applauded, these fine vocal activities could not dominate his *gayaki* and as per his nature, he maintained the importance of tranquility in his *gayaki*. That is why, weaving the descending *swara* phrase with melodious *murkis*, staying on a particular *swara* with dexterity, he pacified all the excitement and impatience. During improvisation, a pause of few seconds [silence] was a purposeful object to save basic theme of *gayaki* from waves of excitement. Especially in *vilambit khayal* set in *jhumra tal*, the duration of rotation being extensive, the portion of *mukhda* [opening profile] and *sam* [first beat] comes later, therefore the pauses falling in the middle, save the *alap* from unwanted continuity. During these moments of pause, sound of *Tanpura* coming from the background, provides enough tranquility. Probably this was the reason that he did not accept assistance or *swara* application by disciples and others, during his performances. As in his technique of *swara* application, *kan* comes in a natural way; the same position is of *meend*. During *alap*, whether a *swara* phrase belongs to an ascending order [*arohi*] or descending order [*avrohi*], he did not break his voice in between, nor did he accept change of *swara* in striking manner. Thus in such condition, *meed* is automatically included in *swara* phrases. He had his own method of applying *meed* also. Some times his *meed* moves from one *swara* to another in such a slow and melodious manner that an impression of some other *swara* is created in between. For example in *swara* phrase of *raga jayjayvanti*: '(d g m g r)', while coming from *ga* to *re* with *meed*, an impression of *komal gandhar* is also felt in the middle. He Had unique method of presenting a *swara* with stressful *khatka*, and from the same moment applying a descending *swara* phrase with *meed*. For example, see the *swara* notation of *raga darbari* and refrain of *raga jayjayvanti* in *vilambit khayal* as follows:

Swara phrase in *raga darbari*:

n̲ n̲ p m p, n̲, ([p] g̲ – m r s).

Refrain of *vilambit khayal* of *raga jayjayvanti*:

3

'ʳsdn̲ᵍr,-gmp'	'([m]gr)'
'Ay---,-maaee-'	'saa--'
	X

Khan Saheb applied *andolan* to the *swaras* very gently to prevent them from any jolt or roughness. This is the reason that his application of *komal gandhar* in *raga darbari* and *komal rishabh* in *raga ahir bhairav* [even keeping the tradition of *andolan*] seems different from others.

Khan Saheb also used *khatka* [a musical embellishment noted in bracket in Bhatkhande Notation System] as usual, but he provided it a special form by joining it with *sam* [the first beat of *tal* rotation]. That is with the emphasis of *sam*, giving stress on a *swara* by *khatka* effectively, and going down on descending *swaras*, was his method. For example, such applications of *khatka* can be observed in *bandishes* of *raga darbari [mori aali], raga charukeshi [laaj rakho tum mori], raga darbari [mori palakan son mag jharun]* etc.

The qualities of other fine embellishments of *swaras* have already been mentioned.

5-*Alap*, *Sargam* and *Tan*: -
Alap and *Badhat:* - Among the different elements of khayal gayaki, based on extempore improvisation, *alap* is supposed to be most effective in expressing the basic theme of *raga* and in presenting its form. Especially in swara dominant gayaki, it becomes necessary to pay more attention to refinement of *alap*. If looked from another angle, it appears that a *gayaki* becomes *swara* salient on account of giving more importance to *alapchari*. In the above matter, *alap* means an *alap* falling under a *nibadha gayaki* [within the composition and *tal* accompaniment]. It does not mean *alap* or *nom tom* etc, being presented before a *bandish*.

In the opinion of Pt. Bhimsen Joshi: "Alaap is the life-force of the song. It is only the Alaap that is capable of capturing the temperament of the artist. If the artist is Shaant [at peace] and Gambhir [serious], like Amir Khan was, the Alaap will represent the core of his very being."[86]

---

[86] India Today-15 Sept. 1987, P.124, 'Bhimsen Joshi- The Master's Choice', Writer: Inderjit Badhwan

Mr. Vaman Hari Deshpande writes: "Like Kirana and Patiala *gayaki*, this [Amir Khan's] gharana also belongs to *tantkar* [players of stringed musical instruments]. Shahmir Khan, father of Amir Khan, was a famous Sarangi player and Amir Khan himself is fond of Sarangi. That is why stretching of strings can be found in the three *gharanas* equally. - - -

Therefore giving greater emphasis on *alap* by *tantkars* is quite natural. Because of this, all the *gharanas* having quality of stretching strings are devotees of *alap bazi*. Predominance of application of fine *kans* is generated on account of pull of the string and all these things are found in the *gayaki* of Amir Khan Saheb in prominence."[87]

In this context, Dr. Prabha Atre opines:

"The style of Khan Saheb was nearer to Kirana, yet his improvisation and presentation of *raga* was quite different. - - - His very first *swara* appeared to be coming from inner apartment of a temple as if it was coming out with its sacredness. It made the listener spell bound. Then started the weaving of *swaras*. Every *swara*, in the context of *raga*, came forward with its whole beauty and stabilized. With the support of *kans*, stuck to *swara*, and complex forms of *meed*, his *alap* blossomed."[88]

As much importance Khan Saheb gave to bass octave under *alap*, was different from the prevalent *khayal gayaki* of that period. Nevertheless, in the *alap* of *dhrupad*, lower octave was improvised. Reaching of his *alap* to *mandra gandhar* several times, was usual thing. The *alap* in lower octave was the foundation for the building of his improvisation. *Bhatiyar* is supposed to be an *uttarang* dominated *raga*, and from the very beginning, it rises with 's – d, d n p, d m, p g,' etc, in such a way it goes towards *uttarang*, and usually the notations of *bandishes* are also of the same pattern. Even adopting the traditional *bandish* of *raga Bhatiyar*, [*Barni Na Jaye*], Amir Khan Saheb easily performs *alap* of lower octave in few rotations of beginning in his well known method, whose form is as follows:

---

[87] 'Gharanedar Gayaki'-P.93, Chapter-'Indore Aur Amir Khan', Author: V.H. Deshpande.
[88] 'Swarmayee'-P.28-29, Chapter-'Amir Khan Saheb', Author: Dr. Prabha Atre.

s n d, p p d n d n p, d n p g, g m d p, m m p d n p, p p d n r̲ n d, n d s. [Except *sa* and *re*, all are of lower octave.]

He started *alap* around *madhya shadja* with the discipline of progression. He used to begin improvisation of *alap* with *bol alap*. Once the *bandish* was started, he did not perform wordless *alap* by making *akar* etc as medium. The movement of *alap* generally reached the *rishabh, gandhar* or *madhyam* of treble octave and in the end; he stabilized *alap* on *shadja* of treble octave. In between these *bol alaps*, he artistically mixed *behlavas, zarab* and *swara alap* [*alap* with *swara* names in the form of *sargam*], which was helpful in maintaining attraction of his *gayaki*.

According to Ms. Bindu Chawala: "Its [of Amir Khan's style] movements have been compared to the telling of a story-with structuring of commas and full stops, sentences and chapters."[89]

The comparison of Amir Khan's *gayaki* with a story can be meaningful in another sense also. As the climax of a story occurs at the end, but its real pleasure can be derived only when the reader goes through all the events described previously. Similarly the real effect of *raga* presentation by Ustad Amir Khan can be appreciated by a listener, when his mind is constantly tuned with all the stages of gradual development of the *raga*.

"Ustad Amir Khan has compared *khayal gayaki* to mountaineering. He said: patience is required in mountaineering and continuous climbing is also essential. On stopping, foot will slip and on running, one will roll down. Those who clapped on your running would also clap on your helplessly falling down. They would ridicule you. Instead, one should climb the mountain with patience. There is pain but the pleasure is also

---

[89] Hindustan Times-30th Oct. 1988, 'The Journey of Gharanas', Author: Bindu Chawala.

immense. Get delighted and be happy. Every one will come to taste that pleasure. Seeing cheerfulness in your eyes, they would also like to share it."[90]

In sum, there should be gradual and patiently unfolding of *raga* during improvisation. As in mountaineering, running and halting, both are dangerous; similarly, neglecting orderliness in *raga* presentation in haste and monotonous repetition, both inflict damage to the *raga-rasa*.

All the qualities of *alap* and *raga* progression of Ustad Amir Khan mentioned above can be summed up on the following points: -

1) <u>Brief *alap* before *bandish*</u>: - Before presenting *bandish* of a *raga*, he performed brief *alap* through *akar*.
2) <u>*Bol alap* within *nibadh gayaki*</u>: - When he improvised a *raga* under the *bandish* of *khayal*, he always blended the *alap* with the words of *bandish*. In *nibadh gayaki*, he did not take wordless *alap* by *akar* only.
3) <u>Improvisation centered on lower and middle octaves</u>: - First, the gradual improvisation reached to the bass octave, and then the *raga* was slowly improvised into middle octave. He hardly emphasized *alap* presentation over *shadja* of treble octave.
4) <u>Selection of thought provoking *ragas*</u>: -Especially he liked generally known *ragas*, having infinite scope for improvisation and having definite and independent form, such as: *darbari kanhada, abhogi kanhada, malkauns, marva, Shuddha kalyan, multani, todi, lalit, yaman* etc.
5) <u>Reign of *shadja* [keynote]</u>: - The *alap* style of Khan Saheb was such that *swara* phrases got complexity with different *varnas* and were eliminated on *madhya shadja*. *Marva* is the only exception; otherwise there is reign of keynote in most of the *ragas*. Coming on *shadja* only at the end of *alap*, before taking the refrain, such formality was not applicable to his style.

---

[90] 'Sangeet'-Dec. 1973, P.26, 'Sangeet Jagat Ke Amir-Ustad Amir Khan', Writer: Madanlal Vyas.

6) Clear status of *swaras*: - Under the gradual movement with every *swara* of a *raga*, light is thrown through different *swara* combinations, because of which the status of every *swara* becomes clear. Instead of *phirat* by lengthy ascending and descending, he created *alap* by making the main *nyas swaras* as center. That was the specialty of his *gayaki*.

The *alap* of initial five rotations in *raga darbari* and *marva*, available in LP records, have been provided below in *swara* notation. It will help to understand the practical aspect of Khan Saheb's *alap* and movement system.

Raga Darbari Swara Vistar: -
Alap/badhat of the *raga* in initial five *avartans* of *vilambit khayal* presented in LP No.EALP-1253, side B:

1. m p, $^n\underline{d}\,\underline{n}$ p, m p $\underline{n}$ g, m p, $\underline{d}\,\underline{n}$ p, ^{n}m $\underline{n}$ p $\underline{n}$ g, g m p $^n\underline{d}$, $\underline{n}$, $\underline{d}$ $^s\underline{n}$, ($\underline{n}$ s).

2. ^{P}m p $\underline{d}$, $\underline{d}$ ($\underline{n}$ p), $^d\underline{n}$ m p $^n\underline{d}$, ($\underline{n}$ p), m p $^n\underline{d}$, $\underline{n}$ s ($^d\underline{n}$ p), ^{n}m p g m p, $^n\underline{d}\,\underline{n}\,\underline{n}$ s $^d\underline{n}$ p, m p $^n\underline{d}$, $^s\underline{n}$, ($\underline{n}$ s).

3. m p $^n\underline{d}$ $^s\underline{n}$ s, $\underline{d}\,\underline{n}$ s, $\underline{d}\,\underline{n}$ p s, m p $^n\underline{d}\,\underline{n}$ s ($^d\underline{n}$ s) p m p $\underline{n}$ p g m p $^n\underline{d}$, ($\underline{n}$ s), $\underline{d}\,\underline{n}$ p s, $\underline{d}$, $^s\underline{n}$ s.

4. $\underline{d}$ $^s\underline{n}$ r, s, r $^s\underline{n}$ [s] ($^n\underline{d}\,\underline{n}$ p s), $\underline{d}\,\underline{n}$ (r, s $\underline{n}\,\underline{d}\,\underline{n}$ r) - $\underline{n}$ r s, $\underline{d}\,\underline{n}$ s r r s ($^n\underline{d}\,\underline{n}$ r $\underline{d}$ r $\underline{d}\,\underline{n}$ s), m p $\underline{d}$, r r s ($\underline{d}$ $^s\underline{n}$ s) $\underline{d}\,\underline{n}$ (p r s).

5. $\underline{n}$ s r r g, (m r), s, ^{m}r $^s\underline{n}$ [s] $\underline{n}$ s r r $^s\underline{d}$, $\underline{d}$ ($^s\underline{n}$ ^{m}g), r [s] $^n\underline{d}\,\underline{n}$ r, s, $\underline{d}\,\underline{n}$ s r g m r [s] ($^n\underline{d}$ $^s\underline{n}$ m $\underline{d}$ $^s\underline{n}$ r - s r, [s] $^s\underline{d}$, $\underline{d}\,\underline{n}$ s r g m $\underline{d}\,\underline{d}$ ^{m}g $\underline{n}$ (r $\underline{d}$) $\underline{n}$ p, ^{P}s, $\underline{n}$ ^{s}r, ^{m}r $^s\underline{n}$ [s] $^n\underline{d}$, $\underline{d}\,\underline{d}\,\underline{n}$ s r g m [s], $^s\underline{d}\,\underline{n}$ s r ($^r\underline{d}$ r) s.

Raga marwa Swara Vistar: -

Alap/badhat of the *raga* in initial five *avartans* of *vilambit khayal* presented in LP No.EALP-1253, side A:

1. m̲ d, m̲ d m̲ g r̲ g m̲ d, g m̲ g d, m̲ n d, m̲ ᵍr̲ g m̲ (d r̲ d), g (m̲ n m̲ d), n ᵈm̲ d m̲ n d, (n d s).

2. m̲, n n d, n d m̲ d, m̲ ᵈn n d, g g m̲ d n n d m̲ g m̲ d, m̲ n d, ᵈr̲ g ᵐn d, n m̲ d - m̲ d n m̲ d, g d - m̲ d n m̲ d - m̲ n - d, n n d d m̲ d n - d, n ᵈm̲ ⁿd s.

3. ᵈn - d ᶠn r̲ - ⁿd n d, ⁿd ᶠn r̲ - n d, ⁿr̲, ⁿd, m̲ n d, ᶠn r̲ n r̲, n d, m̲ d n r̲ [n] - d m̲ d m̲ r̲ - n d, m̲ g r̲ g m̲ d n r̲, ᵈn ᵈr̲ - ᶠn d, m̲ n d s.

4. d ᶠn r̲ - r̲ r̲, n d, n r̲ n r̲, n d, d n r̲ r̲ n d, m̲ d, n r̲, n d, (r̲, d n m̲ n, d r̲ n r̲), n r̲ n d, n r̲ d n d r̲, n r̲ ⁿd, r̲ n ᵈn d, (m̲ r̲) n m̲ d m̲ n m̲ d - n (r̲ - s).

5. d n r̲ g (r̲ - ᵍd) n r̲ g, ⁿr̲ d, d n r̲ g g r̲, g r̲, g g r̲ n n (d g r̲), n d, d n r̲ g, r̲ n d n d r̲, n r̲ g, r̲, 'g r̲ n d n r̲,' r̲ ᵍr̲, n d, ᵐn d, r̲ n g n r̲ d g r̲ - n d ᵈs.

Role of *Sargam* in the *Gayaki*: - The word '*sargam*' is derived from first four notes [*swaras*], *sa, re, ga, ma,* of the seven notes of *saptak*. To sing *swaras* by pronouncing their brief names is called '*sargam*'. Sargam occupies a traditional role in training of music, because for the knowledge of *swaras* and the form of *raga*, *paltas* [vocal exercise of scale notes] were taught in the form of *sargam*. '*Sargam*' or '*swara malika*', brief and poetry less music compositions, are still used in teaching of music. But, this is the teaching side of '*sargam*', which has nothing to do with actual vocal performance.

The *sargam* got entry in *khayal* as a part of *gayaki* in 20th century. The credit for this is given to Ustad Abdul Karim Khan. Thereafter it grew sufficiently in the middle *laya khayal gayaki* of Bhindi Bazaar Walas. On other hand, Ustad Bade Ghulam Ali Khan of Patiala Gharana, adopted it as a form of *tan*. Then, in the style of Ustad Amir Khan, various usage of *sargam* were included, from *ati vilambit* to *drut ang*.

Khan Saheb gave sufficient importance to *sargam* in his *gayaki*. The main reasons for this are worth consideration.

Sargam is very convenient in the creation of different permutations of *swaras* based on *merukhand*. In such a place, if the words are applied, their pronunciation is likely to become senseless or opposite to sense. On the other hand, the *akar* also does not seem to be natural and attractive. The abbreviated name of every *swara* consists of one letter only and if they are put in any order, there is no problem of any damage to lyric. In *bol bat*, expressing spontaneous rhythmic variations, the words become instrument to indicate *laya khand* [partitions in rhythm] and *aghat* [stress]; there is no significance of their meaning and sense. Such misuse of words was not acceptable to Khan Saheb. That is why he kept the lyric apart from the part of *swara* permutations combining with rhythmic variations.

Sargam has a method of its own, according to which the *swara* pronounced should not differ from its basic form [pitch]. So it is expected that both the actions should occur simultaneously and the *swaras* should be applied in flat manner. In order to make the *sargam* competent to express the *raga* sentiment, Amir Khan Saheb relaxed this rule to some extent and increased the possibility of applying *meed, gamak, kan* and *khatka* there in.

Relaxing the strict rule of equality between the *swara* name and *swara* pitch, the application of *meed, kan* and *khatka* in *sargam*, their mutual encroachment to some extent has to be accepted. Dr. Prabha Atre, who did her doctorate on subject '*Sargam in the Khayal Gayaki*', has described three possibilities of application of *meed* in *sargam* in her book: -
1. Joining two *swaras* with *meed*, reaching to the pitch of the second *swara*, after pronouncing the second *swara's* name at the first pitch. For example: -

    Swara pitch -   g   n
    Swara name -   *ga | ni [i]*---->

2. Extending the first *swara* name, reaching to second *swara* pitch, and then pronouncing the second *swara* name: -

   Swara pitch   g   n

   Swara name   *ga [a]----->ni*

3. Changing swara name between the two *swara* pitch: -

   Swara pitch   g   n

   Swara name   *ga[a]------>ni[i]------>*

Ustad Amir Khan did not apply the second of the above three types of *meed* in *sargam* in the ascending order [*arohi varna*]. Except this, all the possibilities of *meed* in *sargam*, in ascending or descending order, have been used by Khan Saheb.

Amir Khan Saheb has applied *kan* in *sargam* sufficiently, but the *Swara* name of only main *swaras* has been pronounced and not of *kan swaras*.

While applying *gamak* in *sargam*, a peculiar thing in the singing of Khan Saheb is seen that at the time of showing repetition [*dana*] of the same *swara* with *gamak* two or three times, he does not repeat the *swara* name of that *swara* two or three times. There, only by the strokes of *gamak*, it can be realized that how much the *swara* has been repeated. It can be understood by following example of *sargam* with *swara* name: -

Swara pitch-   d̲ d̲d̲m m m g̲ g̲m m m

Pronounced *swara* name-   *dha - - ma - - ga - ma - -*

Various applications of *sargam* by Khan Saheb can be classified mainly in three categories: -

     a) During improvisation of *raga* by *alap*, application of *sargam* in the way of *alap* – that can be called *swaralap*.

     b) As an alternative to the application of *layakaries* by *bolbat* – in traditionally accepted form of *khayal gayaki*, *bolbat* with *layakari* finds place as a link between tranquil *alap* and *drut* [fast] *tans*. As he did not accept *upaj* [secondary phrase derived from basic *swara* structure of a *raga*] with *layakari* by words, Khan Saheb changed this link of the middle and gave this place to *sargam* with *laya*. The Pace of *sargam* falling in this part increases gradually. Thus a background for *tans* is prepared after *alap*.

c) To express *tans* in the form of *sargam* – that is called *tan* of *sargam*. There is a difference between *tan* of *sargam* and *tan* of *akar* or *boltan*; as it helps in creating strange *swara* combinations of distant *swaras*. In this part, beauty and delicacy of pronunciation of Khan Saheb's musical expression can be seen particularly.

In today's prevalent *khayal gayaki*, some other applications of *sargam* can be considered applicable. These applications are not available in the *gayaki* of Ustad Amir Khan. Main such applications are: -

1. To reach on *sam* by *tihayees* [the technique of three tier method] in *sargam* (to be observed: Pt. Jasraj, Salamat Ali/Nazakat Ali Khan's *gayaki*).
2. Application of *jhala* part of Sitar [to be observed: *gayaki* of Pt. Jasraj].
3. Peculiarity by change of the keynote [to be observed: *gayaki* of Ustad Bade Ghulam Ali Khan].

Among available audio recordings of Khan Saheb, LP of *raga chandramadhu* is the only exception, where, making the *pancham swara* the keynote by *murchhana* method, Khan Saheb presented some *swara* phrases of *sargam*. In this way he created reflection of *raga chandra kauns*.

Some of the main qualities of *sargam* presentation of Ustad Amir Khan can be understood by the following points: -

1. Application of *swara* phrases beyond imagination, inspired by *khandmeru* – regarding *khandmeru*, a detailed description along with examples of *swara* notations, is given in chapter 2.
2. Application of *swara* phrases, showing combination of distant *swaras* and different octaves, has been mostly accomplished in *sargam*.
3. Many a time, in *drut khayal*, Khan Saheb comes to refrain and *sam* by slowing down speed of the last portion of *sargam tan*. The method of slowing down the speed of *tan* and adjusting it with *bandish*, is called '*neem-bat*'. It is helpful in keeping *tan* of *sargam* expressive.
4. He starts many descending *tans* of *sargam*, directly by any *swara* of treble octave, which ends around *madhya shadja*. In the *bandish* of *raga yaman kalyan*, available with Akashvani Indore [*Aiso Sughar Sundarva Balamva*], following descending *tan* can be observed: -
P M̲ G R S n d p m̲ g r s n d.
5. Under all the parts of *gayaki* based on extempore improvisation of *raga* [*upaj*], opportunity has been given to *layakari*, only in *sargam*, to play its effect.

After unfolding of a *raga* being completed by the improvisation of *alap*, or after *antara*, Ustad Amir Khan applied *sargam* on the basis of *laya*, without taking *bolbat* or *layabat*. It is worth mentioning that on the one hand giving *alap* the form of *bol alap*, he kept it joined with the words of the *bandish*; on the other hand he did not use words as a link of *layakari,* falling between *alap* and *tan*. Instead, he gave this role to *sargam*. Onwards, *gamak* is mixed with this *sargam*. By speeding up, *sargam* assumes the form of *tan*.

Tan-Form and Characteristics: - In the vocal style of Ustad Amir Khan, his *tans* at their climax, had effect of stimulating emotions. The part of excitement and stimulation could be felt in his *tans*, instead of in other parts of his *gayaki*. In the *ati vilambit khayal*, his tranquil improvisation was the one end, whereas his speedy and bright *tans* were the climax of his *gayaki* at the other hand. In *raga* presentation, the *tan* aspect of his *gayaki* was effective and attractive from both points of view: *swara* aesthetic and *layakari*. "In *raga* presentation, the *sargam*, entering with the speed of *alap*, reached the speed of *tan*, and then the *tan* started. These *tans* were crystal clear, beautiful, propagating in the three octaves , made surprising formations giving different forms to the *laya*. If the audience fail to pay attention, they are likely to miss them."[91]

The real range of his voice in the three octaves becomes clear in his *tans*. His straight *tans* could not be named '*saral tans*' [easy *tans*], because to combine the three octaves easily in single straight *tan* and to maintain the voice natural as usual, makes difficult to imitate his straight *tans*. In the available audio recordings, *raga shuddha kalyan* presented in a stage performance, the climax of his *tans* could be observed. In this presentation, the lowest point [*swara*] of his *tans* is *mandra rishabh* and its highest point [*swara*] is *ati tar shadja*. The rapidity of *tans* in treble octave is common, even the speed of his *tans* is not affected in bass octave at all. As in his *vilambit gayaki* – the thick *gamak* and *lahak* of his *tans*, in *drut khayal* – *tan* having two *swaras* in every beat, in *drut tans* – three or more *swaras* in every beat, thus also in the speed of *tan*, he made different usage according to requirement.

Swara phrases influenced by *khandmeru*, and complex stresses of *laya* variations there in, made his *tans* very complicated. It was beyond the capability of each and every accompanist to give exact accompaniment on Sarangi or harmonium. Another reason of increasing the complexity of his *tans* was that, no sooner one phrase of a *tan* was over, the other phrase would start with which of the *swaras* and what form would it take? It was impossible to predetermine. This quality of his *tan* style can be observed in following *palta* in *raga hansadhvani:* -

p p **n** s r g p **n** r g p R S n r g n p g r s **n** p s

---

[91] 'Swarmayee'-P.30, Chapter-'Amir Khan Saheb', Author: Dr. Prabha Atre.

In both type of *ragas*, curved and straight, this complexity of *tan* or zigzag movement can be seen in equal proportion.

In case of *tans*, the style of Khan Saheb does not follow formality of any gradual movement. That is, few *tans* to be presented as *sapaat*, few *alankarik*, few *vakra*, few *ragang*, few *firat* and few on the basis of *zarab* – any such planned gradual method of application is not found in his *tans*. On the contrary, all the above mentioned movements of *tans* [*sapaat, alankarik, vakra, ragang, firat* etc] are available in mixed way in most of his *tans*. The *tan* which goes to treble octave, straight in ascending order, comes to middle octave joining complex phrases. On the other hand, the *tans* which appear to be going ahead in curved manner, suddenly end in the form of descending *chhoot tan*. Besides this blended form of *tan*, he used many fast descending *tans*, beginning from any *swara* of treble octave independently, and in a unique manner. In sum, his *tans* can be called such free flight of imagination, for which no law of physics creates any obstacle in change of direction. In spite of all these, his voice culture for *swara* application [in the context of crystals of *tan*] remains the same. He did not applied *jabde ki tan* [the *tan* with jaw movement] or *halak ki tan* [the *tan* with throat stretching].

He effectively carried out the tradition of *tan* presentation as the final part of *khayal gayaki*. In addition to these, he used special *tan* application also in many *bandishes* of *drut khayal* and *tarana*. Unique *tans* are woven also in the *swaras* of basic composition. The best examples for it are *drut khayal* of *raga bilaskhani todi* and *malkauns*, and the *tarana* of *hansadhwani*.

Before the refrain of many *vilambit khayals* or within it, Khan Saheb used some *swara* phrases as *zarab* with *tan ang*. For example, see the presentation of *megha* and *darbari* in LP record No. EASD1331, EALP1253. Even during *alap*, in the last portion of rotation [*avartan*], this type of application of refrain along with phrase of *tan*, used to be continued.

6-*Laya* and *Tal* Aspect: -

Ustad Amir Khan accepted *laya* as an instrument to keep the speed and its stability under discipline, in his *swara* salient *gayaki*. That is, *swara* is the medium of expression for him and *laya* is the means to keep its form balanced on the basis of *kal* [time]. It is not in itself a medium of expression. Both extremes of *laya* [*ativilambit* and *atidrut*] are covered by *raga* improvisation in Ustad Amir Khan's style. As his *bada khayal* set in *jhumra* moves in *ativilambit laya*, his *tans* in *chhota khayal* and *taranas* moving in *drut laya*, reach *atidrut laya*.

Khan Saheb contributed a lot in *embellishing ativilambit gayaki* and getting it venerated in music concerts. He ventured to present *ativilambit gayaki* at such a time, when exciting vocal styles, playing with *layakaries* and making the audience spell bound by collision of *tal*, were presented and heard.

Approximately one fourth *laya* of normal *laya* of *vilambit ektal* or *jhumra* in *bada khayal* is known as '*ativilambit*'. That is why, originally *ektal* of twelve beats and *jhumra* of fourteen beats, are used on the basis of forty eight and fifty six beats respectively, in *vilambit khayal*.

Although before Ustad Amir Khan, Ustad Abdul Wahid Khan had applied this *laya*, it could acquire the status of a recognized style only due to Ustad Amir Khan Saheb. Being influenced by the popularity of his style, other forthcoming artists also adopted it.

For the success of singing in *ativilambit laya*, capacity to stay on *swaras* and patience is required. Khan Saheb had this capacity. When duration of rotation of *tal* is increased, opportunity for flight of imagination in *alap* and *tan* etc is obtained. As the duration between beats is increased, its hold on *swaras* is comparatively relaxed. Hence the stability of *swara* gets boosted. Thus the *gayaki* based on imagination and deep contemplation gets ideal ground to grow.

Because of above reasons, Ustad Amir Khan adopted *ativilambit laya* in most of the *bada khayals* and applied *jhumra tal* befitting this *laya*. In those days, generally *ektal, tilwada* and *trital* were in vogue for *bada khayal*. *Jhumra* had become a non prevalent *tal*. Only few traditional *bandishes* were sung in it. But Ustad Amir Khan selected *jhumra tal* for *ativilambit laya* and the reasons for which he used it mostly, in this regard following points are worth consideration: -

1. The form of *jhumra tal* is such that, in order to maintain actual form of *tal*, the Tabla accompanist has to restrict on basic *bol* [sound] of *tal* [called *theka*] and there is not much scope to fill the gaps between beats with variety of fast *bols*. With Khan Saheb, only that Tabla accompaniment was successful, where the Tabla player, instead of showing jugglery of his hands, has the capability to maintain the *laya* and *tal* with controlled and melodious sound of Tabla.

2. The initial ½ part of the second beat of *jhumra tal* is left vacant. That is, after *sama*, the silence of 1½ beats can be better adjusted with previously described 'pause'.

3. In this *tal*, four times the *bol*: '*ti ra ki ta*' [on 3rd, 7th, 10th and 14th beat] comes, which is helpful to the Tabla player to maintain the *laya*. As has already been mentioned, in *ativalambit laya*, one beat is divided in four internal beats, which makes it easy to understand. Every syllable of *ti ra ki ta* of *jhumra* [1 *ti*, 2 *ra*, 3 *ki*, 4 *ta*] naturally play the role of four internal beats.

4. In the last two beats of this *tal*, 1 *dha ge*, 2 *ti ra ki ta* are present. So, there the internal beats are available naturally. Hence the accompanist is not required to fill the refrain with secondary phrase, nor is there any scope for it. Thus, the refrain of *khayal* and its *sama* are presented according to the convenience of the vocalist.

5. There are 12 beats in *ektal* and 14 beats in *jhumra*. Comparatively there being two more beats, the period of rotation is increased and within which sufficient scope is available for *raga* improvisation. Besides it, it is necessary that period of rotation of *tal* should be increased for Khan Saheb's system of setting up the

whole *sthayi* in one rotation. According to the Tabla player, Ismail Daddu Khan, one rotation of *jhumra* took 70 to 75 seconds, in the *laya* applied by Khan Saheb. But, in audio records issued by HMV, Khan Saheb did not use such *vilambit laya*. The time of one rotation of *jhumra* could be assessed as 65 seconds in these records.[92]

Generally the conservative supporter of *bada khayal* having *vilambit laya* near the *madhya laya*, allege that there is no relation between *tal* and singing in *ativilambit bada khayal*. To show *sama* in miraculous manner, to high light every beat by stress on *swaras*, to demonstrate mathematical dexterity by *tihais* [three tier method] and to entangle words with *tal* beats; if these are supposed to make relation between *tal* and singing, then certainly it can be said that these were missing in Khan Saheb's *gayaki*. In an interview, when Khan Saheb was asked about the criticism on *ativilambit laya*, he replied as under: -
"Every one has his own nature. Some one is inclined towards *drut* and the other is inclined towards *vilambit*. Generally it has been seen that those who could not adorn *ativilambit*, called it bad. For them, grapes are sour."[93]

Instead of putting a question mark on the competence of each other, it is better to relate using or not using *ativilambit laya* with the nature of the style.

In the *gayaki* of Khan Saheb, those factors which show the relation of singing with the *tal* in *ativilambit laya* are as follows: -
1. Because the whole *sthayi* falls in one rotation, the words of *bandish* have not to be unnecessarily prolonged and though they may not be fully parallel to the beats, still their relation with *tal khand* remains constant.[94]

---

[92] Observe: LP No.EASD-1331 – *vilambit khayal* of *raga megha* and Cassette No. STC-04-7504 – *vilambit khayal* of *raga chandani kedar*.
[93] 'Sangeet'-January/February 1980, P.19, 'Meri Gayaki, Meri Awaz Hai', Writer: Ravindra Visht.
[94] See the Swara notation of Bada Khayal of Raga Malkauns in chapter IV/[3].

2. Usually he presented *sthayi* two times in the very beginning, and in spite of some difference in the *swara* composition in both presentations, the similarity in division of words in *khali-bhari*, proves the setup with *tal*.

3. In *ativilambit bada khayal*, only the *laya* of *tal* is reduced, not of *bandish*, that is why it becomes possible to bring traditional *sthayis* of *bada khayal* in *jhumra* in single rotation, which usually take three or four rotations. The traditional *vilambit khayals* in *raga puriya kalyan [Aaj Sobana], raga nand kalyan [Ai Vare Saiyan]* and *raga bhatiyar [Barni Na Jaye]* are the grand examples of this among the audio records of Akashwani. Pt. Amarnath has thrown enough light on the above matter in his lecture demonstration delivered at Bharat Bhavan, Bhopal. A part of that lecture is as follows: - "The *vilambit* which is sung now a day, which is being called *ativilambit*, it is nothing else but we have brought down the *theka* [basic form of *tal*] four times, the *laya* of *khayal* is the same. The *khayals*, which we had sung in four rounds, now we sing in one round. Still beats are 48 [in the context of *ektal*]. But why we did so? It is a question related to the aesthetics. When we improvise the *raga* in detail and sing it enjoying deep Samadhi [concentration] and minute points there in, then when beat of the *tal* intervenes, it disturbs us a little. The *khayal* has not been done more *vilambit* [slower], *laya* of the *khayal* is the same; we brought down *theka* four times, which has come to 48 beats. Thus, this is an aesthetics, which started with Kirana Gharana. Followers of Kirana and Indore Gharanas use it. Now others are also using it because it is a good thing. Consider it as a progress."

On the *laya* and *tal* aspect of *gayaki* of Ustad Amir Khan, Dr. Prabha Atre throws light as follows: -

"It is said that Khan Saheb knew the Tabla well. Its reflection can be observed in his *gayaki*. But very few people could realize it. In his *gayaki*, the movement of *laya* used to be as refined as that of *swara*, touching lightly. Does the vocalism of Khan Saheb have any relation with the *tal*? What is to be said about them who made such remarks? Falling forcefully on the *sama*, striking a *tihayi*, confronting with the *tal* all this shows relation with *tal*. This might be their [critics] conception."[95]

In fact, the purpose of application of *ativilambit laya* in *bada khayal* is that, *raga* must have scope to establish its full effect through *swaras* even in *nibaddha gan* [set up of song]. The famous vocalist and expert of Rampur-Sahaswan Gharana, Hafiz Ahmed Khan says in an interview about *ativilambit laya*: "In *ativilambit laya*, *tal* is not salient. Hence, the contribution of *tal* should not be expected there. There the *swara* is most important. The delight produced by salient '*swara* usage' with secondary '*laya*' can be realized only when prejudice is given up."[96]

The extempore improvisation of *bol ang*, based on *layakari*, which is basically a part of *dhrupad gayaki*, was not included in the vocal style of Ustad Amir Khan. Its alternative was available to him in the form of *sargam*. That is why, where as the form of his *sargam* is inspired by *khand meru*, there is also expression of *layakari* in its movement.

In Khan Saheb's *tans,* application of *swara* stress, produced complex *laya* types. The different combinations of *laya* type appear peculiar sufficiently. *Laya* parts of 3-3, 4-4 are not to be seen parallel in his *laya* application. Instead he used *laya* types in a mixed manner. Amir Khan Saheb himself says: "previously much jugglery was performed with the Tabla player in singing, which is reduced in my *gayaki*. Much soberness has been brought in it. Although *layakari* in it is so tough that people are unable to understand how the tan reached to *sama*. Because different type of divisions are in it. People never went ahead of *tristra jati* [division of three units] and *chatastra jati* [division of 4 units], or if they ever sang any *tan* in *khand jati* [pattern of combining divisions of 3 and 4 units], they sang a *palta* of the whole *khand jati*. That is whatever *bal* [stress] was applied, was maintained completely till the end of

---

[95] 'Swarmayee'-P.31, 'Amir Khan Saheb', Author: Dr. Prabha Atre.
[96] 'Sangeet'-January/February 1976, Khayal Edition, P.193, 'Khayal-Kuch Sangeetagyon Ke Khayalat' [Khayal-views of some musicians], Author: Mukesh Garg.

tan – to show that they were singing *khand jati*. But, the division I make in *laya*, I have changed the method. If I sing one *bal* of *tistra jati*, I sing the second *bal* of *khand jati* and the next *bal* of *mishra jati*. [Then he sings to give an example]: -

g g r s, s n n d m, d G G, G R S n, d m g r s.
*   *   *   *   *

s g, s g g r s, s n m d, G G R, G R S n d m g r s."[97]
*   *   *   *   *

In above *tans* '*' sign represents the place of *bal* [stress]. The long and short *swara* phrases, joining together, produce *laya* variations on the basis of stress.

So far as the application of *tal* is concerned, besides *jhumra* in *ativilambit laya*, few *bada khayals* or *madhya vilambit* compositions were sung by Khan Saheb in *ektal, trital, jhaptal* and *roopak*, and *chhota khayals / taranas* were presented in *ektal* and *trital*.

7-*Raga* Profile: -

Every *raga* has its own profile from the point of view of *swara* application. The form of *raga* is decided by some factors of *raga* grammar, like the position of *swaras* omitted or applied in ascending or descending, their *shuddha* or *vikrat* form, *ragang* or *raga* introductory *swara* combinations or *swara* phrases, *alpatva* [rarity] or *bahutva* [frequent use] of a note, *nyas sthan* [place of stabilizing], *vadi* [most important], *samvadi* [consonant of *vadi*], *purvang pradhanta-uttarang pradhanta* [the lower or upper tetra chord dominance] etc. Observing these principles of grammar, the vocalist has to find out the ways of his artistic expression. Ustad Amir Khan combined the tradition and his own thinking in the context of *raga* profile. That is why in most of the *ragas* presented by him, the traditional *raga vachak* [that gives identity to a *raga*] *swara* combinations and *swara* phrases, are easily available,

---

[97] Audio recorded interview, April 1973, Sangeet Academy, Bhopal.

whereas his own imagination generated quite new impact in *raga* presentation. Dr. Prabha Atre writes: -

"There was thinking of *merukhand* system in *swara* creation, but its presentation was very artistic. It was not merely mathematics; there was also his self discretion in the context of *raga*. That is why the *ragas* presented by him appear different from prevalent profile and ahead of tradition."[98]

Khan Saheb used to give importance to the thought as to what profile a *raga* should have in presentation. That is why he didn't sing *raga bilaskhani todi*, until he reached to his own conclusion about *raga* profile. Similarly to what extent a *raga* should be improvised in bass octave, he had his independent opinion. For example, he has sufficiently improvised *raga lalit* and *bhatiyar* in bass octave, whereas it is prevalent that these *ragas* are to be kept in *uttarang* [upper tetra chord] from the very beginning. Such applications by Khan Saheb remained controversial among critics too. For example, Mr. Chetan Karnani, in his book 'Listening to Hindustani Music', does not consider it proper to apply the method of *badhat* [gradual movement] in *raga lalit* by Khan Saheb. From available audio recordings of Ustad Amir Khan, on the basis of some *ragas*, the *raga* profile in his vocal style can be analyzed as follows: -

Raga Marwa: Ustad Amir Khan has sung *raga marwa* in serious mood, joining *swaras* with *meed*. Avoiding the *shadja*, stabilizing more and more on *rishabh* and *dhaivat*, he has produced heart touching emotion of compassion. If the traditional profile of *marwa* is compared to that of Khan Saheb's *marwa*, the impact of both would be different. As Pt. Vishnu Narayan Bhatkhande in his book, Kramik Pustak Malika Vol.2, has stated about *raga marwa*: "Generally *meed* is not applied in this *raga* and it also doesn't look nice."[99]

---

[98] 'Swarmayee'-P.29, 'Amir Khan Saheb', Author: Dr. Prabha Atre.
[99] 'Hindustani Sangeet Paddhati-Kramik Pustak Malika'-Vol.2 [Hindi version], P.282, Author: Pt. Vishnu Narayan Bhatkhande.

That is in absence of *meed*, application of *swaras* in flat manner can not produce effect of pathos [*karun rasa*]. On the other hand, the quantity of avoidance of *shadja* by Khan Saheb was more than that was in tradition. Khan Saheb's improvisation in *raga marwa* have been quoted previously in this chapter, under the topic: '*Alap* and *Bhadat*'. For comparative evaluation, Pt. Bhatkhande's *swara vistar* in *raga marwa* is as follows:

1. "g, r, s, **n**, r, s, **n** r g, r g, m g, r, s.
2. **n** r g, m g, d m g, r g m d n d, m g, r, d, m g, r, g, r s, **n** r, s.
3. **n** r g, m d m g, n d, m g, n R n d m d, m g, d, m g, m g, r, s, **n**, r, s.
4. s, **n** r n d, **m** d s, r, g r, m g r, d m g r, n d m, g r, g m d, m g r, g r, s, **n**, r s.
5. **n** r s, **n** r g r s, **n** r g m g r s, **n** r g m d m g r s, **n** r g m d n d m g r s, **n** r g m d n d m g r s.
6. d m d m g r, g m g r s, **n** r s, **n** r n d, **m** d s, **n** r g m g r s, **n** r g m d n R n d m g r s.
7. **n** r g, r g, m g, d m g, n R n d m g, n n d d m m g g, R R n n d d m m g g, r g m d n d m g, n d m g m g r s.
8. m g, m d m, S, S, n R S, G R S, M G R S, n R S, n R n d, m d, n d m g, r g m d n d m g, d m g, m g, r s.
9. s d; d, n d, m d, n d, m g r, g m d, n d, m g, r, g, r s.
10. m g, m d, m, S, S, S R S, n R G M G R S, M G R S, R S, R n d, m d, n d m g, r, g m d m g, r, g, r, s, **n** r, s."[100]

Pt. Ravi Shankar has considered *raga marwa* presented by Khan Saheb in LP, as an ideal of *khayal gayaki*. In this regard, his ideas have been expressed in a Marathi article, written by Mr. G.N. Joshi as under: -

"That night, I [G.N. Joshi] got a very beautiful audio recording done in *raga marwa* by him [Ustad Amir Khan]. It is not necessary to tell the knowledgeable people, what a worth listening presentation of this *raga* was by Ustad Amir Khan. Two years ago

---

[100] 'Kramik Pustak Malika: Vol. II'-P.494-495, 'Marwa-Swara Vistar', Author: Pt. Vishnu Narayan Bhatkhande.

[some time in 1972], Pt. Ravi Shankar delivered a lecture before the students of department of music of Bombay University. For this, he had taken 5-6 LPs from me, from which he played *raga marwa* of Khan Saheb, as an ideal of *swara* application, *raga* presentation and *alap*, and made the students understand the artistic qualities of Khan Saheb."[101]

Pt. Ravi Shankar, in his book 'Rag Anurag', has himself accepted Khan Saheb's presentation of *raga marwa* as extract of Khan Saheb's vocal style and Kirana *gayaki*.

Raga Bilaskhani Todi: Khan Saheb maintained the profile of this *raga* with the help of *todi-ang* and in application of *swara* combinations he assumed sufficient imaginative freedom. That is why, 'r̲ g̲ p m, p m m p d̲ p m' etc *swara* phrases he applies in *raga* improvisation, also he applies them in the basic *bandish* of *vilambit khayal*.[102] Thus, departing from the prevalent profile, the *pancham swara* has been generally taken in descending and *madhyam swara* has been given importance as *nyas*. Such usage brings this *raga* near *komal rishabh asavari raga* but if *komal rishabh asavari*, presented by Khan Saheb is kept in mind, the difference becomes clear; because he has maintained *alpatva* [rareness] of *gandhar swara* in *komal rishabh asavari*. Whereas the *sama* of *vilambit khayal* of *raga bilaskhani todi* too falls on *gandhar*.

Khan Saheb had presented *raga bilaskhani todi* also in Radio Music Conference of 1972. On that occasion, he made a new experiment by including *tivra madhyam*, due to which the lower tetra chord of the *raga* in descending became much similar to *todi raga*. Acharya Brihaspati was also present in that concert. His reaction to this experiment was as follows: -

---

[101] Maharashtra Times-22nd Feb 1974, 'Ustad Amir Khan', Writer: G.N. Joshi.
[102] See the *swara* notation of *bandish* of *vilambit khayal* of *raga bilaskhani todi* in chapter IV/[3].

"Two years ago, he [Ustad Amir Khan] has rendered *bilaskhani* in Radio Music Conference. He used *tivra madhyam* in it and maintained fully. Though I would not like to do so, but I had to appreciate his genius."[103]

It is to be noted that in HMV LP, No. ECLP-2765, there is no use of *tivra madhyam* in *bilaskhani todi*.

Raga Charukeshi: An example of his experimentation with the *raga* profile can be found in *raga charukeshi*, wherein he has freely applied *rishabh* in *aroha*. Due to this reason, he has also included the *swara* phrases like 'r g m p, s r g m p'. So some impression of *raga natbhairav* is possible. With such *swara* phrases, joining the upper tetra chord, and by abundance of *komal nishad* in it, he protects *charukeshi* from *natbhairav*.[104]

Raga Darbari Kanhada: Special discipline is required to vocalize *raga darbari*, looking to its profile and gravity. During the movement of *raga*, Khan Saheb improvises it from every possible angle, with the controlled *andolan* [tonal glide] of *ati komal gandhar* and *dhaivat*. He does not mix *swara* phrases such as 'r m p' or 'p n̲ S' in ascending, with *sarang ang*, for making the movement of *raga* easy and accessible. Even under the *tans*, *gandhar* and *dhaivat* remain in *aroha*. After establishment of profile of the *raga* fully, some non prevalent usage are seen in his vocalism. For example, in the audio recording of Akashvani Indore, 'd̲ n̲ g̲ m' and 'd̲ n̲ r g̲ r', such usages are found in *tarana* of *darbari*. Considering such new experiments being made by Khan Saheb in *darbari* as proper, Acharya Brihaspati writes: - "Amir Khan intelligently used freedom in *raga* like *darbari*, but it was very scanty. It was his own specialty."[105]

---

[103] 'Sangeet'-March 1974, P.10, 'Do Shraddhanjaliyan', Writer: Acharya Brihaspati.
[104] Observe-HMV Cassette No.STC-4B-7371 Side A.
[105] 'Sangeet'-March 1974, P.10, 'Do Shraddhanjaliyan' Writer: Acharya Brihaspati.

Raga Malkauns: *Madhyam* and *shadj* as being *vadi [dominant]* and *samvadi* [subdominant] respectively, are generally used emphatically in *malkauns*. Since Khan Saheb wanted expression of devotion and pathos in *malkauns*, he gave a new dimension to this *raga* by laying stress in various ways on *komal gandhar* and the *komal nishad* of bass octave. Also the *sama* of his *vilambit khayal* falls on the *komal nishad* of bass octave.[106]

Raga Hansadhwani: *Raga hansdhwani* of South Indian Music was adopted for *khayal gayaki* and Khan Saheb has added *swara* combinations in it, according to the interest of prevalent North Indian Music. Such worth mentioning *swara* combinations are as follows: -
1. p s **n** r, 2. r **n** p s, 3. **p n** r g r, 4. g p r s, 5. n R n p g r, 6. **n** r g p, 7. g r g p, 8. p g n p.

In the above *swara* phrases, '**n** r', 'g r' and 'p r', *swara* combinations may appear to be influenced by *kalyan ang* from the point of view of *ragang*, but in the presentation by Khan Saheb, the purpose of avoiding *shadja swara* for some time was to produce a peculiar beauty there in. On avoiding the *shadja*, appearance of *swara* combinations, like '**n** r' or 'r **n**' is quite natural. Afterward, the *swara* combinations of 'g r' and 'p r' were accepted as included in *raga hansadhwani* by most of the musicians of North India.

In this way, on the basis of some selected *ragas* in the *gayaki* of Khan Saheb, we understood his own experiments amidst the prevalent trends of *raga* profile. Some other qualities of his *gayaki* regarding '*raga*', can be summed up in the following points: -
1) What *swaras* should be applied to raise the *raga*, in this regard he had his own style, which some times appeared to be different from the prevailing modes.

---

[106] See notation of *vilambit khayal* of *raga malkauns* in chapter IV/[3].

For example, raising *bageshri* with bass *dhaivat*, with bass *dhaivat* and *rishabh* in *puriya* and in *darbari* with bass *dhaivat* and *gandhar*.

2) He did not take much interest in mixed and non prevalent *ragas*, but has vocalized mixed *ragas* such as *kafi kanhada, bageshri kanhada, kaunsi kanhada, hemkalyan, nandkalyan, puriyakalyan, bhatiyar* etc.

3) He did not aim to show his dexterity in *tirobhav* [concealment] and *avirbhav* [unfolding]. In different dimensions of expressing emotions, the shadow of *samprakritik* [similar] *raga* can be seen naturally and the entire profile of basic *raga* being clear, no special effort is required for *avirbhav* [unfolding].

4) Khan saheb has avoided some prevalent *swara* usage in certain *ragas* too. As in *raga bhatiyar*, the *swara* combination 'm d S', coming as part of *marva ang*, Khan saheb applies *shuddha madhyam* only, in place of *tivra madhyam*. In his *bhatiyar* presentation preserved with Akashvani Indore, there is no *tivra madhyam* and because of this there is no *lalit ang* also. The second example can be given of *raga ahirbhairav*, wherein he never applied *shuddha rishabh*, which is commonly done. Similarly in his presentation of *raga lalit*, the *swara* combination of '*sa ma*' has not been applied any where.

8-*Sangat* [Accompaniment]: -

For the base of *swara* and *tal* in *khayal gayaki*, accompaniment of Tanpura and Tabla is essential. Khan Saheb used to keep accompaniment of two Tanpuras in his performance. Before the performance, he paid special attention to Tanpuras being tuned properly and its *jawari* [resonance set by thread] being kept balanced. The first string of at least one Tanpura [which is generally tuned with *pancham swara*] was tuned in *nishad*. It can be supposed as the influence of *gayaki* of Kirana Gharana. But in the context of Khan Saheb, this fact must be mentioned that in the *ragas*, where there is no role of *shuddha nishad*, therein too *shuddha nishad* remained on Tanpura, such as *raga malkauns, darbari* etc. Khan Saheb got prepared a Tanpura having five strings for him, in which the additional string was used for *nishad*; whereas he had also used prevalent Tanpuras having four strings and six strings. He did not like that his disciples who gave accompaniment on Tanpura, to give him vocal support or assist him in singing.

For *swara* accompaniment in singing, Khan Saheb considered harmonium more fit for him compared to Sarangi. In his accompaniment, the sound of harmonium was kept low so that it could not suppress the effect of Tanpura.

Khan Saheb accepted accompaniment of Sarangi from some selected artists only, such as Sultan Khan, who was a disciple of Ustad Shahmir Khan and who had been taking training from Ustad Amir Khan also. Besides him, Munir Khan and Pt. Gopal Mishra had also accompanied Khan Saheb on Sarangi. The reason for not accepting accompaniment of Sarangi was the tendency of Sarangi players to confront and surpass the vocalist in art demonstration, exceeding the task of accompaniment, and this created obstacles in the meditative and introspective vocalism of Khan Saheb. In unwanted efforts to compete with complex *sargam* and *tan* of Khan Saheb, it was not surprising that the Sarangi became out of tune and discordant. In many radio programs, Khan Saheb had taken accompaniment of neither harmonium nor Sarangi. In such audio recordings, only the sound of Tanpura can be heard.

In Tabla accompaniment, Khan Saheb liked the accompaniment, forming basic rotation of *tal* in definitive tempo. It has already been mentioned in given material regarding *tal* and *laya*.

9-*Rasa* and *Bhava* Aspect [Aspect of Aesthetic Expression of Sentiment and Mood]:- The vocal style of Ustad Amir Khan is the result of talent and sense of aesthetics. Along with quality of his voice, emotional depth made his *gayaki* heart touching. On the basis of grammar and technique, only purity can be evaluated, not the aesthetics of his *gayaki*. As the trends of aesthetics, while being developed and stabilized, take the form of principles and technique in the fine arts. So the *gayaki* of Ustad Amir Khan played both roles- 1 the follower of prevalent trends, 2 the setter of trends. That is why he has been called 'Trend Setter' in reviews. Also Acharya Brihaspati, accepting 'expression of emotions' in a *raga* as most important, writes in his book 'Sangeet Chintamani': - "A *raga* is an instrument, not the goal. The goal is expression of emotions."

Whatever Khan Saheb adopted from the prevalent music and whatever he left, or whatever he produced new by his imagination, in the back ground of all that, his aesthetics was at work and its aim was expression of emotions. He did not do any thing in *gayaki* with the aim to demonstrate his genius or capability. Although there was peculiarity in his *gayaki* too, but it was full of aesthetics and not miraculous. Mr. V. H. Deshpande, writes in his book, first published in 1961: "One more worth mentioning quality of Ustad Amir Khan is that, he is totally free from prevalent trend of miraculous presentation, which disbanded the enjoyment. Wrangling in *jugalbandi* [duet] prevalent in today's big music concerts and the desire to spellbound the audience; he is exception to all these. Bade Ghulam Ali, Pt. Ravi Shankar the Sitar player, Ustad Ali Akbar Khan the Sarod player or Vilayat Khan the Sitar player, all these people have become Musical gods of music concerts. Similarly Amir Khan also gets invitations from the whole of India. From this point of view, if he has also fallen in the line of miraculous ness, there could have been no objection. But his honesty to his art is so strong that in the midst of this cacophony, he never allowed his art to fall least. - - - Despite so much popularity and so much opportunity to become corrupt, he never allowed his art to degenerate. Howsoever his artistic integrity is applauded, it will remain scanty. - - - If the coin is genuine, such slow *gayaki* too can get currency in big societies. They listen to it with pleasure and can enjoy it. Does this fact is not proved by honest *gayaki* of Amir Khan Saheb? - - - Amidst unseemly and insipid trend of miraculous ness of today, there is at least one ray of hope and this is the matter of satisfaction in it."[107]

---

[107] Book 'Gharanedar Gayaki'-P.93-94, 'Indore and Amir Khan', Author: V. H. Deshpande.

Prof. C.L. Das, a writer of reviews and articles, specially on the art of Ustad Amir Khan expresses the same in following words: - "This fact is worth mentioning that the sense of aesthetics, the view of synthesis, refinement and artistic balance produced by *khayal* singing style of Ustad Amir Khan, should be considered as an important achievement in the Hindustani music of today. - - - The most important subject in the vocalism of Khan Saheb is his emotion dominated style, that is why the importance accorded to *vilambit khayal* by him, was perhaps not given to it by any one else before him. By this, I don't mean that there had been no other vocalist more melodious than Ustad Amir Khan. But as an ideal example, his vocalism definitely proves that the vocalist can express the emotion, generated by *raga*, maximum in *vilambit* rendering."[108]

In vocalism of Khan Saheb, mainly the expression of sentiment of tranquility [*shant rasa*], pathos [*karuna rasa*], devotion [*bhakti rasa*] and romance [*shringar rasa*] is found. For the first time, the *gayaki* of Khan Saheb proved that the mode of *vilambit khayal* was most suitable for the expression of sentiment of tranquility. Remaining within the frame work of sentiment of tranquility, other auxiliary sentiments can also enter, as in *raga todi* pathetic *vilambit khayal* "*sagun vicharo bamana, jo begi aan mile more sai*" and in *raga marva* "*piya more anat des gayilawa, na janu kab ghar avenge*". On the other hand, *vilambit khayal* in *raga megha*, expressing beauty of rainy season, "*barkha ritu aai, boondan jhar layee, chamkat bijariya jiyara larjayee*", provides direction to *raga* sentiment by means of lyric. In this *bandish, while* presenting the words '*boondanjhar layee*' impression of falling rain drops is created by means of *gamak*; and in the words '*jiyara larjayee*' trembling can be experienced. In the *drut khayal* of Khan Saheb, all those *rasas* [moods] are included which are possible in the music.

---

[108] 'Sangeet'-May 1973, article: 'Ustad Amir Khan Aur Unki Kala' [Ustad Amir Khan and His Art], Writer: Prof. C.L. Das.

Ustad Amir Khan tried to keep in limit, the *shringar rasa* [romantic expression] in the lyric of *bandish*. He shunned the *bandishes* having exciting and obscene poetry and preferred to sing his self composed *bandishes* and *taranas*.

In *vilambit khayal*, Khan Saheb's *shant rasa* [tranquility] finds the greatest flourish in *bandishes* having devotional lyric. The best examples of it are, in *raga malkauns* "*Jinke man Ram biraje, vake safal hove sab kaj. Jo mange so det padarath, vo aiso garib navaz*" and in *raga shuddha kalyan* "*Karam karo kripalu dayalu, tum ho sab jag ke data*". He considered some of the *ragas* especially suitable for *shringar rasa* and kept the form of his *gayaki* comparatively playful and delightful. As in *raga shahana* "*Sunder angana baithi nikas ke, moh lio man mero hans ke*" and in *raga nand kalyan* "*Man ber-ber chahat hai, tumhre daras ko balma*" etc.

In an LP, Ustad Amir Khan has presented two compositions in *raga malkauns*: 1. '*Jin ke man Ram biraje*' [*vilambit*], 2. '*Aaj mere ghar aaila balma*' [*drut*]. In *drut bandish* of *malkauns*, application of romantic lyric and there being so called no adjustment in *vilambit* and *drut* compositions, Mr. Chetan Karnani has criticized Amir Khan Saheb on the basis of sense of *rasa* as follows: -

"- - - - the singers of this form show an astonishing indifference to the text. Not only is the text not enunciated correctly, but occasionally, in *drut khayal*, the poetic theme does not correspond to the musical theme. Even Ghulam Ali and Amir Khan were not free from this fault. Their renderings of *malkauns* are a clear instance of carelessness towards the content of the text. While Ghulam Ali starts with a romantic composition in slow tempo, he ends with a religious composition in a fast one. On the other hand, Amir Khan reverses the process by starting with a religious composition and ending with a romantic theme. The result would have been happier if both had suitably interchanged their compositions. As it is, both the artists make nonsense of *raga-bhava* by ignoring the poetic content of their music."[109]

---

[109] 'Listening to Hindustani Music'-P.59, 'Dhrupad and Khayal', Author: Prof. Chetan Karnani.

The *drut khayal* of Ustad Amir Khan *"Aaj moray ghar ayeela balma, karungi Adarang son rang-raliyan"* has been described as 'romantic' in the above criticism; in fact its romance too is devotional. It is a composition of Adarang, who was a *Sufi* saint. In *Sufi* philosophy there has been a tradition to express love for God, *peer* [saint] and *guru* [teacher], which is called '*ishquay-haquiqui*' [true love]. About philosophy of Adarang, Pt. Amarnath writes: -

"Adarang: Pen-name of Feroz Khan, *khayal* composer in the court of Mohammad Shah 'Rangeele' [who reigned during 1719-1748]. All the compositions of Adarang available today reflect Sufi thinking"[110]

There is difference of effect between *vilambit khayal* and *drut khayal* sung in the same *raga*. So it is not necessary to expect the same *rasa* from the lyric of both the *bandishes*. The conclusion is that however the *raga* being same, *vilambit* and *drut khayals* are independent on the basis of their peculiarity.

In the vocal style of Ustad Amir Khan, his view is manifested to a great extent that music is a medium of communication of expressing and experiencing sentiments. In his own words- *"Gana wohi hay-jo rooh kahay aur rooh sunay."* [The singing is only that which is said by the soul and listened by the soul.]

Due to posture of Khan Saheb, unconcerned and unmoved by the surrounding and overwhelming effect of *shant rasa* on the mind of audience, many experts and critics have described his *gayaki* as Yoga, Dhyan [meditation], Samadhi and Sammohan [hypnosis] etc. The recollection of former Secretary of Culture, Govt. of Madhya Pradesh, Mr. Ashok Vajpayee is worth mentioning, who had actively contributed in organizing music conferences sponsored by the state government. In his lecture *'Sunanay Se Gunanay Tak'* [From Hearing to Understanding], delivered at Kalidas Academy, Ujjain, on 23-04-1991, he said: "In concerts, even before the thousands of

---

[110] 'Living Idioms in Hindustani Music: A Dictionary of Terms and Terminology'-P.19, Author: Pt. Amarnath.

listeners, the vocalism of Ustad Amir Khan was like a contemplation of a Yogi. With closed eyes, he continued to sing in his own mood. In between there would be a break; while he had a glance at the audience, opening his eyes and if he had an eye to eye contact with a known person, his expression would be like this, as he is saying – 'Oh! You are also present here'.

Generally the purpose of expressing such reactions is that the audiences of Khan Saheb want to consider his vocalism of higher level than that of entertainment. All this confirms the thinking of Amir Khan Saheb also. Hence following words of Mr. Chetan Karnani are relevant: -

"He believed that the function of classical music is not only to please and surprise, but to soothe and elevate mind. Since not many contemporary vocalists have realized this principle, Amir Khan's contribution is greater than is generally realized."[111]

About creation of *rasa*, opinion of Pt. Bhimsen Joshi is worth mentioning. It has been written by Prof. Shankar Abhyanker: -

"Amir Khan was his [Bhimsen Joshi's] favorite vocalist. Sweetness of Amir Khan's vocalism and its presentation is worth learning. The *shant rasa* [tranquility] of Amir Khan's *gayaki* is heart rendering. Due to this *shant rasa*, his *gayaki* acquired a sort of depth and gravity. According to Panditji's opinion there was an ocean like depth in his *alapi*."[112]

The *gayaki* of Ustad Amir Khan proves that if singing is performed keeping in mind the basic concept of *khayal* style, this style is capable to create such *shant rasa*, wherein the vocalist and the audience are absorbed fully.

---

[111] Book 'Listening to Hindustani Music'-P.89, 'Ustad Amir Khan', Author: Prof. Chetan Karnani.
[112] Book 'Swara Bhaskar'-Chapter-'Kalavantamadhil Athavani', Author: Prof. Shankar Abhyanker.

10-Adjustment between *Swara, Laya* and Lyric: -

In any vocal style, inclusion of *swara, laya* and lyric [verse], all the three elements are essential. In their mutual proportion, there may be difference of importance, quantity and variation.

As has already been mentioned, *gayaki* of Ustad Amir Khan was '*swara* salient'; because in his *gayaki swara* was the medium of expression. *Laya* and lyric are the factors to adorn expressive capability of *swara* in his *gayaki*. Thus, from the point of view of importance, first the *swara*, second the lyric and third the *layakari*-in this order the three elements can be placed. Though words are few in *khayal gayaki*, Khan Saheb considered correct presentation of words very essential for manifestation of *raga*. In this context, the opinion of Khan Saheb has been written by Mr. Mohan Nadkarni as follows: -

"Amir Khan had paid much attention on application of words. Often he used to say- 'Singing the words with emotion, music becomes more expressive. The lyrical element of *raga* is as much important as its element of *raga*. If an artist has to become a good musician, it is necessary to have poetic imagination."[113]

Khan Saheb did not include *layakari, bolbat* and *tihayee* etc, the parts based on *laya*, in his *gayaki*; because he did not want to see negligence of verse and its sense in demonstration of *layakari*. Considering this fact, it can be said that lyric was given more importance than the *layakari* in his *gayaki*.

Because of *swara* being most important, *ati vilambit laya* was adopted in *bada khayal*, so that stability and continuity of *swara* could not be affected by the beats of *tal* coming rapidly. His *gayaki* is so much centered on *raga* improvisation by movement of *swaras* that very often *antara* [the second section of composition] of

---

[113] Nai Dunia-29th March 1987, P.5, 'Unhone Lokranjan Ki Sharton Se Samjhota Nahin Kiya', Writer: Mohan Nadkarni.

bandish is left out. That is because of *swara* dominance, like *laya*, also the lyrical aspect had to compromise to some extent.

After accepting the sovereignty of *swara* aspect in *khayal gayaki*, confluence of *swara*, lyric and *laya* in Khan Saheb's vocal style and justification of their mutual priorities can be understood. That is why Dr. Prabha Atre, a follower of *swara* dominant style of Kirana Gharana, applauds the confluence of *swara*, lyric and *laya* in Khan Saheb's style in the following words: -
"Importance of lyric in word formation, pronunciation of words and attention to their emotional value, these things prove uniqueness of Khan Saheb's style. He often used to sing his own compositions. In one word it can be described as 'Sarvangsunder' [beautiful in all aspects]. Lyric, Swara creation and *laya*, all these three parts came to the fore."[114]

11-View about Other Modes of Singing: -
In concerts of classical music, Khan Saheb focused only on *khayal gayaki*. Generally the vocalists, after presentation of one or two *ragas*, present *thumri, dadra, bhajan* etc to change the taste of audience and ordinary listener too may be satisfied. The specialty of Khan Saheb's program was that from the beginning to the end the mode of *khayal* and *tarana* continued by means of different *ragas*. Despite the tradition, he did not consider it necessary to end the program with *raga bhairvi*. He wanted to see *khayal* as popular; he did not accept to deviate from his objective in order to become popular himself.

Parallel to *khayal gayaki*, *thumri* also acquired an honourable place among the classical vocalists [especially of Kirana Gharana] in the twentieth century. As Khan Saheb did not sing *thumri*, it did not mean that he considered it to be of low-grade, but he considered that all kind of sentimental expression was possible in *khayal gayaki* by means of *swara*. As far as relevance of *thumri* is concerned, he thought it

---
[114] 'Swarmayee-P.30, 'Amir Khan Saheb', Author: Dr. Prabha Atre.

fit to be associated with dance. *Khayal gayaki* proved most suitable for his tranquil nature. He recollected in an interview with Akashwani about the first music concert at Mirzapur: - "I had not been much fond of *thumri*. It does not mean that I consider *thumri* to be of low grade. I had never such view. *Thumri* also has its own place; but my inclination was not towards it. That is why I did not sing *thumri* till today." It is to be noted that Khan Saheb also could sing *thumri* well. It is known only to those who had opportunity to listen *thumris* from him in informal home sittings. Among musicians, Ms. Nirmala Arun and Dr. Prabha Atre confirm it. An interview of Ms. Nirmala Arun, famous for *thumri* singing, with Vividh Bharati was broadcast on Sunday, 28th March 1988, in the program 'Sangeet Sarita'. In this program she was asked "whether the voice of a vocalist becomes attuned to a particular *gayaki* and does it become difficult for him to sing any other style?" In reply to this question, she gave the example of Ustad Amir Khan and said: - "From very beginning, a learner should be taught in such a way that he could sing all types of *gayakis*. I often requested Amir Khan Saheb to sing *thumri*. But mostly he sang *khayal*. But I know that he could sing *thumri* also very well."

In the professionally released audio recordings of Khan Saheb, the only *thumri* available is that which was sung by him for the Bangla movie 'Kshudhit Pashan'. This *thumri* is set in *raga khamaj*, whose wordings are: '*piya ke avan ki main sunat khabariya*'. Mixing of *ragas* of different moods or *shudh* or *vikrat* form of *swaras* has not been adopted in it for peculiarity of expression, as is generally done in singing of a *thumri*. Audio recordings of *thumris* in *raga mishra pilu, jhinjhoti, tilak kamod, gara* and some *ghazals*, presented in domestic *mehfils*, are preserved with Goswami Gokulotsavji Maharaj. Khan Saheb some times sang *ghazals* also in private sittings. His favorite poet was Mirza Ghalib. He had also sung a *ghazal* of Ghalib for a documentary film.

His inclination to confine himself only to *khayal* in public performances was manifestation of his thinking and ambition. What may be expectations of the audience is a different matter. On this attitude of Khan Saheb, opinion of Pt. Ravi Shankar is worth quoting: -

"Amir Khan Saheb can not be considered to be very popular for a common listener. The reason for this Is that Amir Khan Saheb kept himself away from certain deeds like Abdul Vahid Khan; for example he never sang *thumri* in programs. If he had sung some *thumris* in the concluding part of his programs, e would have become more popular. But he never did so. Whether it was correct or not, I don't want to comment about it. It is a controversial issue. He did whatever he considered best. . . . I don't think that by singing *thumri* one becomes contemptible. . . . What he did was according to his thinking and principles. May be, it was correct for his art. Every individual is the best judge for himself. Hence, it is not justified to evaluate him on the basis of what he did not do. Whatever he did in his music, in my opinion it was the climax of development of music."[115]

12-Effect of Age on His Vocal Style: -

The vocal presentation of Khan Saheb continued from the forties till the end of his life, for about 45 years. Due to influences of *guru* like senior artists, his own experimentations and age, it was but natural that some changes had to occur into his *gayaki*.

In the initial years i.e. till 1945, his presentations were full of vitality, keeping pace with fast movement. He emphasized more on *tans*. At that time, the speed of *tans* was spectacular. It was the climax of influence of Ustad Rajab Ali Khan. Thereafter comes the period of his '*rasvad*' [emotionalism]; when improvisation part of Abdul Wahid Khan and the capability to hypnotize by means of *swara*, gave new dimension to the vocalism of Khan Saheb. During this period because of having good health and vigor, Ustad Amir Khan gave high quality presentation by application of *ati vilambit* movement of *raga,* and by *ati drut tan* and *sargam* in *drut* part. This period could be reckoned between 1948 and 1960. This was the climax of his vocalism, whose

---

[115] 'Rag Anurag'-P.88-89 [translated from original Bangla], Author: Pt. Ravi Shankar.

glimpse can be had from three minutes 78 RPM records and available audio recordings of some programs.

The onward period, after 1960, was affected by old age and disease. Hence, his vocalism continued with certain changes due to circumstances. He comparatively increased the *laya* of *vilambit khayal* and adopted the style of presenting *tans* with less speed and in pieces.

During these days, pain in his liver and stone caused obstacles in his performance; and his voice used to get lax because of cough. During this period, success of his performance depended on his self confidence, contemplation and imagination full of aesthetic sense. The popularity of his LP records made after 1960 and his success in music conferences prove this. The contemplation gave him strength. In later days, the importance of contemplation was more than that of *riyaz* [practice]. In this context, a part of interview written by Ravindra Visht is as follows: - "IN the last days, Khan Saheb had become weak. The disease of stone had become chronic. He said 'I have become empty. Though I practice, it does not show so much effect. As I keep contemplating about singing; through whose force I could sing - - -.' I said: 'Khan Saheb! Why do you think so about yourself that you have become empty? Every thing will be all right.' It is a coincidence that he died not by any disease, but by a car accident. Neither he suffered, nor gave trouble. He sang on the stage until his last breath."[116]

13-Important Reactions about the Style of Ustad Amir Khan: -

The reactions expressed by different artists and critics on the qualities of Ustad Amir Khan's *gayaki*, in midst of prevalent contemporary vocal styles, are given below: -

"A lively debate has been taking place in the world of music about Ustad Amir Khan, when he first got fame during the sixties. In view of the diehard traditionalists, the art

---

[116] 'Sangeet'-January/February 1980, P.19, 'Meri Gayaki Meri Avaz Hai', Writer: Ravindra Visht.

of Amir Khan as an effort to return to ancient music in order to explore again the basic purity of aesthetics. For others his art was a search for new directions of expression and forms. Still others thought that the vision of Amir Khan was not suitable to the commotion and the spirit of twentieth century; and that there were no qualities of exciting expressions. - - - It is not correct to think that the music of Amir Khan is simply an admixture of *'sanskars'* [ordinations] and influences. These *sanskars* helped him to imbibe the worth mentioning qualities of contemporary *gayaki*; because these qualities were in conformity with his musical genius. His style was clearly his own. It is futile to circumscribe it to any one *gharana*. His style was 'Amirkhani style' of singing" – Mohan Nadkarni[117]

"Khan Saheb's singing is like singing after waking from sleep. It does not proceed ahead; There is excess of *sargam*. It has no relation with *tal*. He does not sing *raga*, he sings *swara* – etc; such accusations have been leveled repeatedly against the vocalism of Khan Saheb by critics and those who pretend to have knowledge of music. I would like to say only that there is much exaggeration in it. To understand vocalism is also an art, a *sadhana* [practice]. - - - Khan Saheb's vocalism was not of glittering type. Its intoxication was gradual. A reason for it is that there was no aggressiveness and showmanship. There was a kind of dedication, a meditation [*samadhi*]. Khan Saheb's name can be counted with those who do not run for crowd and fame." – Dr. Prabha Atre[118]

In emotional words Pt. Ravi Shankar writes [translated from original Bangla]: -
"I would say repeatedly that Amir Khan was the vocalist who was dear to me. In case of vocalism, his *gayaki* was ideal for me. Its entirety makes the music grand. Not only *'tayyari'* [sustained speed], not only *vilambit laya*, not only the theoretical aspect of a *raga*; but combining all these and even rising above them, to imbibe music in its entirety should be the goal of every artist. The result of it is that a

---

[117] Nai Duniya-29 March, 1987 'Unhone Lokranjan Ki Sharton Se Samjhota Nahin Kiya' [He did not compromise with conditions for public entertainment], Writer: Mohan Nadkarni.
[118] 'Swarrmayee'-P.30, 'Amir Khan Saheb', Author: Dr. Prabha Atre.

common listener too can enjoy it. Such is the attraction of good music. One, who understands, will surely enjoy it more; but the one who does not understand its classical and theoretical aspect, will also be satisfied with this entirety of music."[119]

Adjustment of classicism, art and sentiment can be observed In Khan Saheb's *gayaki*. "Yet it would be true to say that Amir Khan was virtually a self-taught vocalist who blended talent with imagination, intellect with emotion and technique with temperament, as few masters could." – Printed on the cover of ECLP-2765.

---

[119] 'Rag-Anurag'-P.88-89, Author: Pt. Ravi Shankar.

CHAPTER -IV

EXPERIMENTATIONS BY USTAD AMIR KHAN

[1] *RAGAS, TALS, BANDISHES, TARANAS* ETC-APPLIED BY USTAD AMIR KHAN: -

Applied *Ragas* and *Tals*:

In all kind of his vocal presentations, Ustad Amir Khan applied *ragas* which include both, *shuddha* [pure] and *mishrit* [mixed or complex]. ON the basis of information available, the list of *ragas* presented by him is as under: -

1-Yaman 2-Bhairav 3-Bhoopali 4-Kedar 5-Marwa 6-Purvi 7-Malkauns 8-Bageshri 9-Bihag 10-Jaunpuri 11-Shuddha kalyan 12-Darbari 13-Lalit 14-Miyan malhar 15-Multaani 16-Todi 17-Puriya 18-Jayjayvanti 19- Shuddha sarang 20-Chhayanat 21-Chandrakauns 22-Hansadhvani 23-Kalavati 24-Shahana 25-Jog 26-Vasant mukhari 27-Komal rishabh asavari 28-Gujari todi 29-Megha 30-Ramdasi malhar 31-Abhogi kanhada 32-Suha 33-Bageshri kanhada 34-Jansammohini 35-Priya kalyan 36-Bilaskhani todi 37-Bhatiyar 38-Rageshri 39-Chandani kedar 40-Puriya kalyan 41-Nand kalyan 42-Kafi kanhada 43-Bairagi 44-Charukeshi 45-Kaunsi kanhada 46-Ahir bhairav 47-Chandramadhu 48 Nameless self composed raga 49-Hansakali [*composed* by combining *hansadhvani* and *kalavati*] 50-Kalashri 51-Shankara 52-Vasant 53-Vasant bahar 54-Vibhas 55-Jogiya 56-Puriya dhanashri 57-Desi 58-Sur malhar.

According to the information received from Goswami Gokulotsavji Maharaj, Amir Khan Saheb has performed some non prevalent *ragas* also; such as- *Sarparda, Lachchasakh, Alhaiya, Sawani, Nayaki kanhada, Sugharai, Sampurna malkauns, Megha ranjani, Lalitagauri, Shivmat bhairav, Shri, Maligaura, Bhairvi hindoli* etc.

Among the *tals*, Khan Saheb has particularly applied *Jhumra, ektal, Trital, Jhaptal* and *Rupak*. For *vilambit khayal*, he selected *jhumra*; yet he has presented *bada khayal* in *jhaptal, rupak, ektal* and *trital* also. In comparison to *jhumra*, the *laya* of other *tals* has been kept some what faster. In *chhota khayals* and *taranas*, he has used mostly *ektal* and *trital* in *madhya* and *drut laya*.

Performed *Bandishes* and *Taranas*:

The traditional *bandishes* of all the *gharanas* were applied by Ustad Amir Khan; which include compositions of Sadarang and Adarang of Mughal period. The details of used *bandishes* for the *ragas* mainly sung by him are as under: -

Raga yaman:
1-*Vilambit khayal, tal jhumra*
Kajra kaisay darun
piya nahin aayay meray mandarva.
2-*Drut khayal, tal trital*
Aiso sughar sundarva baalamva,
maika surang chunariya daiho mangaya.
3-*Drut khayal, tal trital*
Avagun na keejiyay. . . .

Raga marwa:
1-*Vilambit khayal, tal jhumra* or *trital*
Piya moray anat des gayilva,
na janu kab ghar aavengay.
Unkay daras dekhabay ko ankhiya taras rahin,
na janu kab ghar aavengay.
2-*Drut khayal, tal trital*
Guru bin gyaan na paavay,
mana murakh soch-soch kaahay pachhataavay.

Satguru ki sangat kar ray,
agyani tab guniyan men guni kahaavay.

Raga malkauns:
1-*Vilambit khayal, tal jhumra* or *trital*
Jinkay mana ram birajay,
vaakay saphal hovay sab kaj.
2-*Drut khayal, tal trital*
Aaj moray ghar aayila balma,
karungi adarang son rangraliyan.
Atar aragaja sugandh phool basan pehru,
phool bin saij bichhaun chun-chun kaliyan.

Raga bageshri:
1-*Vilambit khayal, tal jhumra*
Bahugun kam na aayay sajani,
jab lag karam na jaagay.
2-*Tarana, tal trital*

Raga shuddha kalyan:
1-*Vilambit khayal, tal jhumra*
Ay karam karo kripalu dayalu,
tum ho sab jag kay daata.
2-*Chhota khayal, tal trital*
Mandar baajo - - - [famous *bandish* of Kirana Gharana]
3-*Rubayeedar tarana, tal trital*

Raga darbari:
1-*Vilambit khayal, tal jhumra*
Airee bir ree jako mana chahay,

vo na chahay aapko,
to kaisay ke rain dina bhariyay
2-Vilambit khayal, tal jhumra
Hazarat turkmaan - - -
3-Chhota khayal, tal trital
Jhan jhanakva bajay bichua - - - [prevalent *bandish* of Kirana Gharana]
4-Rubayeedar tarana, tal ektal

Raga lalit:
1-Vilambit khayal, tal jhumra
Kahan jagay raat,
So pyara mora ray.
2-Rubayeedar tarana, tal trital

Raga miyan malhar:
1-vilambit khayal, tal jhumra
Karim naam tero - - - [prevalent *bandish* composed by Adarang]
2-chhota khayal, tal trital
Barsan lagi ray badariya - - -.

Raga hansadhvani:
1-vilambit khayal, tal Ektal
Jai maatay vilamb taj day,
mangan gun day.
Vidya guna amar day janani jag ki.
[Composed by Ustad Aman Ali Khan of Bhindi Bazar, pen name-'Amar']
2-Chhota khayal, tal trital
Lagi lagan pati sati san - - - [composed by Aman Ali Khan]
3-Rubayeedar tarana, tal trital

Raga Shahana:
1-*Chhota khayal, tal trital*
Sundar angana baithi nikas kay,
chhin liyo mana mero hans kay - - - [*bandish* composed by Ustad Aman Ali Khan]

Raga Jog:
1-*Vilambit khayal, tal rupak*
O! balama ab ghar aao,
tumharay bina kal nahin mana men.
Mag jovat moray dinava bitat hay,
baigi daras dikhao.
2-*Chhota khayal, tal trital*
Saajan moray ghar aayay - - - [famous *bandish* of Agra Gharana]
3-Rubayeedar tarana, tal trital

Raga komal rishabh asavari:
1-*Vilambit khayal, tal jhumra*
Jagat sapana,
kaa par karat guman bawaray

Raga megha:
1-*Vilambit khayal, tal jhumra*
Barkha ritu aayee,
bundan jhar laayee,
chamakat bijariya,
jiyara larjayee.
2-*Rubayeedar tarana, tal ektal*

Raga abhogi kanhada:
1-*Vilambit khayal, tal jhaptal*

Charan ghar aayay - - - [famous *bandish* of Kirana Gharana]
2-*tarana, tal trital*

Raga bilaskhani todi:
1-*Vilambit khayal, tal jhumra*
Bairagi roop dharay,
bhabhoot ramaayay,
samaayay meray mana.
2-*Chhota khayal, tal trital*
Bajay neeki ghunghariya,
chalat na chaal saheli.
Anupam chaal chalat matang gati,
maano pag parat paheli.

Raga chandani kedar:
1-*Vilambit khayal, tal jhumra*
Airi tu dhan dhan,
dhan tero bhag,
jo tu chatur sughar piya pyari.

Raga puriya kalyan:
1-*Vilambit khayal, tal jhumra*
Aaj su bana byahan aaya,
lad ladavan day maayee.
2-*Rubayeedar tarana, tal trital*

Raga nand kalyan:
1-*Vilambit khayal, tal jhumra*
Airi varay saiyan,
tohay sakal bana-bana dhundu - - - [famous *vilambit khayal* of Agra Gharana]

Raga ahir bhairav:
1-*Vilambit khayal, tal jhumra*
Jaagray banday rab sumarlay,
yason hovay nistar tero.

Raga chandra kauns:
1-*Rubayeedar tarana, tal ektal.*

After the age of fifty, Ustad Amir Khan became specially inclined towards *bhakti rasa* [sentiment of devotion]. He has also sung compositions of Vallabha sect, which are set in *raga darbari; as the lyric of Mahaprabhu Hariraiji* – 'meri palakan son mag jharun'. He has also sung a lyric of Dhondhi, set in *raga darbari* – 'Chalo sakhi sautan kay ghar jaihen'.

[2] Self-Composed Compositions under Pen-Name 'Sur Rang': -

Ustad Amir Khan was a composer also. He had assumed his pen-name 'Sur Rang'. In some of his self-composed *bandishes*, he has used this pen-name; and also some of them are without pen-name. Following are the available *bandishes* composed by him.

Self-Composed *Bandishes* in Self-Composed *Ragas*: -

A *raga* named *chandra madhu* and an untitled *raga* based on *swara mel* of *vachaspati* – these two *ragas* also were composed by Ustad Amir Khan. The description of untitled *raga*, has been given under the material about Karnatak Music, in chapter II.

Raga chandra madhu:
1-*Vilambit khayal, tal jhumra* or *trital*
Bairan bhayee raina,
maika piya bhavan na bhavay.

Bin daikhay pee kay rahiyo na javay,
'sur rang' kab lag tarsavay.

It is to be noted that this *raga* of *audav* type is also composed by Khan Saheb. He has considered a mixture of *chandra kauns* and *madhukauns* in it. By considering the *pancham swara* of *madhu kauns* as keynote and by improvisation of *chandra kauns*, this *raga* is produced. Generally the difference of this *raga* from *madhukauns* can not be experienced clearly. The dominance of *tivra madhyam* in *chandra madhu* distinguishes it from *madhu kauns*; because as *nishad swara* is salient in *chandra kauns,* while *pancham swara* being accepted as *shadja* [keynote], the *tivra madhyam* replaces *nishad*. Besides this, in *uthav* [raising] of the *raga* and for the final note of *avaroha*, the *pancham swara* should have to be given that much importance which is generally accorded to the *shadja* in other *ragas*. That is, keeping the *swaras* of *madhu kauns*, generating emotions like that of *chandra kauns* is the specialty of this *raga*. The ascending [*aroha*] and descending [*avaroha*] of *chandra madhu* are as follows: -

p n̠ s, g m̠, p, n̠ S.
S n̠ p, m̠ g s, n̠ p.

Self-composed 'Untitled *raga*':
1-*Chhota khayal, tal trital*
Paar karo gun nahin momen,
ham murakh tum chatur khiwaiya.

Creating Compositions in Other *Ragas*:
Raga charukeshi:
1-*Chhota khayal, tal trital*
Laaj rakho tum mori gusaiyan,
dhyan dharun aur laagun paiyan.
Tumhari baat kay dhang nyaray,

dukhiyan kay ek tum hi sahaaray,
'sur rang' tum par bal-bal jaiyan.

During his stay in Bombay, Ustad Amir Khan used to visit the main temple of Pushti sect. At that time, he composed this composition for Shri Vitthalnathji son of Mahaprabhu Vallabhacharyaji. This information was obtained from Goswami Gokulotsavji Maharaj.

Raga bairagi:
1-*Chhota khayal, tal trital*
Mana sumarat nis din tumaro naam,
ab tum hi sudharo sagaray kaam.
Hon avgun kachhu gun nahin momay,
tumaray sharan ab liyo vishraam.

Raga abhogi:
1-*Chhota khayal, tal trital*
Laaj rakh leejyo mori,
saheb sattaar, nirakar jag kay daata.
Tu rahim raam tu hi,
teri maya aprampar,
mohay tero karam ko aadhar jag kay daata.

Raga rageshri:
1-*Vilambit khayal, tal trital*
Baigun ko gun deejay daata,
tumharay karam ki hay mohay aasha.

Raga ahir bhairav:
1-*Chhota khayal, tal trital*

Piya parbeen [praveen] param sukh chatur,
mohini murat natnagar.
Rom rom chahay baran na jayay moson,
aiso shyam sundar natnagar [gun sagar].

Raga ramdasi malhar:
1-*Chhota khayal, tal trital*
Chhayay badara karay-karay,
umad ghumad ghan garajat barasat,
taison jiyara umado hi aayay.
Nisi andhiyari karee bijuri chamakay,
pavan chalat sanananananananana,
piya bin jiyara nikso hi jayay.

Raga nand kalyan:
1-*Chhota khayal, tal Ektal*
Mana bair-bair chahat,
tumharay daras daikhan ko o! balma.

Raga malkauns:
1-*Chhota khayal, tal trital*
Laagila manva tum sang,
moray mitva surjanva.

According to Pt. Amarnath, Ustad Amir Khan had not composed *antara* of above *bandish* of *malkauns*.

Raga basant mukhari:
1-*Vilambit khayal, tal jhaptal*
Prabhu daata vidhaata saban kay,

jap ray mana ghari pal chin.

Raga lalit:
1-*Chhota khayal, tal trital*
Jogiya moray ghar aayay,
ghar-ghar alakh jagayay.
Kaanan kundal garay bich saili,
ang bhabhoot ramayay.

Raga bhimpalasi:
1-*Chhota khayal, tal jhaptal*
Chinta na kar ray,
rab ko sumar ray.

Raga priya kalyan:
1-*Vilambit khayal, tal jhumra*
Sarmad! gham-e ishque bul-hawas ra na dihand.
Soz-e-dil-e-parwana magas ra na dihand.

The wordings of above composition in *priya kalyan* are originally of the Persian poet, Sarmad. Khan Saheb made this *rubayee* of Sarmad worth singing by giving it *swara* composition in the form of *bada khayal*.

Raga darbari:
1-*Vilambit khayal, tal jhaptal*
Mori aali ree,
jab say bhanak pari piya kay aavan ki.

Raga jansammohini:
1-*Chhota khayal, tal trital*
Kaun jatan son piya ko manaun,
mora piya monsay ruth raho ray.
Na aavay na patiyan pachavay,
kab lag yeh dukh paun.

Pt. Amarnath, in his lecture demonstration at Bharat Bhavan, Bhopal, in 1987, has confirmed that above mentioned *bandishes* of *raga bairagi, ahirbhairav, rageshri, lalit, malkauns, nand kalyan, bhimpalasi,* and *ramdasi malhar* were composed by Khan Saheb.

The following *bandish* of *raga darbari* was jointly composed by Khan Saheb and his wife, Sharifan.

Raga darbari:
Sthayee- Kin bairan kaan bharay, mora piya mosay bolat nahin.
Antara- Hun to vaki charanan dasi, charanan sees dharay.
The *sthayee* was composed by Sharifan and *antara* by Ustad Amir Khan.

It is to be noted that under the title 'Performed *bandishes* and *taranas*', mentioned previously, the *taranas* of various *ragas* were self-composed by Khan Saheb. The Persian *rubayees* coming there in, were taken from the literature of famous Persian poets, such as Amir Khusro, Hafiz, Sarmad etc, and were set in *swaras* by Khan Saheb. The information about different *rubayees* of *taranas* has been provided in chapter II [under 'Influence of Hazrat Amir Khusro and his Literature'].

[3] Notations of *Bandishes:* -

Introduction of IMSOC Notation System: The author has formed a new modified notation system, which is applied in presenting the notations of *bandishes* in this book. This notation system is a modification to prevalent notation system in North Indian classical music to make it suitable for international readers and also to make it compatible for generally used Microsoft Office Program with normally available fonts and formatting tools. So, this innovation can be called IMSOC Notation System [Ibrahim's Microsoft Office compatible Notation System]. The following detail of IMSOC Notation System will be helpful to introduce its rules and to make the presented Notations easily understandable.

Function	Method	Example
shudha swaras of *madhya saptak*	small letters [single character]	for *sa, re, ga, ma, pa, dha* and *ni*, respectively s, r, g, m, p, d and n
vikrit swara	for *komal re, ga, dha, ni* and also for *tivra ma*, initial letters with underline	*komal*: r̲, g̲, d̲, n̲ *tivra*: m̲
kan swara	super script *kan swara* on the left side of main *swara*	^{s}r ^{r}g ^{g}m ^{m}p
mandra saptak	bold letters	**n, d, p, m, g, r, s**
taar saptak	capital letters	S, R, G, M, P, D, N
vikrit swara in *mandra* or *taar saptaks*	underlined bold letters or underlined capital letters respectively	*komal mandra ni*: **n̲** *komal re* of *tar saptak*: R̲
khatka [stress by touching the upper and lower *swaras*]	the *swara* Inside []	[S]
meend	included *Swaras* inside ()	(d m)

Function	Method	Example
insertion of more than 1 swara or syllable of words, in a *matra*	In side ' '	*swara*: 'gm' word: 'rama'
extending duration of *swara* or syllable to next *matra* or unit	'-' in the cell of *swara* or word	*swara*: p - g m words: jaa - vo re
vibhag or *tal*-division	visible vertical border of the column	|
sama, tali and *khali*	X, number of *tali* and 0 respectively	*trital*: X 2 0 3

- 154 -

Raga-Megha
Vilambit Khayal-Tal Jhumra

Wordings: Barakhaa ritu aayee, boondana jhara laayee,
Chamakata bijariyaa jiyaraa larajaayee.

Sthayee

		'ᵐnsrm,ᵈpᵐr,sᵈs,rs,'	'ᵖnp'	'-ˢn.r'
		'Ay--,-ba,rakhaa,ritu'	'aa-'	'-,-,'
			X	
'(ᵐns)'	-	'ʳmʳmrˢˢrsnsrs'	'rs'	'ˢnˢmʳrm'
'yee-'	-	'jha------ra'	'laayee'	'chamakata'
2			0	
'p,ᵖmm'	'p,pnpmrsnsr'	'ˢnsrm,ᵈpᵐr,sᵈs,rs,'		'ᵐrrᵖmp'
'yaa,jiya'	'raa,la-ra-jaa---'	'Ay--,-ba,rakhaa,ritu'		'bijari-'
3				

Raga-Megha
Tarana-Tal Ektal
Sthayee

r	r	r	-	^{r}s	(r	p)	^{m}r	-	^{s}n	-	^{r}s
di	mta	di	-	mta	de	-	maa	-	-	-	Ta
X	0	2	2	0	0	0	3	3	4	4	
r	r	r	-	^{r}s	(r	p)	^{m}r	-	^{s}n	-	^{r}s
di	mta	di	-	mta	de	-	maa	-	ta	-	ta
X	0	2	2	0	0	0	3	3	4	4	
r	(^{s}n	-	^{p}p	^{p}n)	n	-	n	-	^{p}n	-	^{p}S
na	de	-	maa	ta	de	-	maa	-	ya	-	la
X	0	2	2	0	0	0	3	3	4	4	
n	-	^{s}R	S	^{p}n	p	-	p	m	'rs'	'la-'	'ns'
yee	-	ya	la	la	la	-	la	la	'la-'	'la-'	'la-'
X	0	2	2	0	0	0	3	3	4	4	
r	r	r	-	^{r}s	n	-					
di	mta	di	-	mta	de	-					
X	0	2	2	0	0	0					

Antara

p	ᵖn	-	p	ˢn	-	S	S	S	-	ᵃp	ᵖm
bre	ta	-	-	rse	-	ne	cha	man	-	bul	A
3		4		X		0		2		0	-
p	p	n	-	n	S	n	R	S	-	0	-
bu	lo	gul	-	fa	sa	le	ba	haa	-	-	-
3		4		X		0		2		ˢn	-
p	m	'rs'	'ns'	ˢn	s	ᵐr	ᵖm	p	-	-	-
-	-	'_'	'-ra'	saa	-	ki	yo	-	-	-	-
3		4		X		0		2		0	-
S	(n)	-	p)	ᵃp	-	p	ᵖR	R	-	ˢn	n
ri	bo	-	me	yaa	-	ra	ba	se	-	mu	ta
3		4		X		0		2		0	-
S	-	'mm'	'pm'	'pp'	'nS'	'MM'	'RS'	'nn'	'pm'	S	-
gul	-	'zaa'	'_'	'_'	'_'	'_'	'_'	'_'	'_'	ne	-
3		4		X		0		2		0	-
'mp'	'mm'	'rs'	'ns'	r	-	r	r	-	ʳs	'pn'	'nn'
'_'	'_'	'_'	'-ra'	di	-	mta	di	-	mta	'_'	'_'
3		4		X		0		2		0	-

- 157 -

Raga Malkauns
Vilambit Khayal-Tal Jhumra

Wordings: Jinake mana raama biraaje,
Vaake saphala hove saba kaaja.

Sthayee

				$^m\underline{\mathbf{n}}$	'$\underline{\mathbf{d}}$'	'$^s\underline{\mathbf{n}}$s'
		'^{s}g,mg,$^s\underline{\mathbf{d}}$,^{m}gm'	'^{s}g,$^s\underline{\mathbf{g}}\underline{\mathbf{s}}\underline{\mathbf{n}}\underline{\mathbf{d}}$'	raa	-	'je-'
		'ke-,-ma,naraa,mabi'	',Ji-na---'	X		
'$\underline{\mathbf{n}}$sggss$\underline{\mathbf{n}}$sg'	'$^s\underline{\mathbf{d}}$'	'$^s\underline{\mathbf{n}}$s'	'$^m\underline{\mathbf{n}}\underline{\mathbf{d}}$'	'$\underline{\mathbf{n}}$s^{m}gm'	'g$\underline{\mathbf{n}}$gs'	'$^s{}^m$gmd'
'vaa-------'	'ke'	'la-'	'sapha'	'ho-ve-'	'----'	'sabakaa-'
'-,m$\underline{\mathbf{d}}\underline{\mathbf{n}}$'	'($\underline{\mathbf{d}}$m[m])g'	'^{s}g,mg,$^s\underline{\mathbf{d}}$,^{m}gm'	'^{s},$^s\underline{\mathbf{g}}\underline{\mathbf{s}}\underline{\mathbf{n}}\underline{\mathbf{d}}$'	0		
'-,---'	'ja---'	'ke-,-ma,naraa,mabi'	'-,Ji-na---'			
3		3	2			

- 158 -

Raga Malkauns
Chhota Khayal-Tal Trital

Wordings: Aaja more ghara aayeelaa balamaa,
Karungi adaaranga sau rangaraliyaan.
Atara aragajaa sugandha basana perun,
Phula bina seja bichhaaun chuna-chuna kaliyaan.

Sthayee

-	'ʂS'	-	S	'SG̱'	'Sṉ'	'ḏm'	'gm'	ṉd	-	ṉ	ḏ	ᵐg̱	m	g̱s	-
-	Aa	-	ja	'mo-'	're-'	'gha-'	'ra-'	aa	-	yee	laa	ba	la	maa	-
0				3				X				2			

'gs'	'**ṉd**'	**ṉ**	s	ᵐg̱	m	ṉd	ṉ	'ṉṉ'	'ḏm'	'ḏṉ'	'SG̱'	'Sṉ'	'ḏṉ'	'ḏm'	'gs'
'ka-'	'ru-'	ngi	a	daa	-	ra	nga	'sau-'	'—'	'ra-'	'—'	'nga-'	'ra-'	'li-'	'yaan-'
0				3				X				2			

'**ṉ**s'	'ʂS'	-	S
'—'	aa	-	ja
0			

- 159 -

Antara

'ᵐdd'	'mg'	'md'	'mg'	s	ᵐg	ᵈm	ⁿd	ˢn	S	-	S	ⁿd	-	n	S
'A-'	'_'	'_'	'ta-'	ra	a	ra	ga	jaa	-	-	su	ga	-	ndha	ba
0		M	'GS'	'GS'	ⁿd			X				2			
ᴹG	na	'pe-'	'_'	'_'	run	-	-	s	ᵐg	m	(g	-	s)	ˢd	ⁿn
sa				3				phu	la		bi	-	na	se	-
0	ᵍS	ᵈm	ⁿd	ˢn	S		'nn'	'dm'	'md'	'nS'	'GG'	'Sn'	'dG'	'Sn'	'gs'
ᵍS	bi	chhaa	-	un	-	'chu-'	'na-'	'chu-'	'chu-'	'_'	'_'	'na-'	'ka-'	'li-'	'yaan-'	'_'
0	ˢS	-	S	3		X	X					2			
'ns',	Aa	-	ja												
'_',															
0															

Raga-Darbari Kanada
Chhota Khayal-Tal Trital

Wordings: Kina bairana kaana bhare, moraa piyaa moso bolata naahin.
Hun to vaaki charanana daasi, charanana sisa dhare.

Sthayee

$^m\underline{g}$	m	r	s	-	$^s\underline{n}$	s	r	$^n\underline{d}$	-	$^s\underline{n}$	'gm'	-	^{n}S	r
bai	-	ra	na	-	kaa	na	bha	re	-	-	-	-	Ki	na
0				3				X				2		
-	$^s\underline{d}$	$\underline{n}$	p	^{p}S	-	-	'sr'	$^m\underline{g}$	'-m'	p	'gm'	-	'sn''	'^{n}sr'
-	mo	raa	pi	yaa	-	-	'so-'	bo	'-la'	-	'ta-'	-	'hin-'	'kina'
-				3				X				2		

Antara

^{p}m	p	-	-	$^n\underline{d}$	-	(n	p)	^{p}S	S	S	S	-	S	-
Hun	to	-	-	vaa	-	ki	-	cha	ra	na	na	-	si	-
0				3				X				2		
$^s\underline{n}$	$^s\underline{n}$	S	'RS'	'^{n}S'	'np'	'mp'	'np'	'^{n}p'	$^p\underline{g}$	-	m	^{s}r	'$^s\underline{n}$'	^{n}sr
cha	ra	na	'si-'	'--'	'sa-'	'--'	'dha-'	re	-	-	-	-	ki	na
0				3				X				2		

Raga-Lalit
Vilambit Khayal-Tal Jhumra

Wordings: Kahaan jaage raata, so pyaaraa moraare.

Sthayee

'ⁿrgm̲.grs.nr̲.gm'	ᵐm	'gmgmm̲.mg'	g
'Ay---,kahaan-,-,jaage'	raa	'-,---,-,'	ta
	X		
'ˢn,ʳg,md,m'	'ᵈm̲ⁿd'		'ᵈS,nR̲n'
'so,pyaa,-,-'	'raa-'	S	'mo,--raa'
	0	-	
'ⁿrgm̲.grs.nr̲.gm'			
'Ay---,kahaan-,-,jaage'			

3

'nrgm'	'ʳg,mrg'	'-,gmgmm̲'	'g,ᵐr̲ gmrgrs'
'raa---'	'ta,---'	'-,-----'	'-,-----'

3   2   3

'(dmdmm)'
're---'

Raga-Lalit
Chhota Khayal-Tal Trital

Wordings: Jogiyaa mere ghara aaye, ghara-ghara alakha jagaaye.
Kaanana kundala gare bicha seli, anga bhabhoota ramaaye.

Sthayee

ᵣg	ɾ	g	m̲	g	ɾ	s	(ˢn	'-d'	-	m	(d	m	m)	-
Jo	gi	yaa	-	me	re	gha	aa	'-'	-	-	-	-	ye	-
0				3			X				2			
m̲g	m̲g	gha	m̲g	a	d̲m̲	d	n	R	-	-	[m]	-	-	m̲m
gha	ra	ra	ra	a	la	kha	-	-	-	-	ye	-	-	-
				3			X				2			
g	ɾ	g	m̲											
Jo	gi	yaa	-											
0														

Antara

m̲d̲	-	g	d	dS	-	S	S	ⁿS	S	S	-	(ˢn	R	n	d)
Kaa	-	na	na	ku	-	nda	la	ga	re	bi	cha	se	-	-	-
0				3				X				2			
m̲g,	g	g	g	d̲m̲	d	'nR'	n	d̲m̲	-	-	-	[m]	-	-	m̲m
li,	an	ga	bha	bhoo	-	'ta-'	ra	maa	-	-	-	ye	-	-	-
0				3				X				2			

Raga-Ahir Bhairav
Vilambit Khayal-Tal Jhumra

Wordings: Jaaga re bande raba sumir le,
Yaason hove nistaara tero.

Sthayee

'ᵈsm'	'mgm[m]'	'ᵐɪ,**n**g̱'	'-,**nd**,s,s'	'g̱ɪ'	'g̱rs'	-
'raba'	'su-mira'	'le,--'	'-,jaa-,ga,re'	ba	'nde-'	-
3				X		
'ᵈsm'	'ᵈpd[ᵍm],gmg̱'	'ᵗmᵍpm,gmg[m]g̱'	's,s,**nd**,s,s'	'ᵈsm'	'ᵍmgpp'	'mgmd,pdṉ'
'raba'	'--,--ra'	'te--,---ro'	'-,jaa-,ga,re'	'yaason'	'ho--ve'	'ni--,---'
2				0		
'(ᵖd,pm)'						
'staa,--'						
3						

- 164 -

Raga-Ahir Bhairav
Chhota Khayal-Tal Trital

Wordings: Piyaa parabina parama sukha chatura,
 Mohani moorata natanaagara.
 Roma-roma chaahe barana na jaaye moson,
 Aiso shaama sundara natanagara.

Sthayee

(ⁿs)	'dp'	ᴾd	n	(ᴾd	'dp'	m)	m	ᵐg	g	m	[m]	ᵐr	r	ⁿs	s
yaa	'_'	pa	ra	bi	'_'	na	pa	ra	ma	su	kha	cha	tu	ra,	Pi
3				X				2				0			
(ⁿs)	'dp'	p	'dn'	(ᴾd	'dp'	m)	m	ᵐg	g	m	[m]	ᵐr	r	ⁿs	s
yaa	-	pa	'ra-'	bi	'_'	na	pa	ra	ma	su	kha	cha	tu	ra	pi
3				X				2				0			
ˢn	d	n	s	(ⁿs	S)	n	d	p	m	g	[m]	ᵐr	'dn'	ᵍr,	s
mo	-	ha	ni	moo	-	ra	ta	na	ta	naa	-	ga	'_'	ra,	Pi
3				X				2				0			

Antara

ᵐg	-	m	'ᵐd̠'	S	S	S	S	ˢṉ	ṉ	S	'RG'	ᴳR	S	ˢṉ	d
Ro	-	ma	'ro-'	-	ma	chaa	he	ba	ra	na	'na-'	jaa	ye	mo	son
0	-	ᵈd	-	3	ṉ	S	ṉ	X	p	m	-	2	m	'g[m]'	ᵐr̠
ᵈm	-	so	-	ᵈS	-	ma	su	d	ra	-	-	g	ta	'_'	naa
ai	-	s,	s	shaa				nda				na			
0	ᵍr̠	ra,	Pi	3				X			2				
'ⁿd̠'	ga														
'_'															
0															

Raga-Bilaskhani Todi
Vilambit Khayal-Tal Jhumra

Wordings: Bairaagi roopa dhare, bhabhoota ramaaye, samaaye mere mana.

Sthayee

	'srgpdn,dm,$\underline{g}^s\underline{r}\underline{n}$,^{r}s$\underline{r}$'	'$^r\underline{gr}$'	'rgm,m'	'-,[m]$\underline{g}^g\underline{r}$s'
	'Ay----,--,bai-'	'raa-'	'gi--,roo'	'-,---'
3		X		
'$^n\underline{srg}(\underline{g},\underline{r}s)$'	'^{n}s,$\underline{r}^{gs}\underline{n}$'	'$^r\underline{gr}$'	'($^g\underline{r}^m\underline{g}$pm)'	'm[m]g,$\underline{g}$,^{g}p'
'pa--dha,-re'	'bha,bhoo-'	'maa-'	'ye---'	'samaa-,ye'
2		0		
'm,mp$\underline{d}$'	'$\underline{d}^p$m,pmgrgpm'	'([m]$\underline{g}^g\underline{r}$,g$\underline{r}$s)'	'srgpdn,dm,$\underline{g}^s\underline{r}\underline{n}$,^{r}s$\underline{r}$'	
'-,me--'	're-,------'	'ma--na-'	'Ay----,--,bai-'	
3				

Raga-Chandramadhu
Vilambit Khayal-Tal Trital[120]

Wordings: Bairana bhayee rainaa, maikaa piyaa bina bhavana naa bhaave.
Bina dekhe pee ke rahyo naa jaave, 'suraranga' kaba laga tarasaave.

Sthayee

'p**n**sg'	'mp'	'**n**pm**gm**'	'-pS**n**S'	'[p]**m**'	'mp'	'mg'	s
'Bai-rana'	'-'	'-----'	'-bhayee--'	'rai-'	'-'	'naa-'	-
3				X			
's**gm**-'	'gs'	's**n**'	's**gm**-'	[p]	'mg'	's**np**'	'**n**s'
'----'	'-'	'mai-'	'kaa---'	-	'piyaa'	'----'	'--'
2				0			
n	-	p	-	'**pn**'	'sgm-'	g	'gmpnS'
bi	-	naa	-	'bhava'	'na---'	-	'naa---'
3				X			
n	p	[p]	'mgs-'	'sgm-'	'gsnp'	'pns-'	'**np**'
bhaa	-	-	'----'	'----'	'----'	'----'	've-'
2				0			

---
[120] 'Sangeet'-December 1976, P.28-29, 'Ustad Amir Khan Saheb Ka Raga-Chandramadhu', Swara notation: Dilip Chakravarti.

CHAPTER-V

THE PLACE OF INDORE GHARANA IN THE TRADITION OF KHAYAL SINGING

CHAPTER-V

THE PLACE OF INDORE GHARANA IN THE TRADITION OF KHAYAL SINGING

[a] THE GHARANAS OF KHAYAL SINGING:

Different styles develop for presentation of a mode of singing and the followers of these different styles form separate schools or sects. In ancient times there were sects like *Shivmat, Brahmamat* and *Bharatmat*. In *dhrupad* singing there were four *Vanis* [voices] e.g. *khandhar, Gobarhar, Dagur* and *Nohar*. Similarly in *khayal* singing there were separate *gharanas*. "*Gharana*: a school, by style and tradition of Hindustani *Sangeet*."[121]

"The traditional advent of different styles of singing is called *gharana*. The *ragas* of many gharanas are the same, but the mode of their singing is different. The mode of singing the *raga* is called style, and the style of separate *gharanas* is different. Regarding the style, following points should be considered: 1) the composition [bandish] of a song. 2) the mode of voice culture. 3) the improvisation of the *raga* or *alapchari*. 4) the use of *tan* and *boltan* [*tan* with words]. 5) *tal* and rhythmic variations. 6) choice of the *raga*."[122]

Although all the above mentioned elements of formation of style are found in all *gharanas*, the mode of their quantum and application provides identity to a particular *gharana*. In Indian music the method of teaching under the tradition of teacher and taught, has been there since ancient times. The birth of *gharanas* takes place from the tradition of a particular teacher [*guru*]. When a great singer develops a particular style and his disciples in propagation of that style give a permanent shape to it, then a

---
[121] 'Living Idioms in Hindustani Music'-P.48, Author: Pandit Amarnath.
[122] 'Sangeet Shastra Darpan'-Volume-2, P.74, 'Gayan Ke Vibhinna Gharane' [The Different Gharanas of Singing], Author: Ms. Shanti Goverdhan.

separate *gharana* comes into existence. The initiator of the style becomes founder of the *gharana*. Generally, name of the *gharana* is given on the basis of the place of residence of the founder.

Traditionally, there are five main *gharanas* of *khayal gayaki*. They are: [1] Gwalior, [2] Agra, [3] Patiala, [4] Jaipur, [5] Kirana. Besides these, some other *gharanas* also came in existence. They are: Delhi, Lucknow, Bhindi Bazar, Indore, Rampur-Sahaswan, Mewati, Shyam Chaurasi etc.

The brief introduction of main five *gharanas* is as follows:

[1] Gwalior Gharana:
Gwalior Gharana is the oldest amongst all the *gharanas* prevalent at present. It was started by Natthan Peer Buksh [1800 A.D.]. The ancestors of Natthan Peer Buksh belonged to Lucknow Gharana, which is not prevalent today. Hence it can be said that Gwalior Gharana is the off-shoot of Lucknow Gharana. Ghulam Rasool [Lucknow] was the grand father of Natthan Peer Buksh and Bade Mohammed Khan was his cousin. Natthan Peer Buksh left Lucknow and came to Gwalior. Hassu Khan and Haddu Khan of the court of His Highness Gwalior, were grand sons of Natthan Peer Buksh, whose disciple propagated *gayaki* of this *gharana*.

Some learned persons do not accept Natthan Peer Buksh to be founder of Gwalior Gharana, because he belonged to Lucknow Gharana. Besides it, he lacked the gayaki of *dhrupad ang*, where as *gayaki* of *dhrupad ang* can be clearly seen amongst the artists of Gwalior Gharana, such as Miyan Tansen, Baiju Bawra, Gopal Lal, Mohammed Khan, Haddu-Hassu Khan to Pandit Krishna Rav Pandit.

Ashtang *gayaki* [consisting of eight aspects] is said to be specialty of Gwalior Gharana. In Ashtang improvisation [*vistar*] *alap, bahlava* and *tan* and its different types, *layakari, gamak, khatka, kan, murki, meend* and *soot* are included. But these are the specialties which are used by people of all *gharanas*. Hence the specialties of *gayaki* of this *gharana* can be listed as follows:-

"[1] Singing with loud and open voice. [2] *khayal* of *dhrupad ang*. [3] Straight and smooth *tans*. [4] *layakari* in *boltans*. [5] Application of *gamaks* [grace]."[123]

The main singers of Gwalior Gharana are Natthan Peer Buksh, Hassu Khan, Haddu Khan, Natthe Khan, Nisar Husain Khan, Gul Imam, Mehdi Husain, Nazir Khan [Jodhpur], Ram Krishna Buva Vajhe, Rehmat Khan Bavle [died in 1922], Shankar Pandit [1863-1917], Rajabhaiya Poochvale, Krishnarao Shankar Pandit, Vasudeorao Joshi, Baba Dikshit, Devji Paranjpe [Dhar], Balkrishna Buva Ichalkaranjikar, Vishnu Digambar Paluskar, B.R. Deodhar, Anant Manohar Joshi, Gajananrao Joshi, Faiz Mohammed Khan [Baroda], Bhaskarrao Bakhle [Poona], Narayan Vyas, Vinayakrao Patwardhan, Pandit Omkarnath Thakur, Dattatraya Vishnu Paluskar etc.

At present the singers who are presenting the *gayaki* of this *gharana* are Bala Saheb Poochwale, Lakshman Krishnarao Pandit, Malini Rajurkar, Veena Sahastrabuddhe, Vidyadhar Vyas etc.

[2] Agra Gharana:

This *gharana* of *khayal gayaki* has been born from a family of *dhrupad* singers. This *gharana* is supposed to be related to Sujan Khan's family tradition, who was son-in-law of Tansen, and court singer of King Akbar. A descendent of this family, Ghagge Khan, started the tradition of *khayal* singing. In addition to *dhrupad gayaki* which he inherited, he received training of *khayal gayaki* from Natthan Peer Buksh, the founder of Gwalior Gharana, by becoming his disciple. Ustad Fayyaz Khan [1886-1950], the grand son of Ghulam Abbas Khan, and Vilayat Husain Khan [1862-1962],

---

[123] 'Sangeet Visharad'-P.278, 'Gayakon Ke Gharane-Gwalior Gharana' [Gharanas of Singers-Gwalior Gharana], Author: Prabhulal Garg "Vasant".

son of Natthan Khan, have been modern and ideal representative singers and *vagyakar* [composer of music and lyric] of this *gharana*. As *vagyakar*, Ustad Fayyaz Khan was nicknamed "Prem Piya", and Ustad Vilayat Husain Khan was nicknamed "Pran Piya". Followers of this *gharana* generally sing their compositions. Maternal grand father of Ustad Fayyaz Khan was in patronage of the court of Mughal King, Mohammed Shah Rangile. That is why this *gharana* is known as Rangila Gharana.

The stylistic specialties of this *gharana* are: "[1] Singing with open voice, like Gwalior Gharana. [2] *Alap* in *nom-tom*, like *dhrupad* singers. [3] Special structure of compositions. [4] Specialties of *boltans*. [5] Singing of *dhrupad-dhamar*, besides *khayal gayaki*. [6] Special authority on *laya* and *tal*."[124]

The main artists of this *gharana*, from beginning till today, have been-Ghagge Khuda Buksh, Natthan Khan, Ghulam Abbas Khan, Fayyaz Khan, Vilayat Husain Khan, Jagannath Buva Purohit, Pandit Shri Krishna Narayan Ratanjankar, Ataa Husain Khan, Ram Marathe, Sardar Sohan Singh, Asad Ali [Pakistan], Dilip Chand Vedi etc.

At present, Sunil Bose, Yunus Husain, M.R. Gautam, Sumati Mutatkar etc are engaged in presenting the *gayaki* of this *gharana*.

[3] Patiala Gharana:

Vocal style of Delhi gharana has been in the root of Patiala Gharana, but being influenced by regional styles of Punjab and being developed in Patiala state, this *gharana* came in existence. Main styles influencing this *gharana* are- *tappa*, *shabad*, *sufi vani* and *Quavvali*. In those days *khayal* singers used to get patronage in different states of Punjab and the most important of them was Patiala. During reign of Maharaja Narendra Singh, many artists of Delhi court came to Patiala. One reason of

---

[124] 'Sangeet Shastra Darpan'-Volume-2, P.79, 'Gayan Ke Vibhinna Gharane-Agra Gharana' [Different Gharanas of Singing–Agra Gharana], Author: Ms. Shanti Govardhan.

this exodus was the mutiny [Ghadar] of 1857, which forced them to leave Delhi. Main singers who came from Delhi were Tanras Khan and his disciples, Kalu Miyan, Ali Buksh, Nabi Buksh and Fateh Ali. Hence the origin of Patiala Gharana is said to be from Tanras Khan, who basically belonged to Delhi. After death of Haddu Khan, Tanras Khan became court singer of Gwalior, and thereafter, he went to Nizam of Hyderabad. Famous duo of this *gharana*, Ali Buksh [Titled: General] and Fateh Ali [titled: Tan Kaptan] came to be known as Aliya Fattu. In their *gayaki*, there was a blend of Delhi, Gwalior and Jaipur. The *bandishes* of *khayal* and the *thumries* full of amorousness and variety, composed Alyafattu, are very reputed. Nabi Buksh and his two sons, Miyan Jaan and Ahmed Jan, of this generation learnt *gayaki* systematically from Haddu Khan of Gwalior Gharana.

In modern time, the representative singer of this *gharana* has been Bade Ghulam Ali Khan [alias Sabrang] about whom enough information is given in chapter VI. Ustad Bade Ghulam Ali Khan was son of Ali Buksh and nephew of Ashik Ali.

The specialties of singing style of this *gharana* are: "[1] Artistic *bandish* of *khayal*. [2] Brief *khayal*. [3] Application of figurative *[alankarik]*, curved *[vakra]* and *firat tans*. [4] Artistic application of *drut* [fast] and *ati drut* [extremely fast] *tans*. [5] Besides *khayal*, special ability to sing *thumri* with *tappa ang*. [6] Special exercise for voice culture."[125]

Main singers of this *gharana*, from beginning to date, have been- Tanras Khan, Kalu Miyan [Sarangi player], Umrao, Ali Buksh, Nabi Buksh, Fateh Ali, Pyar Khan, Akhtar Husain, Miyan Jaan, Ahmed Jaan, Ashik Ali, Kale Khan, Munavvar Ali, Barkat Ali Khan, Abdul Ahmed Khan [Patiala] etc.

---

[125] 'Sangeet Shastra Darpan'-Volume-2, P.80, 'Gayan Ke Vibhinna Gharane-Patiala Gharana' [Different Gharanas of Singing–Patiala Gharana], Author: Ms. Shanti Govardhan.

At present, main artists presenting this *gayaki* are- Pandit Jagdish Prasad, Ajaya Chakravarti, Prasun Banerjee, Meera Banerjee, Ghulam Ali [disciple of Barkat Ali, Pakistani Ghazal singer] etc.

[4] Jaipur Gharana:

Now-a-days, *gayaki* of this *gharana* finds prevalence, especially in Maharashtra, because it mainly developed in Kolhapur. Beginning of this *gharana* is supposed to be from Karamat Ali and Mubarak Ali [Lucknow Wale], who were court singers of Maharaja Ram Singh of Jaipur. Mubarak Ali was son of Bade Mohammed Khan, a famous singer of Lucknow. Late Allahdia Khan [1855-1946] was also representative of this *gayaki*. He was related to the family of Dagur Vani *dhrupad* singers. Ustad Allahdia Khan received training of *dhrupad* singing from Jahangir Khan, who was a disciple of Khwaja Ahmed Khan, father of Allahdia Khan. Singing style of Ustad Allahdia Khan was very much influenced by above mentioned Mubarak Ali Khan [court singer of Jaipur]. In course of time, by the tradition of disciples of Allahdia Khan, this *gayaki* gained popularity.

Besides, being based on singing style of Lucknow, the singers of Jaipur Gharana were also associated with Gwalior Gharana. Brother of Ustad Allahdia Khan, Haider Khan, was influenced by Rahmat Khan, a singer of Gwalior, and son of Allahdia Khan, Badruddin Khan's [Manji Khan, died 1937] *gayaki* was also influenced by Gwalior Gharana. This matter was a cause of controversy between father and son.

The stylistic qualities of *gayaki* of this *gharana* are – "*Vilambit alap* with *gamak*, *tans* with *balpench* or curved shape, *mukhbandi tans*, *alapchari* in more than one *avartan* in single breath, *bolbanav* of *laya*, new *bandishes* and rendering of non prevalent *ragas*. In *khayal* rendering, this *gharana* prefers *vilambit teental*. In *Khayal*, words are dominated by *swaras*. Like *tappa*, short *tans* and *murkis* with *drut laya* are used in slow *alaps*. The straight and long *tans* of Gwalior Gharana are generally nonexistent. Non prevalent *ragas* are mainly sung in this *gharana*, such as – *Kafi Kanada, Nayaki Kanada, Rayasa Kanada, Bihagada, Khokhar, Triveni, Patbihag, Patmanjari, Jaitshree* etc."[126]

Main artists of this *gharana* from beginning to date, have been – Karamat Ali, Mubarak Ali, Allahdia, Badruddin [Manji Khan], Mogubai Kurdikar, Mallikarjun Mansoor, Shankar Rao Sarnaik, Nivrattibua Sarnaik, Vamanrao Sadolikar, Govindrao Tembe, Bhailal, Master Krishna etc.

At present, main singers of this *gharana* are – Rajshekhar Mansoor, Kishori Amonkar, Ashwini Bhide Deshpande, Sarla Bhide, Shruti Sadolikar Katkar, Arati Anklikar Tikekar etc.

[5] Kirana Gharana: -

This *gharana* is born out of the tradition of Binkars. Main singers of this *gharana* belong to Kirana, a town of District Saharanpur in Uttar Pradesh.
The initial artists of Kirana Gharana were *bin* players, Sadik Ali and his son, Bande Ali. Bande Ali was also a good *dhrupad* singer. He was married to daughter of Haddu Khan of Gwalior. The Sarangi player of Kolhapur court and main companion of Allahdia Khan, Haider Khan, received training of music from Bande Ali Khan.

The main representative singers of this *gharana* were Ustad Abdul Karim Khan [1872-1937] and Ustad Abdul Wahid Khan [died at approximate age of 78 years in 1949], in whose tradition of disciples, this *gayaki* remained protected. Abdul Karim Khan was basically resident of Kirana. Father Kalu Khan and uncle Abdulla Khan taught him music. Abdul Rahaman Khan of Kirana taught him *khayal gayaki*. He propagated his *gayaki* by living in Baroda, Mumbai, Meeraj, Pune and Madras.

---

[126] 'Sangeet Bodh'-P.192, 'Sangeet Men Gharana-Jaipur Gharana' [Gharana in Music–Jaipur Gharana], Author: Dr. Sharad Chandra Shridhar Paranjape.

Rambhau Kundgolkar [Sawai Gandharva], Ganesh Ramchandra Behre Bua, Roshanara Begum and Kapileshwari Bua were his main disciples. The second representative singer, Ustad Abdul Wahid Khan, has already been Introduced in second chapter. His main disciples have been – Hirabai Barodekar, Saraswati Rane, Suresh Babu Mane, Firoz Nizami [Pakistan], Shakoor Khan [Sarangi player], Pran Nath etc.

The specialties of *gayaki* of this *gharana* are: - "[1] *Alap* dominated rendering. [2] Sentiment expressive application of *swaras*. [3] Making *gayaki* interesting by extending *swaras* one by one. [4] Specialties of *thumri ang*."[127]

From beginning to that, main singers of this *gharana* have been – Bande Ali Khan, Haider Khan, Murad Khan [Jawara], Nanhe Khan, Abdul Rehman Khan, Kale Khan, Abdul Wahid Khan, Abdul Karim Khan, Faiz Mohammed, Suresh Babu Mane, Hirabai Barodekar, Sawai Gandharva, Behre Bua, Roshanara Begum, Kapileshwari Bua etc.

At present, main exponents of this *gayaki* are – Saraswati Rane, Bhimsen Joshi, Prabha Atre, Firoz Dastoor, Gangubai Hangal, Mashkoor Ali Khan Keranvi etc.

The Tradition of Khayal Gayaki and Indore Gharana: -

The childhood and adolescence of Ustad Amir Khan passed in Indore. He received his training in music from his father, Shahmir Khan, at Indore. Hence, his name is associated with Indore.

Ustad Amir Khan did not like sectarian tendencies of Gharanaism and mutual recriminations. Although he accepted different styles of singing, yet he wanted to

---

[127] 'Sangeet Shastra Darpan'-volume-2, P.82, 'Gayan Ke Vibhinna Gharane-Kirana Gharana' [Different Gharanas of singing-Kirana Gharana], Author: Ms. Shanti Govardhan.

keep the whole Hindustani Music in one sphere. In this context, he expressed his views in an interview with Akashwani Indore thus: "In fact I want only one gharana in classical music, which should be termed as Hindustani Music, and it should have different departments. These are gharanas. If the main thing is kept in this form, then our mutual recriminations with respect to music will be reduced. Many separate styles were formed out of one style of a gharana, as in the case of languages. Many languages came out of one language, similarly styles and gharanas were formed in music. Now a days, I am singing in the name of Indore Gharana."

A book, "Gharanedar Gayaki", was published in 1961 by a famous music reviewer, Shri Vaman Hari Deshpande, in which he wrote a broad commentary on all prevalent *gharanas* of music. There, he has extensively written on Indore Gharana of Amir Khan. In this book he has evolved a principle to explain *gharanas*, on the basis of mutual ratio between *swara* and *laya*. According to this principle, Agra and Kirana Gharanas are two opposite extreme points, because Agra *gayaki* is increasingly *laya* salient and Kirana *gayaki* is increasingly *swara* salient. The *gayaki* of Gwalior and Jaipur Gharana is said to follow the golden mean, because in these, so called equal importance is given to *swara* and *laya*. In the area of *swara* salience, 1-Patiala, 2-Indore, and the point of climax has been assigned to Kirana.

According to this principle, Shri Deshpande draws a straight line to represent the position of all these *gharanas* as under: -

Blending of Swara and Laya [128]

Laya Salient	Jaipur			Swara Salient
......x............................x...........x............x..................................x......				
Agra	Gwalior	Patiala	Indore	Kirana

---

[128] 'Gharanedar Gayaki'-P.95, 'Sambhavniya Aakshep', Author: V.H. Deshpande.

In review of each *gharana* in this book, chapter eight [P. 90-94] is devoted to Indore Gharana, titled as 'Indore And Amir Khan'. Considering Patiala, Indore and Kirana, as *swara* salient *gharanas*, comparatively position of Indore Gharana has been described as under: -

"Now, it is necessary to pay attention towards *gayaki* of Indore Gharana of Ustad Amir Khan, in order to complete the line joining two ends of music-*swara* and *laya*. In this view, place of this *gayaki* lies between the *swara* salient *gayaki* of Abdul Karim Khan of Kirana, and Bade Ghulam Ali Khan of Patiala or Panjab. Kirana Gharana is fully bent towards intoxication of *swara*; therefore it is indifferent to *layakari*. But, it has to be accepted that in comparison to that, Indore Gharana has paid sufficient attention to *layakari*. But this attention is less than that in *gayaki* of Bade Ghulam Ali Khan of Patiala, this should also be understood. In Kirana Gharana, *tal* was paid attention at the period of coming to *sama*, while Indore *gayaki* kept caution to *layakari* in between also. Not only this, he maintained it constant in compositions of *Madhya laya*. But, he did not maintain delight of *layakari* or its climax along with delight of *swara*, in his *vilambit khayal*. In comparison to that, Bade Ghulam Ali Khan's Patiala gayaki gave prominence to *bol ang* and *bol tan* sufficiently. In *gayaki* of Ustad Amir Khan, there is no *bol ang*, nor *bol tan*. In this view, place of this *gayaki*, shall lie between Patiala and Kirana, in the mentioned straight line."[129]

The above mentioned principle of Mr. V. H. Deshpande, and the review based on it, throws light on the position of *gharanas* from one angle only, i.e. the ratio between *swara* and *laya*, and balance between the two, is the basis of his evaluation. Besides this, to maintain a certain ratio between *swara* and *laya*, is not the aim of any artist or style, and the idea of an ideal ratio can be different for different persons. Nevertheless, this principle, though being one sided, keeps its importance among different dimensions of evaluation.

---

[129] 'Gharanedar Gayaki'-P.90, 'Indore Aur Amir Khan' [Indore and Amir Khan], Author: V.H. Deshpande.

Actually, Ustad Amir Khan was an opponent of narrow mindedness of Gharanavad [Gharanaism]. According to his view, this narrow mindedness impedes receptivity of an artist to adopt virtues of others. He believed that all *gharanas* have their own virtues. In fact, expertise in different virtues is the reason for development of *gharanas*. Instead of any pride on the brand of *gharana*, he assumed achievements to be the basis of evaluation. He thought that instead of expressing pride on one's family, one should make himself so able as to make his family proud of him.

If Ustad Amir Khan had desired, in initial stage of his progress, he could have associated his name with Kirana, Bhindi Bazar or any other recognized *gharana*, and he could have taken his rightful place among musicians. Looking to Influence of Abdul Wahid Khan and proximity to Kirana style, some persons have tried to place Ustad Amir Khan under Kirana Gharana. For example, in special issue, 'Gharana', of Sangeet monthly, it is written – "In present age, among representatives of Kirana Gharana, names of Gangubai Hangal, Ustad Rajab Ali Khan, Ustad Amir Khan, Roshanara Begum, Hirabai Barodekar, Bhimsen Joshi, Basavraj Rajguru can be mentioned."[130]

While mentioning different *gharanas*, Ms. Shanti Govardhan writes, "Nowadays, main representatives of this [Kirana] gharana are Hirabai Barodekar, Saraswatibai Rane, Gangubai Hangal, Rajab Ali Khan [Dewas], Ustad Amir Khan, Behre Bua, Roshanara Begum of Pakistan etc."[131]

When enquired about his *gharana*, Amir Khan mentioned Indore Gharana. As conservative musicologists want to keep number of *gharanas* limited, and want to classify all the singers under them, it is not surprising that they want to place *gayaki*

---

[130] 'Sangeet'-January/February 1982, Gharana Visheshank [Special Issue on Gharana], P.49, 'Gayan Ke Vibhinna Gharane Aur Unki Visheshtayen' [Different Gharanas of Singing and their specialties], Writer: Miss Alka Ashtekar, Vandana Chaube.
[131] 'Sangeet Shastra Darpan'-volume-2, P.82, 'Gayan Ke Vibhinna Gharane' [Different Gharanas of Singing], Author: Shanti Govardhan.

of Ustad Amir Khan in Kirana Gharana, instead of giving recognition to any new *gharana*.

Prabha Atre has not included *gayaki* of Ustad Amir Khan in Kirana Gharana, due to quality of voice. She says: "Comparatively the *gayaki* of Kirana Gharana is of *Madhya* [middle] and *tar saptak* [treble octave], whereas the *gayaki* of Ustad Amir Khan is that of *kharaj* [bass octave]. *Mandra sthan* [bass octave], more or less rough and uneven, but Khan Saheb made the *gayaki* of *Kharaj* green and soft as much as that one does not wish to come out of it. Therefore his *gayaki* obtained three dimensional structure."[132]

According to V. H. Deshpande's book 'Gharanedar Gayaki', to recognize any style of music as a specific *gharana*, there are three criteria: -
[1] Continuation of a tradition of music for three generation, either by family inheritance or by the teacher and taught tradition.
[2] Clearly recognized musical elements, tendencies or regulations.
[3] Any influential singer and quality of his voice culture - an ideal of that *gharana*.

Ustad Amir Khan is known as The founder of Indore Gharana. The fact is that, the singers who consider the style of singing and ideology of Ustad Amir Khan as their ideal, get a place in Indore Gharana. Inheritance, *ganda bandhan* or being residence of Indore etc, any such formality has no importance here. In the family of Ustad Amir Khan, nobody came forward to continue tradition in field of music. Some of his disciples and followers have been continuing his style. It must be accepted that the branches of the tree of Amir Khan's *gharana* could not get sufficient opportunity to develop under his guidance, because of his death in early age. That is, as a guru [teacher], he could not contribute as much as is expected from a senior artist.

---

[132] 'Swarmaye'-P.29, 'Amir Khan Saheb', Author: Prabha Atre.

So far as question of the musical elements which give clear recognition to the style of singing, they can be seen in the performance of his disciples and followers. Available records, cassettes etc of Ustad Amir Khan, also offer a grant testimony to this. It has already been mentioned that being influenced by the musical elements of Ustad Abdul Wahid Khan, Ustad Rajab Ali Khan and Aman Ali Khan, Ustad Amir Khan created his own style of singing. Undoubtedly this style proved to be so effective that many great singers were drawn towards it. It became such a distinct style that it could not be placed in any already prevalent *gharana*.

The specialties which give clear identity to style of singing of Ustad Amir Khan can be classified in following points, which are recognized as the style of Indore Gharana: -

[1] Detailed *badhat* [improvisation], [2] emphasis on *mandra* [bass] and *Madhya saptak* [middle octave], [3] application of *jhumra tal* in *ati vilambit* [ultra slow] *laya*, [4] *swara* combinations motivated by *merukhand* system, [5] complex *sargam* and *tan* structure giving full opportunity to imagination, [6] to accept voice of Ustad Amir Khan as ideal in voice culture and application of notes, [7] application of *nishad* on Tanpura like Kirana Gharana, [8] Khayal like *rubayeedar taranas* of middle *laya*.

In order to confer the status of a *gharana*, third criteria is assumed to be the quality of voice culture of an influential singer. In context with quality of voice culture of Ustad Amir Khan, a quotation of Dr. Prabha Atre has been cited above, and this topic has already been discussed previously.

In a book titled 'Living Idioms in Hindustani Music', written by senior most disciple of Ustad Amir Khan, Pandit Amarnath, mention has been made [P. 55] about Indore Gharana, its style and its follower artists. Similarly, in an article written by Ms. Bindu Chawala and published in Hindustan Times, dated 30-10-1988, titled as 'The journey of the Gharanas', along with other *gharanas*, there is an introduction of Indore Gharana also. It must be noted that this article is based on research in Indian Music

Education System, conducted in direction of Pandit Amarnath for I.C.S.S.R. In the above two references regarding Indore Gharana, Pandit Amarnath, Shrikant Bakare, Singh Brothers, Purvi Mukharjee and Goswami Gokulotsavji Maharaj, have been recognized as the followers of this *gharana*. It must be mentioned that in addition to the singers, who come under the tradition of disciples by *gandabandi*, those singers who do not fall under the tradition of disciples, but are the followers of the style of Ustad Amir Khan, have also been recognized. For example, Goswami Gokulotsavji Maharaj, a resident of Indore, comes in this category.

Ustad Amir Khan himself did not become follower of any particular *gharana*, but due to his work and contribution, he became a legend, worth to be followed by the coming generation. Therefore his distinct *gharana* developed. According to Acharya Brahaspati, "Amir Khan himself was a *gharana*, he came and has gone."[133]

[b] INTRODUCTION OF DISCIPLES:

Those vocalists / instrumentalists, who took lessons in music from Ustad Amir Khan and obtained guidance in developing their *gayaki*, and are proud of being his disciple, their brief introduction is given below: -

[1] Pandit Amarnath [1924-1996]

Pandit Amarnath was born in Jhang, District of Punjab [Pakistan] in 1924. He was interested in music since his childhood. In beginning, Pandit Amarnath used to try to follow the vocal style of Ustad Abdul Karim Khan of Kirana Gharana. Prof. B.N. Dutta, a well known singer of Lahore, was also the follower of the same style. Therefore, it was natural to desire to become his disciple. Pandit Amarnath began receiving training in music from Prof. B.N. Dutta, in 1942. The process to receive lessons from Mr. Dutta continued till 1947. Coincidently, Pandit Amarnath listened

---

[133] 'Sangeet'-March 1974, P.10, 'Do Sraddhanjaliyan, Ek Patravyavahar Tatha Ek Patra' [Two Homages, One Correspondence and One Letter], Writer: Acharya Brahaspati.

to a performance of Ustad Amir Khan on radio. At that time, Ustad Amir Khan used to sing from Akashwani Delhi. He was very much impressed by this *gayaki*. Despite his financial difficulties, some how he purchased a radio, and listened regularly and attentively vocal performances of Ustad Amir Khan, broadcast by All India Radio, Delhi. Because of this, the singing of Pandit Amarnath started having similarity with the style of Ustad Amir Khan. In 1944, in a music conference at Lahore, he heard live performance of Ustad Amir Khan for the first time. Since then, he desired heartedly to become his disciple. In 1947, after partition of the country, he had to migrate from Lahore to Delhi. There he tried to become disciple of Ustad Amir Khan. He used to meet him very often and after a long wait, his desire was fulfilled. In this context, Pandit Amarnath said in an interview – "In 1947, when political upheaval took place, I left Lahore and came to Delhi. Here I expressed my desire to learn music from Amir Khan Saheb. I received a straight reply from him. He told me that he did not teach any one, and that he had no time to spare. I was not frustrated by these words and continued practicing music. At that time, I used to sing from Delhi station of Akashvani. Ustad Amir Khan heard my program on radio, and coincidently meeting me, all of a sudden he said that I should become his disciple and that he would teach me singing. Hearing this, I was overjoyed and since then I have been learning singing from him."[134] Until passing away of Ustad Amir Khan, Pandit Amarnath received his guidance.

Pandit Amarnath began singing on radio in 1942 and through out his life, he used to sing for radio and television. Under the auspices of All India Program of Music, Akashwani has broadcast his performances also. On 31st January 1987, an All India program was broadcast, whose sound recording is preserved with the author. In 1949, Pandit Amarnath was appointed as supervisor at Akashvani Delhi. After eight years, he left this job and became fully active in the field of music. Also he had been Head of the Department of music at Triveni Kala Sangam, Delhi, for seventeen years.

---

[134] 'Sangeet'-March 1955, P.52, 'Sangeet Sadhakon Se Bhent: Amarnath' [Interview with Musicians: Amarnath], Interviewer: Harish Chandra Shrivastava, M.A., Sangeet Prabhakar.

Besides it, he served as *guru* at Shri Ram Bhartiya Kala Kendra, Delhi. He delivered lecture demonstration in several Indian and foreign Universities and Institutions. His one lecture demonstration was held at Bharat Bhawan, Bhopal, in 1987. In music conferences, he made recognition as a representative of Indore Gharana. Although he adopted all the special qualities of singing style of Ustad Amir Khan in true manner, he did not sing *tarana*. He performed successful singing in 1987, in the function, which is held every year at Indore in memory of Ustad Amir Khan.

He was also a *vaggeyakar* [poet cum music composer]. He has created about 200 *bandishes* [compositions], under the penname of "Miturang". Pandit Amarnath has given music direction in films and dramas also. 'Papi' [1943], 'Dasi', 'Panchhi', 'Irada' [1944], 'Kaise Kahun', 'Dhamki', 'Ragini', 'Shirin Farhad' [1945], 'Jhumke', 'Shahar Se Door', 'Shalimar', 'Sham Savera' [1946], 'Mirza Saheba' [1947], 'Rooprekha' [1948], 'Ek Teri Nishani' [1949], 'Garmkot' [1955', 'Mirza Ghalib' [Documentary] etc, were the films wherein he had been music director. In the film, 'Garmkot', and documentary, 'Mirza Ghalib', his music was highly appreciated. The well known music director, Husnalal Bhagatram was his younger brother and Khayyam was his disciple. He was director of a research project on *gharanas*. In 1989, his book in English, 'Living Idioms in Hindustani Music: A Dictionary of terms and terminology' was published. He had two daughters and a son. The son is a physician by profession. One daughter, Ms. Bindu Chawala, is active in music research and writing. One of his disciples, Ms. Shanti Sharma, representing his *gayaki*, has made his name shine.

[2] Singh Brothers

Presenting vocal performances in *jugalbandi* [duet], these two brothers, Tejpal Singh and Surender Singh duo, are known as Singh Brothers. Tejpal Singh was born on July, 24, 1937, at Lahore and Surender Singh was born on August, 16, 1940. During childhood, they received their education in music from their elder brother, Mr. G.S. Sardar, who was blind and was music teacher by profession. G.S. Sardar himself received training in music from B.N. Datta, who was also the first *guru* of Pandit Amarnath. The elder brother motivated his two brothers to study the styles of other musicians by living in their close contact. Consequently, Surender Singh received guidance from *dhrupad* singer, Ustad Nasir Aminuddin Dagur for some time. In 1961, both brothers became disciples of Ustad Amir Khan and started learning music from him. Before being influenced by the style of Ustad Amir Khan, their *gayaki* was mostly influenced by Kirana and Patiala styles. In most of the *ragas*, they sing *bandishes* created or used by Ustad Amir Khan and they try to apply *swara* phrases, born out of *merukhand*, into *sargam*, like him. Nevertheless, their *gayaki*, in its entirety, is quite different from that of Ustad Amir Khan. Singh Brothers do not sing *thumri, dadra* etc, supposed to be semi classical, but they are active in the field of Panjabi devotional music.

They sing in India and abroad in different music programs and conferences. In 1987, during the Ustad Amir Khan memorial function, along with other disciples of Ustad Amir Khan, Sing Brothers also gave their performance. They are also Artists of Akashwani and Doordarshan. In 1988, under the chain broadcasting of music conference of radio, on 9th December, their performance was broadcast on all India level. Its sound recording is preserved with the author. During eighties, HMV released an LP of Shabad of Sikh Gurus, wherein Singh Brothers were music directors and songs were sung by Ms. Lata Mangeshkar.

Younger brother, Surender Singh, is no more alive.

[3] Shrikant Bakare

Shrikant Bakare was born at Nagpur. Pandit Manoher Barve of Nagpur gave him initial music lessons. Afterwards he was influenced by the gayaki of Ustad Amir Khan. He became his disciple and was taught by him regularly. Influence of Ustad Amir Khan can be seen clearly in his *vilambit* improvisation and *drut tans* and his *tarana* also appears to be influenced by Ustad Amir Khan. At the same time, he had an open mind to adopt specialties of other *gharanas*. In presentation of *ragas*, his selection of *bandishes* was different from Ustad Amir Khan. He used *layakari* based *bolbat* in *khayal*, which is against the style of Ustad Amir Khan. His *vilambit khayals* were not very often in *jhumra tal*. Basically, being a *khayal* singer, he also presented devotional music based on Ramcharit Manas and poetry of Guru Granth Saheb. He had been singing for Akashvani and Doordarshan for forty years. Audio cassettes of his performances have also been released. In cassette No. SB 001 released by 'Swarashree', *raga purya dhanashree, khayal* and *tarana* presentation have been worth to be noticed. He gave his performance in Ustad Amir Khan Memorial Function held at Indore, in 1988 and 1989. He had represented India in World Peace Festival held in USA. He is no more alive.

[4] A. Kanan

Mr. Arkat Kanan [known as A. Kanan] was born in 1921 at Chennai [Madras]. His family was molded in South Indian cultural milieu and Karnatak music prevailed in his home. Despite this, later on, A. Kanan achieved success in North Indian music. His childhood passed in Hyderabad. There, besides his school education, he used to take lessons in music from Lanu Baburam. Thereafter, he took training as signal inspector in Railways, and was appointed to that post. In 1941, he was transferred to Calcutta. There, his ambition to go ahead in the field of music got encouragement by the environment of music prevailing in Calcutta. He started taking lessons in classical music from a famous singer of Calcutta, Mr. Girija Shankar Chakravarti. After some time, Mr. Chakravarti passed away. In those days, Ustad Amir Khan resided in Calcutta. In programs, A. Kanan heard his performance, which appealed to him, confirming to his interest. He requested Ustad Amir Khan to give advanced training in music, which Khan Saheb accepted, considering his talent. Mr. Kanan wanted to learn music with enthusiasm, but service in railways and frequent transfers, appeared to him as hindrance in his devotion. Therefore, he left service and started his own business. This process of taking lessons from Ustad Amir Khan continued for 1-2 years.

In 1945, he presented his public performance for the first time in a music concert, in Calcutta and thereafter his performance on stage continued. On 17th July, 1954, and 14th September, 1963, his all India programs were broadcast by Akashvani. HMV has also made records of his singing.

He considers his style to be based on the style of Ustad Amir Khan and Ustad Bade Ghulam Ali Khan. Gradual improvisation of *swaras* in *vilambit khayal*, and to avoid *mudra dosh* [distortion in facial expression], *ladant-bhidant* [push and pull between singer and accompanists], and mathematical miracles, his opinions are similar to ideals of Ustad Amir Khan. Practically, in his application of *swaras* and in the effect of his *gayaki*, style of Ustad Amir Khan is not visualized.[135]

Besides *khayal gayaki*, he sings *thumri* also. He also sang for Bangla Films. His wife, Mrs. Malvika Kanan is also a famous singer.

[5] Kankana Banerjee:

She was born in Calcutta in 1946. Though she was born in the family of businessmen, she inherited music from her mother. Mother received the training of music from Pandit Tarapad Chakravarti and late Mr. Ratan, as the teacher and taught tradition. The first teacher of Ms. Kankana Banerjee was her mother. At an early age of nine years, she started learning music from Ustad Amir Khan. In those days, Ustad Amir Khan was a permanent resident of Mumbai, but very often he used to come to Calcutta and Kankana Banerjee took advantage of his guidance.

The voice of Ms. Kankana Banerjee is very sweet. The characteristic features of her singing are application of *jhumra tal* of *ati vilambit laya* in *vilambit khayal*, singing the famous *bandishes* and *rubayeedar taranas* of Ustad Amir Khan and *laya* blended *sargam*. These are the features which show the training given by Ustad Amir Khan.

---

[135] Instance: HMV Record 7 EPE 1002/Side 1 Raga Bageshri Vilambit and Drut Khayal. Side 2 Thumri.

She is the artist of Akash Vani and Doordarshan. She participates in music conferences also. In 1988, she participated in Ustad Amir Khan Memorial Function held at Indore. HMV and Rhythm House PVT LTD Bombay have issued her cassettes. In the two cassettes issued by Rhythm House, Kankana Banerjee has tried to present *bandishes* of Ustad Amir Khan in his style.[136]

At present, she lives at Bombay and is receiving guidance from Mr. Pratap Narayan, brother of Pandit Jasraj. Hence, the *bandishes* and fine vocal activities of Mewati Gharana have been included in her *gayaki*.

[6] Dr. Ajeet Singh Pental:
He received his initial training in music from Mr. S.N. Ratanjankar. Then he started learning music from Ustad Amir Khan and was guided by him for about 15 years. He has been presenting his performance on radio since 1954. His vocal programs have been broadcast from Doordarshan also. In music competition organized by Akashvani in 1960, he won the gold medal. Mr. Pental was awarded Ph.D. in music by Delhi University in 1970. The subject of his research project was- "The nature and place of music in Sikh religion and its affinity with Hindustani Classical Music". Presently he is working as a reader in music in Delhi University. He is supervisor for M.Phil. And Ph.D. degrees. His music programs are also held in India and abroad. As he has made his identity as a disciple and follower of Ustad Amir Khan, he was invited to present his performance at "Sur Rang" Music Conference held in Delhi, in May 1988 and Ustad Amir Khan Memorial Function held at Indore, in 1990.

Depth in voice, the mode of applying *swara*, and *chaindari* [patience] in gradual improvisation, reflect the influence of Ustad Amir Khan.

---

[136] Rhythm House Cassette No.240, 344 A- Shuddha Kalyan Vilambit Jhumra, Drut Trital, B- Jog- Vilambit Rupak, Tarana Trital. No. 240, 352 A- Komal Rishabh Asavari, Vilambit Jhumra, Tarana Trital, B- Darbari Kanada, Vilambit Jhumra, Drut Trital.

[7] Dr. Prem Prakash Johari:

Dr. Prem Prakash Johari is resident of Merut [U.P.] and he is active in the field of teaching music. He also performs for Akashvani Delhi.

He heard Ustad Amir Khan for the first time, in a music conference held at Jaipur in 1969. There he was very much influenced by the presentation of *raga shuddha kalyan* and he intensely desired to learn music from him.

His second meeting with Ustad Amir Khan took place at Shrinagar. Ustad Amir Khan was there to participate in a music conference and Dr. Johari had gone there to conduct examination at Shrinagar University. There he expressed his desire to become his disciple, which Ustad Amir Khan accepted.

On 9th April 1970, at the residence of Dr. Johari [328, Shivranjani, Kabadi Bazar, Merut Cant.] his *ganda bandhan* [string tying] ceremony was held. There, in the presence of invited prominent persons of Merut, first Dr. Johari and then Ustad Amir Khan presented their *gayaki*. Under the circumstances in which Ustad Amir Khan reached there to attend the program, is mentioned in the recollection of Dr. Johari, in Chapter 8.

Dr. Johari has been awarded Doctorate in music. His articles on music and *bandishes* are published in music journals.

[8] Mrs. Purvi Mukarjee:

The classical music prevalent in Calcutta was also influenced by *gayaki* of Ustad Amir Khan. Among the musicians influenced by him one is Mrs. Purvi Mukarjee. Mrs. Mukarjee was in his company until he breathed his last.

Mrs. Mukarjee performs for Akashvani and Doordarshan. In the serial of music programs broadcast by All India Radio on every Saturday, a program of Mrs.

Mukarjee was broadcast on 18th January 1988, which was relayed by all stations of All India Radio. The audio recording of this program is preserved with the author. In this program, Mrs. Mukarjee presented *raga yaman* and *bageshri*, wherein the style of Ustad Amir Khan can be observed clearly. In *raga yaman, bandish* in *vilambit jhumra* '*kajara kaise darun*' and *khayal* in *raga bageshri* '*bahugun kam na aye*' and *taranas* in both *ragas*, all these *bandishes* were in conformity with those of Ustad Amir Khan. She has participated in many music conferences in the country. In 1987, she performed in Ustad Amir Khan Memorial Function at Indore.

Living in Calcutta, she has kept alive the *gayaki* of Ustad Amir Khan.

[9] Gajendra Bukshi:
His training of music began in an institution of Rajkot named Sangeet Natya Bharati. His elder brother, Mr. Surendra Bukshi, was proficient in classical music. So, under his guidance, he practiced singing and became a rising artist. At this time, he had an opportunity to come in close contact with Ustad Amir Khan. Listening to his performance attentively and understanding his views and principles during discussions on music, Mr. Gajendra Bukshi became follower of his style. His method of applying *swaras* appears to follow the voice culture of Ustad Amir Khan sufficiently. His *raga bihag* [*vilambit- kaise sukh soye, drut- ali ri alabeli*], broadcast on 30th May 1989, is an example of this. Its audio recording is preserved with the author. He has performed in music conferences also. In March 1989, his program was held in Ustad Amir Khan Memorial Function at Indore. His performances are broadcast regularly from Rajkot station of Akashvani.

[10] Ustad Muneer Khan:
Besides vocalists, some instrumentalists have also received training in music from Ustad Amir Khan. One of them is Ustad Muneer Khan. Ustad Muneer Khan is a famous Sarangi player of India. He is deft in playing Sarangi as solo, and as an accompanist also.

It is a well known fact that Sarangi is most suitable instrument to follow *gayaki ang* [playing instrument as a replica of vocalism]. His effort to replicate every part of Ustad Amir Khan's *gayaki* and its specialties in Sarangi playing, is praiseworthy. In place of *gat* [composition especially for instrumental], he uses *bandishes* and *taranas* of Ustad Amir Khan. Using the scope of stabilizing *swara* in bow instrument, he unfolds *raga* with improvisation and *chaindari* and he expresses complex *swara* phrases of *khandmeru* on Sarangi.

He is an artist of Akashwani Delhi and resides at Delhi. He has privilege to accompany Ustad Bade Ghulam Ali Khan, Ustad Amir Khan and many other well known singers on Sarangi. In addition to music conferences in India, he has performed abroad also. In Ustad Amir Khan Memorial Function held at Indore, in March 1989, he played Sarangi as solo. On that occasion, by presenting Ustad Amir Khan's *bandishes* and style, in his mixed application of singing and Sarangi playing, he had influenced the audience.

[11] Ustad Sultan Khan:

Ustad Sultan Khan is also a famous Sarangi player. He is son of Ustad Gulab Khan and grand son of the famous Sarangi player, Azeem Khan. He learned music from his father. He had started presenting singing and Sarangi playing effectively from early teen age. Later on he decided to establish himself as Sarangi player. Besides his father, Ustad Gulab Khan, he received guidance in Sarangi playing from Shahmir Khan, father of Ustad Amir Khan. After Shahmir Khan, he received training in music from Ustad Amir Khan and thus attained maturity in the knowledge of music.

He lives at Bombay and is a staff artist of Akashwani Bombay. He is efficient both in solo playing and accompaniment. Including Ustad Amir Khan, he has accompanied several famous singers successfully. He has presented *lehara* in the Tabla performance of renowned Tabla players, Ustad Allah Rakha and his son Ustad Zakir

Husain.[137] He has performed his art in Europe and America also. He has contributed in the field of film music also.

[12] Hridaynath Mangeshkar:

The youngest of the five offspring of the famous singer, Mr. Dinanath Mangeshkar, Mr. Hridaynath Mangeshkar was born on 26th October 1937. The well known play back singer, Lata Mangeshkar, is the eldest of his sisters. When Mr. Dinanath Mangeshkar died in 1942, he was only four years old. After demise of his father, he was brought up under the patronage of his eldest sister, Lata. His father's trend of music was inherited by him through his elder sisters and he started regular practice of classical music.

Lata motivated him to receive training in music from Ustad Amir Khan and due to her insistence, he became disciple of Ustad Amir Khan. About his training of music, Mr. Hridaynath Mangeshkar himself has given following information: -

"I was so young when father died that I could hardly listen to him and learn from him. But I heard Didi rehearsing the *Ragas* and classical songs, she had learnt from him and I picked up whatever I could of Baba's music. - - - - - Although I was sent to school for studies, I could not resist the inherited urge for music and began yearning for it. Didi encouraged me to become a disciple of Ustad Amir Khan, a distinguished vocalist, known for his rich melodious voice and majestic Rag elaboration, so that I could have a proper grounding in classical music."[138]

Being a scholar of classical music and a music director, Mr. Hridaynath is fully confident of tremendous scope of classical music in films and its permanent effect. When he was receiving training in music from Ustad Amir Khan, he composed two songs based on classical music and got them sung by Lataji, in his direction, whose

---
[137] Instance: Magna Sound Cassette No.C 4 H 10241 'Together Ustad Allah Rakha and Ustad Zakir Husain'.
[138] Screen – 22 September 1989, "The Mangeshkars on Lata 'We are proud of Didi'", Writer: R.M. Kumtakar.

records were released by HMV in 1954. One of them is the composition of Surdas, whose wordings are '*nisdin barsat*' and the other is of Meerabai, '*barse bindiya sawan ki*'. This effort of him was appreciated by top artist like Pandit Ravishankar and he encouraged him to go ahead in the field of music direction.

Without surrendering to the demand of commercialism of film industry, he mainly selected the field of directing non film classical and light songs. He has been the music director of most of the non film songs, Ghazals and devotional songs sung by Lata Mangeshkar. Main among them are Gyaneshwari and Bhagwat Geeta, Ghazals of Ghalib, Bhajans of Meera titled 'Chala Vahi Desh', Marathi poems of poet Bhaskar Ramchandra Tambe, etc.

Mr. Hridaynath Mangeshkar has given music direction to many Marathi and Hindi films in his distinct style. Among his Hindi films, 'Prarthana', 'Harishchandra Taramati' [1970], 'Chakra', 'Dhanwan', 'Subah' and 'Mashal' are outstanding. A film made in 1991, 'Lekin' [for which he was given the best music director award], wherein he himself along with Lataji, has sung a traditional *bandish* in *raga gujri todi* [Ja Ja Re Pathikwa][139] It is to be noted that Ustad Amir Khan used to sing *vilambit khayal* in *raga gujri todi* in *jhumra tal*. This *bandish* of Ustad Amir Khan, presented in 'Utsav 1973' held at Bhopal, is preserved with the author. Looking to Hridaynath Mangeshkar's devotion to classical music, Pandit Bhimsen Joshi has awarded him the title of 'Pandit'.

[13] Tom Ross:

Ustad Amir Khan used to perform in western countries during his tours to foreign countries. Working as a visiting professor, there he came in contact with students and music lovers of universities and colleges, having curiosity for Indian music. Many students tried to receive training in music from Ustad Amir Khan systematically. Among them, name of Tom Ross of USA is worth mentioning. He became a disciple

---

[139] Instance: film 'Lekin', HMV cassette No. SPH 044465, side B.

of Ustad Amir Khan and understanding Indian cultural milieu, started learning music. Ustad Amir Khan was impressed by his progress. According to Ustad Amir Khan, merely listening to singing of Tom Ross, one could not imagine that the singer was a foreigner.

In 1969, Tom Ross came to India and participated in some concerts in Bombay. At present, he is not enough active in the field of singing.

[c] INFLUENCE OF USTAD AMIR KHAN'S STYLE ON CONTEMPORARY AND SUCCESSIVE VOCALISTS AND INSTRUMENTALISTS:

The above mentioned vocalists/instrumentalists received their training in music directly from Ustad Amir Khan. In this context, it would be proper to mention those vocalists/instrumentalists who adopted trends of his *gayaki*, simply by listening to him and developed their *gayaki* by its inspiration. Many musicians of different *gharanas* come in this category. The name of Ustad Amir Khan is on the top, among the musicians who influenced the *gayaki* of other *gharanas*. Though, some of them proudly acknowledge this influence, whereas others, in spite of being influenced by him, keep mum about it. Nevertheless, knowledgeable audience can detect this influence. Those who themselves accepted the influence of Ustad Amir Khan are Pt. Bhimsen Joshi, Prabha Atre and Pt. Rasiklal Andharia of Kirana Gharana, Goswami Gokulotsavji Maharaj of Indore Gharana, and Rashid Khan, a disciple of Nisar Husain Khan of Rampur-Sahaswan Gharana. Among the instrumentalists, the names of Pt. Nikhil Banerjee and Budhdevdas Gupta are worth mentioning. In this respect, following few examples are important, which prove his influence: -

Pt. Bhimsen Joshi:

Pt. Bhimsen Joshi had said: "At a certain period, I used to listen only to his recorded tapes at home. If I acquire even fifty percent of his art in my voice, I shall feel fortunate."[140]

In the words of Professor Shankar Abhyankar: "The stamp of Ustad Amir Khan's style Is visible in the *gayaki* of Panditji. The tranquility, sweetness, gravity in presentation of *raga*, all these sanskars have been adopted in the style of Panditji from Ustad Amir Khan's *gayaki*."[141]

Dr. Prabha Atre:

Dr. Prabha Atre writes: "I heard Khan Saheb for the first time through the medium of records. - - - In the same period, I was introduced to Mr. Shrikant Bakare, one of the disciples of Khan Saheb. His view was the same, wise and always thinking about music. Several times, we sang together and discussed. By these sittings, I could get actual view of Khan Saheb's *gayaki*. Unknowingly, I came so near to the *gayaki* of Khan Saheb that I could not realize. 'Prabhaji has changed her trend.' Such comments were reaching to me.

- - - No particular opportunity arrived to come near Khan Saheb personally. Even observing from a distance, one could see his cultured manners during conversation. I had no curiosity to know more about his personal life, as there was a unique place in my mind for Suresh Babu, as a *guru* and as a person also. It was not possible for me to replace him.

- - Even today people ask me 'You have been so much influenced by the *gayaki* of Amir Khan Saheb, why don't you admit him your *guru*?' Always my answer is 'Suresh Babu is my *guru* and Amir Khan is like a *guru* for me.'

---

[140] Jansatta-26th March 1989, 'Ek Raga Ki Kahani', Writer: Vasant Potdar.
[141] 'Swar Bhaskar'-P.283, Writer: Prof. Shankar Abhyankar.

- - The *sargam* between *alap* and *tan* of Khan Saheb was unique. What ever change took place in my *gayaki*, its root was in that *sargam*. After 1960, for the first time I began singing *sargam*. I found a new direction. I began to observe the activity of *swaras* more minutely."[142]

Goswami Gokulotsavji Maharaj:
"When Goswamiji heard late Ustad Amir Khan Saheb, he felt that the ultimate presentation of singing is in this *gayaki*, by which the human soul is enchanted.
The gravity of Khan Saheb's singing, the beautiful application of *swaras* and variety of miraculous *tans*, influenced Goswamiji to such an extent that his singing appeared to be true copy of vocalism of Khan Saheb. Soon he initiated originality in his singing, and now, in spite of being influenced by Ustad Amir Khan, his style has its own specialty. The originality of singing of Gokulotsavji depends on his *alaps*, expression of words and heart touching application of *swaras*. In his singing application of *merukhand* abounds and the image formed by his style of singing leaves clear and deep imprints on mind."[143]

"It is these two traits, his stylistic *tans* and varying *sargam* patterns-which together with *rubayeedar tarana* constitute the essentials of his *gayaki*. And it is these very features which closely identify his singing with these riveting and mystical *gayaki* of the late Amir Khan, who was well known for the use of similar characteristics."[144]

As has already been mentioned that Pt. Amarnath has also recognized Shri Gokulotsavji Maharaj as the follower of the *gayaki* of Indore Gharana. Maharajji is a good *vaggekar* [composer of music and lyric both] and he has composed many *bandishes* under the pen name of 'Madhur Piya'. Without receiving any training from Ustad Amir Khan personally, simply by using audio recordings of Khan Saheb, the

---
[142] 'Swarmayee'-P.27-30, Writer: Dr. Prabha Atre.
[143] Dainik Bhaskar-6 May 1989, 'Bharatiya Sangeet Ke Prakash Stambh Goswami Gokulotsavji Maharaj', Writer: Roop Narayan Dikshit.
[144] From the folder of 'Rhythm House' Cassette No.240-358
Ustadi Gayaki [vol. 2], His Holiness Acharya Goswami Gokulotsavji Maharaj.

presentation of his *gayaki* after his death, is unique in itself. The specialties of *gayaki* of Maharajji are: *bahlava, soot, boltan, meend, gamak,* to present *gamak tan* rapidly with *zarab, lahak, chhoot, sapat,* well balanced *tans* in three octaves, *sargam* of *merukhand* and *gamakdar tans, bal, pench, andolan, daat, khand tan* [which also named as *sakhand tan*], *neembat, firat, murchit* and to present every joint jointlessly. In the *gayaki* of Maharajji, there are some specialties in addition to that of Ustad Amir Khan. Since sixties he has been performing on the stage. His broadcast on radio started in 1975. At present he is Special A Top Grade artist of Akashvani. Not only from Indore, but from other radio stations of Akashvani, his audio recordings are broadcast, e.g. Raipur, Mathura, Delhi, Delhi Urdu Service, Ahmedabad, Rajkot, Mumbai, Pune, Aurangabad, Sangli, Jalgaon, Hyderabad, Jaipur, Jalandhar etc. His All India Programs are being broadcast by radio and television. His vocal recitals have been organized in USA, England, Denmark, Sweden, France and other European countries and also in Arab countries.

Sitar Maestro Pt. Nikhil Banerjee:

Pt. Ravishankar said about performance of Pt. Nikhil Banerjee: "In 1957-58, I observed wonderful form of his performance. There was different type of taste in his performance-playing style like a *gayaki*. In beginning, there was my influence. For some time I had taught him also. Then there appeared the influence of style of Vilayat Khan on him. There after reflection of the style of the great vocalist, Ustad Amir Khan was seen in his Sitar playing. In my opinion, his final hero was Amir Khan."[145]

Mr. Madanlal Vyas writes: "At the end of fifties, in the Sitar playing of Nikhil, there appeared to be influence of such an artist, who in fact can not be called his *guru*. He was the great vocalist Amir Khan. But in his young age, Nikhil was a disciple of Amir Khan just by sentiment. In the performance of Nikhil, development of deep

---

[145] 'Sangeet'-April 1986, P.35, 'Navin Vishisht Wadan Shaili Ke Shrashta Pt. Nikhil Banerjee', Writer: Madanlal Vyas.

spiritualism and thoughtfulness got acceleration by the touch of Amir Khan. In this way, *vilambit khayal* found gradual entrance in the well built and expert instrument technique of Senia Gharana. Similarly, specialty of *merukhand* of Amir Khan was spread in *tan todas*. Perhaps Nikhil was the originator and conveyor of *Merukhand tan* on Sitar."[146]

---

[146] 'Sangeet'-April 1986, P.37, 'Navin Vishisht Vadan Shaili Ke Shrasta Pandit Nikhil Banerjee', Writer: Madanlal Vyas.

CHAPTER-VI

VOCAL PERFORMANCES AND HONORS ACHIEVED

CHAPTER-VI

VOCAL PERFORMANCES AND HONORS ACHIEVED

After obtaining training in music from his father, and with his permission, Ustad Amir Khan started performing his art in different music concerts. Due to success of these programs, his popularity increased gradually. This process continued till the end of his life. He was always recognized as a performing artist. He performed at radio and TV centers and all India music conferences. He performed in foreign countries also. He received many honors. He came in contact with eminent musicians. A detail description of it is being given below.

1-Vocal Performances: -

[a] At the Centers of Akashwani [radio] & Doordarshan [TV]: During the British rule, in the third decade of 20th century, radio broadcast started in India. At the early age of twenty years, Ustad Amir Khan had started singing in radio programs. Though at that time, he had not sufficient experience of performing before the audience in music conferences. By the end of third decade, seven-eight radio stations had been established inn the Indian sub-continent. Even during British age, among radio officials who had special interest in the classical music were Zulfikar Ali Bukhari, Ahmadshah Bukhari, Victor Paranjoti, B.C. Merdekar, K.D. Dikshit, D. Ambel etc, whose contribution was of great importance. In those days, there was no broadcasting center of radio in this region [the area of present Madhya Pradesh]. Hence Ustad Amir Khan started his radio programs from Bombay and Delhi stations.

Still there are many musicians and reviewers who have listened initial radio broadcasts of Ustad Amir Khan. They have expressed their views and recollections with regard to those broadcasts at many places. First of all, recollection of the eminent Sitar maestro, Pt. Ravishankar is worth mentioning wherein he has discussed the vocal style of Ustad Amir Khan of those days on the basis of radio broadcasts: - Translated from original Bangla- "I heard him singing for the first time in 1938. I remember, I continued to listen till 1941. Usually he used to sing from Delhi radio station. It was a quite different vocal style. It was not that vocalism which Amir Khan had been presenting afterward. Besides the training received from his father, he was under the influence of *gayaki* of Ustad Rajab Ali Khan of Dewas. Besides, he was influenced by Aman Ali Khan also. This Aman Ali Khan was a singer of a distinct style. But his fame was limited only to knowledgeable people and vocalists."[147]

At about 1941, when Ustad Amir Khan went to Calcutta to live there, he used to sing from local radio station there. He was paid Rs. 30 as remuneration from Calcutta radio station. Thereafter, on coming to Delhi, remuneration was increased to Rs. 60. Because of the powerful transmission, broadcast of Delhi radio station could be heard easily far and wide. Pt. Amarnath used to listen to Ustad Amir Khan's programs, when he was living at Lahore. Just listening to those radio programs, Pt. Amarnath was influenced by Ustad Amir Khan for the first time. In this context, following recollection of Pt. Amarnath is worth quoting: -

"I was at Lahore. At about 1942 I could sing some what. I used to learn from Datta and was considered as youngest artist of Radio Lahore. Once I heard Amir Khan's performance from Radio Delhi. It struck me. One radio set would have to be bought but there was no money. Any how I could arrange a small radio set of Rs.255. Almost every Sunday, I used to listen Amir Khan from Radio Delhi. Ustad Abdul Wahid Khan was already in Lahore. I used to listen to him also. But I used to listen to Amir Khan Saheb in such a manner that every thing could be absorbed. Not a single drop should fall away; nor someone else should snatch it away. Any heard *swara* should

---

[147] 'Rag-Anurag'-P.63-69, Author: Pt. Ravishankar.

not be forgotten. Evidently my singing was influenced by him. I am telling about those days, when I had not even seen him."[148]

In those days Ustad Amir Khan used to get many programs of 15 minutes duration on Delhi Radio. During the course of conversation, famous vocalist, Goswami Gokulotsavji Maharaj, gave the author following information about one such program. It is to be noted that Goswami Gokulotsavji Maharaj has large collection of Ustad Amir Khan's old radio programs and music concert's audio recorded spools and cassettes preserved with him. More over, when the technique of audio recording on the tape was not introduced, the wire recordings of those days are also preserved with him. He said: -

"Amir Khan liked the *bandish* of *Miyaki Sarang* very much; therefore he got this *bandish* from Babu Khan. Its wordings are *'pratham pyaray ayay'*. In those days, programs of fifteen minutes were used to be broadcast from Delhi; in such a program, Amir Khan had also presented it. It is a matter of forty years old from today [1990]."

The experience of Ravindra Visht was like that of Pt. Amarnath, who became Amir Khan's fan simply by listening to him on radio. He has narrated an event of the fifth decade in following words: -

"I am acquainted with Ustad Amir Khan Saheb from the time when other people were not acquainted with him. Those were the days of Ustad Fayyaz Khan, Ustad Nisar Husain Khan, Ustad Chand Khan etc or Pt. Vinayakrao Patwardhan and Pt. Narayanrao Vyas etc. I often used to listen to radio station of Bombay. One night I heard: 'This is Bombay. Now you are going to listen to *jaijaivanti* by Amir Khan.' In those days, the names of big artists were used to be announced with the prefix of 'Ustad' or 'Pandit'. A unique *jaijaivanti*! After listening to *jaijaivanti* quite different from the usual *jaijaivanti* of Agra Gharana, I said: 'Let Amir Khan be not an 'Ustad' for radio but for me he is an Ustad of Ustads.' With the passage of time, my words became true. The unknown Amir Khan gradually became famous, initiator of an age,

---

[148] 'Kalavarta'-February/March 1989, P.5, 'Aisay Thay Meray Sadguru', Writer: Pt. Amarnath.

Padmabhushan Ustad Amir Khan Saheb and my revered *guru* also. This acquaintance materialized through radio."[149]

The Bombay Radio station [which was the main broadcasting center of Western India, in those days] had for its classical music programs the contemporary senior artists, like Pt. Ramakrishna Bua Vajhe, Ustad Fayyaz Khan, Ustad Abdul Wahid Khan, Sawai Gandharva, Roshanara Begum, Hirabai Badodekar, Ustad Alauddin Khan, Pannalal Ghose etc. Among the radio artists of new generation, besides Ustad Amir Khan, were Mallikarjun Mansoor, Gangabai Hangal, Firoz Dastur, Bhimsen Joshi and D.V. Paluskar, who were arising stars in the horizon of music.

The eminent music critic, Mr. Mohan Nadkarni is also a listener of radio programs of Ustad Amir Khan since past. He has written about his contact with Ustad Amir Khan in his book 'At the Center' in English: -
"I first heard the Ustad on the radio – way back in the early forties. A decade and half had to pass by before I could hear him at an evening concert in Bombay in 1955."[150]

After independence of the country, All India Radio continued those policies for few years, which were prevalent during the British Rule. That time, the Ministry of Information & Broadcasting was under Deputy Prime Minister, Sardar Vallabh Bhai Patel and thereafter under R.R. Divakar. In 1952, when Dr. B.V. Keskar became the Minister of Information & Broadcasting, he brought about wide ranging changes in the policies and criteria of Akashwani. Besides of other issues, the system of audition initiated by him became subject matter of controversy. In order to make retrenchment of inefficient artists associated with Akashwani, under this audition system it was made obligatory for those senior and established artists to appear before the audition board, who were already rendering programs of high quality. For established artists, it seemed to be insulting.

---

[149] 'Sangeet'-January/February 1980, 'Meri *gayaki* Meri Avaaz Hai', Writer: Ravindra Visht.
[150] 'At the Center'-P.16, 'Amir Khan-A Phenomenon', Author: Mohan Nadkarni.

"On a wider plane, one witnessed a near violent reaction from the entire musical milieu, which culminated in a total boycott of AIR by a large number of self-respecting top-notchers and youngsters alike. In Bombay, A Bharatiya Sangeet Kalakar Mandal was formed by celebrities like Moghubai Kurdikar, Amir Khan, Vilayat Khan, Hirabai Badodekar, Gajananrao Joshi and a host of other artists with the avowed purpose of creating public opinion against the new policies of the broadcasting organization."[151]

Due to this boycott the Government had to compromise with the 'Mandal' and a mid-path was adopted whereby the self respect of established artists may not hurt. The audition board was also reconstituted.

The programs of classical music are organized in various ways by Akashwani. For example: All India Music programs which is broadcast from Delhi station and is relayed by all the Akashwani stations of the country; Radio Sangeet Sammelan, wherein musicians are invited and a *mehfil* is organized and thereafter broadcasting is effected on a national scale by using their audio recording; Provincial Sangeet Sabha, where all the centers of the province broadcast simultaneously; regular local broadcast of the centers, where local artists of the area are called to give their performance either directly or through audio recording; a Music concert organized by a particular center at any place in its zone, where artists present their program before the invited audience and thereafter edited parts of the program are broadcast by that center; broadcast of the LPs and cassettes of classical music released by various companies, where Akashwani pays royalty to the concerned company and obtains its rights for public broadcasting.

Ustad Amir Khan's presentation was there in all types of above mentioned programs. Akashwani started the trend of organizing Radio Sangeet Sammelan in sixth decade

---

[151] Times of India-15th August 1987, 'Music from AIR: a Down Hill Journey', Writer: Mohan Nadkarni.

by that time Ustad Amir Khan was reckoned as one of the main vocalists of the country. Only top artists are invited in Radio Sangeet Sammelan and usually they are professional. Ustad Amir Khan usually participated in these Sangeet Sammelans along with other contemporary eminent artists. As example, some published reviews of such Sangeet Sammelans are presented here: -

An audio recorded All India program of Ustad Amir Khan was broadcasted by Akashwani in 1964, wherein Ustad Ismail Daddu Khan was his Tabla accompanist.

The 12th Radio Sangeet Sammelan was held in 1966. In it, top artists like Ustad Bismillah Khan, the eminent Tabla player Ahmadjan Thirakwa and Ustad Amir Khan etc presented their art in Delhi. This Sammelan was held from 29th October to 6th November 1966. After listening to this Sammelan, well known music critic, Prof. C.L. Das wrote a review in 'Sangeet' monthly of December 1966, published from Hathras. It is to be noted that Prof. C.L. Das has written some more important articles on Ustad Amir Khan. From the above mentioned review, part concerning Ustad Amir Khan is quoted below: -

"The third important program was of Ustad Amir Khan, which was held in Delhi. Khan Saheb rendered only one *raga, shuddha kalyan*, because he was allotted one hour only. The *sthayee* of the *raga* was Khan Saheb's own creation, whose initial wordings were, *'Karam karo kripal dayanidhi'*. Khan Saheb often sings this composition. As is usually heard from him, this *vilambit khayal* too was set in *jhumra tal*. In the course of improvisation, a stage arrived where limitless possibility of sentimental expression in the *ragas* of Hindustani music could be realized. As Ustad Amir Khan opined, poetry must confirm to the sentiment of the *raga* and more important than it is that the application of *swara* should have affinity to the sentiment of poetry; so that the *rasa* of that particular *raga* could be relished. No doubt, this idea is fine and many artists do know it but due to conservativeness and lack of talent they perform in such a way, which can not be called music in real sense. The greatness of Amir Khan Saheb lies in the fact he performs according to his high level ideas about music. In *raga shuddha kalyan*, there is dense sentiment of tranquility and listening to his vocalism today, all kind of listeners could feel it. Besides, how artistic and refined *karuna* [pathos] could be expressed so that scope of a great art could be known, a beautiful example of it could be found from the vocalism of Khan Saheb."[152]

The actual wordings of *vilambit khayal* in *raga shuddha kalyan*, sung by Ustad Amir Khan [which has been mentioned in the above quotation] are: '*Karam karo dayalu, kripalu, tum ho sab jag kay daata*'. The author possesses an audio recording of a *mehfil* of Ustad Amir Khan, by which the correct wordings of *raga shuddha kalyan* could be known.

Also in the 13th Sangeet Sammelan held in 1967, Ustad Amir Khan participated. This Sammelan was held from 8th November to 12th November 1967. In this Sammelan, besides Ustad Amir Khan, other senior artists were- Rahimuddin Khan Dagar, Ustad Bismillah Khan, Ustad Ahmadjan Thirakwa, Ustad Mushtaque Ali Khan, Ustad Shakur Khan, Manik Verma, Kumar Gandharva and Abdul Halim Jafar Khan.

A review of above mentioned Radio Sangeet Sammelan was published in the weekly, 'Dinman', published from Delhi. It has been quoted in the December 1967 issue of monthly Sangeet. It mentions about the presentation of Ustad Amir Khan: "Vocal presentation: In the Sangeet Sammelan, Ustad Amir Khan's vocalism of *khayal* and *tarana gayaki* was the finest. One *khayal* and one *tarana* in *raga darbari* and *raga jog* were the best contribution of him to the Sammelan. In *vilambit bandishes* of *darbari* in *jhumra tal* and *jog* in *roopak*, having free self expression, with gradual and unique style of *raga* improvisation and by the refinement of the main *swaras* of the *raga*, it appeared that *ragas* have become alive. The style, complete with all the parts of *khayal gayaki*, attractive *sargam*, *gamak*, *laya* and various *tans*, the method of

---

[152] 'Sangeet'-December 1966, P.57, 'Gagan Sangeet', Reviewer: C.L. Das.

fluent presentation of them was worth adopting. In his original, special and imaginative *taranas* in *darbari* and *jog*, there was good setup and refinement also."[153]

In the above review, the *ragas* presented by Ustad Amir Khan in the Sangeet Sammelan, have been mentioned but their *bandishes* have not been described. Hence, it will be in conformity with the subject matter to tell about the *bandishes*. He mostly sang two *bandishes* of *vilambit khayal* in *raga darbari*, which were set in *jhumra tal*- 1. '*Hazrat turkaman*' 2. '*airi bir ri*'. He used to sing *tarana* of *raga darbari* in *madhya laya ektal*. This self composed *tarana*, based on the literature and philosophy of Amir Khusro, has been mentioned in the part regarding Amir Khusro [chapter-II]. The wordings of the refrain of *bandish* set in *roopak tal* of *raga jog*, sung by him are '*O! balma ab ghar aao, tumharay bina kal nahi mana men*'. *Tarana* in *raga jog*, was his own creation, whose *antara* contained a *rubayee* of Khusro.

For the Radio Sangeet Sammelan of 1969, held at Delhi, Ustad Amir Khan was also invited "This year, the 15th Sangeet Sammelan of Akashwani Delhi started on 25th October and ended on 3rd November. In this Sammelan, many eminent musicians participated, in them, the names of main artists are- Abdul Halim Jafar Khan, Imrat Husain Khan [Sitar], Siyaram Tiwari, Amir Khan, Pt. Jasraj, Nasir Ahmad Khan, Manik Verma, Girja Devi, Lalita Shivram Ubhaykar, Meera Banerjee, Ghulam Mustafa Khan [Sarod], Asad Ali Khan [Veena], Shishir Kanadhar Chaudhari [violin], Karamatullah, Samtaprasad 'Gudayee Maharaj', Munne Khan, Khayamal Bose [Tabla], Ramnarayan, Saghiruddin [Sarangi], Anantlal and companions [Shahnai]."[154]

Ustad Amir Khan participated in the Radio Sangeet Sammelan of 1971 also. Besides him, other artists were- Ustad Bismillah Khan, Ustad Nisar Husain Khan, Jaya Vishwas, Padmavati Gokhale, Gopal Krishna, Amani Shankar Shastri, V.G. Jog, Ali Ahmad Husain, Begum Akhtar, Umashankar Mishra, Pt. Siyaram Tiwari, M.R.

---

[153] 'Sangeet'-December 1967, P.58, 'Gagan Sangeet: Radio Sangeet Sammelan [from 8th to 12th November 1967]'.
[154] 'Sangeet'-December 1969, P.56, 'Sangeet Jagat'.

Gotam, L.K. Pandit etc. This Sammelan was broadcast by Akashwani from 9th October to 17th October. In this Sammelan "Ustad Amir Khan performed *khayal* and *tarana* in *raga darbari*; '*darbari kanhada*' is the favorite *raga* of Ustad. Looking to his voice and vocal style, this *raga* becomes so refined in his voice, which can be rarely heard. Because of subdued voice in the beginning, some laxity was seemed. The verse of devotional *bandish* '*Hazrat turkaman juko bali jaun*' was improvised with tranquility and ease, which was suitable to the sentiment of the lyric. The application of peculiar art of *sargam, murki* and *gamak*, which is found in his vocalism, there was no scarcity of it. By the beautiful presentation of his *tans* and by his vocal style, the heart of a sensitive listener becomes full and so happened too. But there was continued laxity in voice which decreased its effect to some extent. *Darbari-tarana*, '*Yare-mana baya baya*' is his own composition. *Tans* and *sargam* were applied very effectively in it, which created sufficient impact. Prem Vallabh provided attractive Tabla accompaniment in *drut ektal* with *tarana*."[155]

The said *bandish* [*Hazrat turkaman*] mentioned in above quotation, used to be sung by Ustad Amir Khan in *vilambit jhumra tal*. The same *bandish* has been given in '*Kramik Pustak Malika*' written by Pt. Vishnu Narayan Bhatkhande, in Vol. IV [P. 683], which is set in *vilambit ektal*, but there is enough difference in words and *swara* composition. The initial wordings mentioned by Pt. Bhatkhande are '*Hazrat toray kaman*'. It is necessary to draw attention towards a mistake also. The reviewer cited the words of *tarana* as '*Yare man baya baya*', whereas actually it should be '*Yare man biya biya*'. These are the words of Persian language; the meaning of '*biya biya*' is come come.

The laxity of *swaras* and the so called laziness, as depicted in above quotation, might have been due to his deteriorating health. Few years before his death, there was some decline in his health and physical stamina. The reason for it was his old age and diseased body. Also he had chronic problem of renal stone. Some times, sudden pain

---

[155] 'Sangeet'-November 1971, P.63, 'Gagan Sangeet', Reviewer: C.L. Das.

in abdomen also disturbed him and due to cough, he felt difficulty in applying *swaras* in desired manner. Hence, many of his vocal programs could not be as per his expectation.

Many recorded vocal programs of Ustad Amir Khan, presented on radio, are preserved in the National Archive of Akashwani. Even after his death, Akashwani used to broadcast vocal programs of Ustad Amir Khan, in its All India Music Programs. An All India Music Program is broadcast by Akashwani Delhi on every Saturday from 9:30 P.M. to 11 P.M. and is relayed by all stations of the country. After the death of Khan Saheb, the first such program was broadcast on 29th June, 1974. Acharya Brihaspati presented this program after selecting some recorded *ragas* of Ustad Amir Khan from the Archive of Akashwani.

While reviewing this program, Mr. C.L. Das writes: "The first record was that of evening *raga*, *puriya kalyan*, wherein Khan Saheb sang *vilambit khayal* in *jhumra tal*, '*Aaj sobana*'. As was his style to sing refrain with gravity and *zarab*, it was presented in the said *raga* with restrained manner. It is true that for almost last ten years, there was not such smoothness in the voice of Khan Saheb as it was found previously. It was to a great extent due to age. Laxity was seemed in the initial singing. But orderliness in *raga* improvisation and systematic application of *swaras*, which had been a distinctive feature of his vocalism, could be clearly seen in his *puriya kalyan*. The *swara* phrases, 'm̱ ṟ g s n d p n ṟ g' were presented in a unique manner. In applying every *swara* in an orderly and artistic manner, the patience and gravity like him could not be found anywhere else. In *puriya kalyan*, the *swara* phrase of 'n d p' is very attractive, and by applying it Khan Saheb had proved that aesthetics was also fully developed in his *gayaki*. After *khayal*, presenting some fast *tans* in *tarana*, the *raga* was concluded."[156]

---

[156] 'Sangeet'-August 1974, P.57, 'Gagan Sangeet', Reviewer: C.L. Das.

In above quotation, the meaning of the word, 'record' should not be confused with LP disk record, because no LP was made of *raga puriya kalyan* sung by Amir Khan Saheb. In the said quotation, *raga puriya kalyan* is related to the collection of Akashwani itself, which was generally recorded on spool tapes in those days. The audio recording of the same *raga* is available with the author also.

Although Mr. C.L. Das has thrown light on some *swara* phrases of *raga puriya kalyan* in his review, but this fact is to be noted that in this presentation, Amir Khan Saheb has not applied the *swara* phrase 'm r g' independently. Instead he has applied it in the form 'm r g', 'r m g' or 'm r m g'. The *swara* phrase 'm r g' is usually applied in the *ragas* like *puriya, puriya dhanashri, puriya kalyan* etc; but the *swara* phrases like 'm r g r m g, m r m g' are supposed to give a distinctive form to *puriya kalyan*.

After *bada khayal*, the *tarana* presented by Ustad Amir Khan was as usual a *rubayeedar tarana*, whereas there is no mention of *rubayee* in the review. This is a self composed *tarana* of Ustad Amir Khan. But in the said presentation, Amir Khan Saheb made one mistake that in the *antara*, he sang a *rubayee* which was actually for the *tarana* of *shuddha kalyan*. This mistake was only of words, the *raga* form of *puriya kalyan* remained unaffected. A different recording of this *tarana* is preserved with Akashwani [and is available with the author] in which the correct *rubayee* of *puriya kalyan* has been presented. But it is an independent presentation of *tarana*, which does not contain any *vilambit khayal* before it.

"In the All India program of radio, held on 29th June, 1974, after the *raga puriya kalyan*, the second *raga* sung by Ustad Amir Khan was *hansadhwani*, which was his favorite. Though this composition of *hansadhwani* in *Madhya laya ektal*, '*Jay matu vilamb taj day*' was composed by late Ustad Aman Ali [Bhindi Bazarwala], the credit to propagate and popularize it goes to Ustad Amir Khan. Khan Saheb used to render *bandish* of this raga with great sentiment. - - - Khan Saheb presented sargam beautifully in *raga hansadhwani*, which exposed uniqueness of his *gayaki*.

After *khayal*, a *tarana* sung by Khan Saheb of the same *raga* was broadcast. This *tarana* was his self composed *bandish*. Acharya Brihaspati said that Khan Saheb used to sing *tarana* of *khayal ang* [*khayal* type]. In this point of view, he improvised *tarana* in the way of *khayal*; he also applied *tans* in it. The opinion of Brihaspatiji was correct. - - - In the radio record of *hansadhwani tarana*, Khan Saheb didn't sing Persian couplet. Because of *khayal ang* salience, this paucity didn't matter enough; nevertheless if it would have been sung with the couplet, there would be completeness in the *tarana*."[157]

The *tarana* of *hansadhwani* sung by Ustad Amir Khan for the LP of HMV No.EASD1357 contains the stanza of Persian poetry, which was not presented in the said radio program. The Persian wordings are as: '*ibtihadest [ittihadest] miyan nai mano to, mano to nest miyan nai mano to*'.

The next *raga*, '*megha*' sung by Ustad Amir Khan was selected by Acharya Brihaspati for broadcasting. Since the program was being broadcast in the month of June, the selection was suitable for the season. "The '*megha raga*' was also very favorite *raga* of Khan Saheb. He used to sing *bada khayal* in *vilambit jhumra*, '*barkha ritu aaye*' and *tarana* '*tan dir tadir tadim na*' with great delight. These compositions of this *raga*, sung by him for Akashwani Delhi, are beautiful examples of his *gayaki*. While singing *khayal-tarana* in *raga megha*, he improvised *swaras* keeping in view the beauty of *raga* associated to the season. - - - Due to time limit, two recordings of *chhota khayal* sung by Ustad Amir Khan were played in the program and the program concluded. The first composition was a self composed *drut khayal* in *raga abhogi*, '*Laaj rakhlihyo mori*', in *ektal*; the second was a *chhota khayal* of *raga shahana* in *trital Madhya laya*, '*Sundar angina baithee nikas ke*,

---

[157] 'Sangeet'-August 1974, P.57-58, 'Gagan Sangeet', Reviewer: C.L. Das.

chheen liya man mera hans ke'. The *bandish* of *abhogi*, being devotion salient, was presented with sentimental gravity; whereas the composition of *shahana*, which originally belonged to late Ustad Aman Ali, being romantic, was sung by Khan Saheb with ease and merriment. - - In the *chhota khayal* of *shahana*, the clarity of verse, well embellished and combination of *swaras* with *gamak* in *antara*, the best form of *khayal* style is manifested. The dexterity, with which Amir Khan Saheb used to perform this *bandish*, is a shining example of his adoptability and of being a powerful vocalist."[158]

Above mentioned both *bandishes* of *raga megha [vilambit khayal* and *rubayeedar tarana]* are available on side-1 of Lp No.EASD1331. As has been mentioned about the Persian literature of Khusro and other poets, Ustad Amir Khan composed *rubayee* of Hafiz [*Abre-tar sahne chaman - - -*] in the form of *antara* in the *tarana* of *raga megha*. Audio recordings of *raga abhogi* and *shahana*, preserved with Akashwani Delhi, are luckily available with the author. The *bandish* of *raga abhogi*, full of philosophy, is self composed of Ustad Amir Khan. On the occasion of death anniversary of Ustad Amir Khan, on 14th Feb 1990, in a talk broadcast by Akashwani Indore, Goswami Gokulotsavji Maharaj threw light on an important fact concerning this *bandish*. Hence it is reproduced here in his own words: "According Indian philosophy and Geeta, '*Anek baahu darvatra netra*', he did a wonderful job by composing this *bandish* on the basis of this *shlok*. It shows his depth. People didn't have opportunity to ponder about this aspect. How literary and attractive is this aspect! See that *bandish*: -

'*Laaj rakh leejo mori,*
Sahib sattar nirakar jag ke data,
Tu rahim ram tu hi,
Teri maya aparampar,
Mohe tere karam ko adhar, jag ke data.'"

---

[158] 'Sangeet'-August 1974, P.58-59, 'Gagan Sangeet', Reviewer: C.L. Das.

From the point of view of vocal style, under the form of presentation of said *bandish* of *abhogi*, grave improvisation was done applying *Madhya laya* in beginning. Thereafter, fast *tans* were presented by increasing the *laya*. But the chain of *tans* was broken several times in between and joining the next phrase of the *tan* immediately, he skillfully applied *avaroha* till *madhya shadja*.

At the end of All India Music Program of Akashwani held on 29th June 1974, the *bandish* of *raga shahana* was broadcast which has also been rendered by Ustad Amir Khan in a 78 RPM record; that is brief presentation of three minutes. In the radio program, Ustad Amir Khan has rendered it for almost fifteen minutes by improvising it sufficiently. Beginning with *Madhya laya trital*, he applied *badhat* [movement], *sargam* and *tans* by increasing the *laya* gradually. He has repeated *sthayee* and *antara* many times in between. In the audio recording, occasionally sound of coughing could be heard, which might have been caused due to cold. Deviating from his familiar style, a new thing is found in this presentation that after *alap*, without increasing the *laya*, he presented *tans* in the speed four times more than the *tal*; then by increasing *laya*, he presented *sargam* and again by increasing *laya* he presented *drut tans*. Whereas the familiar order of his *gayaki* is –*alap, behlawa sargam* and *tan*.

One more recording of All India Program of Music, broadcast by Akashwani, is available with the author. This program of Ustad Amir Khan was broadcast on Saturday, 8th September 1990, from 9:30 P.M. to 11 P.M. It was also organized by selecting some *ragas* from the recordings preserved with Akashwani. In the selected *ragas* presented by Ustad Amir Khan, which were broadcast, Tabla accompaniment was given by former staff artist of Indore station, Suleman Khan and of Delhi station, Mohammed Ahmed.

This program initiated with the seasonal *raga*, '*ramdasi malhar*'. The *bandish* of *chhota khayal* set in *trital* has the following wordings: '*chhaye badara kare kare, umad ghumad ghan garajat teson jiyara umado hi aaye*'. It is his self composed *bandish*. In this presentation, the words of *bandish* were delivered in very attractive manner. Pronunciation of words with *gamak* for the expression of thunder, seems to be quite effective. Maintaining the basic form of *miyamalhar raga*, some *swara* phrases with *shuddha gandhar*, provide a distinct identity to this *raga*. So much so that, the straight ascending, 's r g m p' [applying *shuddha gandhar*], becomes applicable. In addition to it, Ustad Amir Khan has created peculiarity in lower tetra chord by applying both *gandhars* together as is usually done by applying both *nishads* in upper tetra chord of *raga miyamalhar*. The presentation of this composition broadcast by Akashwani appears to be incomplete. The same composition has been released by HMV having title: 'Festival of India' on side b of cassette no. STC-02b6200. According to the information printed on its folder, it was originally recorded at Akashwani station of Indore in 1965.

After *ramdasi malhar*, *tarana* of *puriya kalyan [purva kalyan]* was broadcast. Although it is the same *tarana* which has already been mentioned, but this time a recording was played, which was made on other occasion. In the *antara*, that *rubayee* was sung which was originally composed by Ustad Amir Khan for *raga puriya kalyan*. At the end of *rubayee*, Ustad Amir Khan has applied fast and well set *chhoot ki tan*, which seems very attractive. This specialty is found in most of his self composed *rubayeedar taranas* that last few words of the last line of *rubayee* are given the form of *tan* and he comes to the refrain of *sthayee* from the decided beat of *tal*. At such a place, the *chhoot ki tan* applied by him, appears to have similarity with the *gayaki* of *Patiala Gharana*. In this presentation of *gayaki*, the *tans* sung by him with *gamak*, are the best example of his style of *tan*, producing effect of *laya* on account of stress and complexity [*bal* and *painch*]. The third *raga*, *rageshri* was broadcast in the program. It is his composition in *Madhya laya trital*, wordings of which are: '*Begun ko gun deeje data, tumhare karam kee hai mohe asha*'. In thirty minute's recording of *rageshri*, which was played in the program, Amir Khan Saheb had rendered only *sthayee*. To express sentiments and emotion of lyric, he has adopted a unique method in his *swara* salient *gayaki*. The emotion of compassion to consider one self mendicant and the *shant rasa* [emotion of peace and tranquility] expressing complete surrender before God with request for one's deliverance, proves the utility of literature in *khayal gayaki* too. *Raga rageshri*, sung by Ustad Amir Khan, was to some extent technically different from its prevalent form. The *swara* phrases, 'g s r s, d **n** r s r **n** d' etc, he considered to be admissible. The short application of *rishabh* in *aroha* 'g – r g m, r s' has been included even in the refrain in this way. From theoretical point of view, *pancham swara* being inadmissible, applying *pancham* as *kan swara* to *dhaivat*, 'd ^{P}d **n** d m', such a *swara* phrase which usually occurs in *bageshri*, he has included it even in basic *swara* composition of the *bandish* of *rageshri*. He hadn't applied *shuddha nishad* at all. Centering on the *madhyam* of middle octave, the improvisation of *rageshri* is generally carried out in middle and treble octave. According to his *badhat* [movement] system, Ustad Amir Khan maintains importance of bass and middle octave in this *raga* also. Various *swara* phrases between *Madhya shadja* and *mandra gandhar*, appears to be effective in his deep voice and help to tend the *raga* towards *shant rasa* [peace and tranquility]. Usually *rageshri* is sung aiming at *shringar rasa* [sentiment of love] and most of the prevalent *bandishes also* belong to *shringar rasa*. At the end of the program, *raga abhogi* was broadcast, which is a recording of 30 minuts. The *bandish* set in *Madhya laya jhaptal*, belongs to Kirana Gharana. Wordings of the *bandish* are: '*Charan ghar aaye, mo pe daya karo ali ri dhan dhan aaj moray bhag*'. The notation of this *bandish* is given in the sixth volume of 'Kramik Pustak Malika' of Pt. Bhatkhande. But there is vast difference between the *swara* compositions of both. HMV has released this *raga abhogi* in its LP No. ECLP-2765, side two, obtaining it from Akashwani collection. Though the same *bandish* is present in that LP, the *abhogi* broadcast in the said All India Program of Akashwani and the recording of Akashwani used in the LP, are recordings of different occasions. The difference appears to be clear from the difference in *bahlawas* generated by imagination under the *gayaki*. In the announcement of radio program, it has been called '*abhogi kanhada*', whereas in LP, it is mentioned simply '*abhogi*'.

Ustad Amir Khan applies *swara* phrases 'g m r s' from *kanhada-ang* also and takes up 'm g r s, g r g m g r' etc in straight *avaroha*; at the same time also applies *swara* phrases like *raga shivaranjani* between bass *dhaivat* and middle *gandhar*. Hence, despite applying *kanhada-ang*, he didn't consider it essential for the *raga*. Hence, it is natural that a state of uncertainty crops up, whether his presentation should be called *abhogi* or *abhogi kanhada*? Nevertheless he Maintained the *gandhar atikomal*, like *darbari kanhada*, whether its application was *vakra* [curved] or *saral* [straight].

In this presentation of 30 minuts, in spite of absence of *atiivilambit jhumra*, he didn't try to make it speedy, parallel to the *Madhya lya* of *jhaptal*; instead he maintained stability and gravity in movement and improvisation of *raga*. Generally such *bandishes* set in *Madhya laya jhaptal*, are presented in *sadara-ang*, along with various *layakaris* and *bolbat* etc. Looking to the speed of *tal*, his movement of *swaras* clearly appears slow. Pt. Bhimsen Joshi has also sung this *bandish* with detailed *badhat* like Ustad Amir Khan, but after the *alap*, he has applied *layakaris* and *bolbat* abundantly. The audio recording of 30 minutes of this *bandish*, presented by Bhimsen Joshi in a radio program is available with the author.

A peculiarity can be observed in *abhogi* of Ustad Amir Khan that he has treated bass *dhaivat* as a place of repose and most of the *swara* phrases of lower tetra chord come to an end towards bass *dhaivat*. As has already been mentioned, his application of *gamak* at such a place points towards Karnataka System.

The recordings of different *ragas* vocalized by Ustad Amir Khan are preserved with various Akashwani radio stations for their local broadcasting and they broadcast them from time to time in their regular programs of classical music. Mainly those stations where particular collection of vocalism of Ustad Amir Khan is available are Indore, Bhopal, Delhi, Bombay, Ahmedabad, Baroda, Calcutta etc. Akashwani Indore has collection of those programs which were recorded at Indore studio, besides it, there being a system of exchange among different Akashwani centers, therefore large collection of Indore station is very important. That is, the programs recorded at other stations are also available at Indore station.

The *ragas* of Ustad Amir Khan archived at Akashwani Indore are: *yaman, ramdasi malhar, bhatiyar, todi [vilambit khayal-'changay naina valiyan'], todi [vilambit khayal-'sagun vicharo'], abhogi, komal rishabh asavari, puriya, basant mukhari, nand kalyan, lalit, rageshri* and *malkauns*.

In 1971, Delhi Doordarshan [TV station] had broadcast a vocal program of Ustad Amir Khan, whose video recording is preserved there and also available with author. In this program, Khan Saheb has presented two *ragas-rageshri* and *malkauns*. In *raga rageshri, vilambit* composition '*Begun ko gun deeje*' in *trital* and thereafter he has presented a *rubayeedar tarana* of *malkauns* set in *Madhya laya trital*. In this program, Tabla accompaniment was given by Ustad Ismail Daddu Khan Saheb.

[b] Vocal Performances at Music Concerts: -
Music concerts [mehfils] plays vital role in Indian classical music. When these *mehfils* are organized on large scale, they are called music conferences [*sangeet sammelan*] or music function [*sangeet samaroh*]. To establish interaction between expression of art and its reception by the audience, has been the specialty of these music concerts. Success in it is the acid test for the artist.

After his training in music, most of the life of Ustad Amir Khan passed participating in music conferences and other programs. His music tours continued to such an extent that he could not remain permanent resident of any particular place or city. Before Independence of India, in the course of native states and Nawabs, artists were extended patronage and they used to organize concerts of music. In such concerts also, Ustad Amir Khan got opportunity to demonstrate his art. But subsequently [particularly after Independence] his art found a clear exposure in the music conferences organized by Central Government, state governments, All India Radio and other institutions. Before Ustad Amir Khan's coming into lime light, Ustad Fayyaz Khan of Agra Gharana reigned supreme in the *mehfils* of music. On the other hand, melodiousness of the vocal style initiated by Ustad Abdul Karim Khan of Kirana Gharana, had a great influence on the receptive audience of classical music, even after his death in 1937.

On the basis of available material of music conferences, wherein Ustad Amir Khan participated, is given in chronological order as follows: -

At the age of 25 [in about 1937], Ustad Amir Khan participated for the first time in a big music conference. His father was alive at that time. This conference was held at Mirzapur [U.P.]. In those days, he was under the patronage of the monarch of Raigarh and was sent to the conference by him. He had bitter experience of failure in this conference, but he was not perturbed. Ustad Amir Khan himself says: "While I was living with the monarch of Raigarh, Sukhdev Seth of Mirzapur organized a music conference. He had modified the Sarangi into an instrument called 'SukhSarangi'. I went to the conference on behalf of Maharaja of Raigarh. At that time, my age would have been about 25 or 30 years. This was the first music conference of my life. The conference was dominated by Inayat Khan, Ustad Fayyaz Khan, Pt. Omkarnath Thakur etc. Before them I was counted as a child. I started singing but was hooted by the audience. One of the organizers asked me to sing *thumri*. I didn't sing *thumri* that time and still I don't sing. Although it was my first program and was hooted in the very program, but it had not affected me much."[159]

In addition to the above mentioned conference, during the time of states before Independence, Ustad Amir Khan demonstrated his art in different states; because his father had granted him freedom to give performances. The main places where Ustad

---

[159] 'Sangeet'-November 1971, P.24, 'Sangeet Sadhakon Se Bhent- Ustad Amir Khan', Interviewer: Shambhunath Mishra.

Amir Khan was invited were Nathadwara, Kankroli, Kishangarh, Rampur, Gwalior, Mysore, Alwar etc.

After the patronage of states, Ustad Amir Khan had to face difficulties in finding place for him in music conferences organized by the government and other institutions. During his first stay at Calcutta, very few of his programs were successful according to his view. When he went to Delhi, there too his struggle continued. He Says: "I came and lived in Delhi. Then I had started to acquire fame. I used to sing in every concert. I used to sing and late Bundu Khan used to play Sarangi. In that period, radio music concerts had just started. Vilayat was about 15 or 16. He and I went to Bhupen Babu, the organizer of the concert, to request that our performance should also be included. In the conference, there were great artists like Fayyaz Khan, Inayat Khan, Kesar Bai etc. Bhupen Babu said that he would not include our name in the list but he would give chance to perform somewhere in between. We would not get time for more than fifteen minutes. I sang, Vilayat played. Both of us got 50 rupees each like extras in a film."[160]

Subsequently, he started getting opportunity in good programs and sufficient remuneration was paid. His fame was spreading far and wide. Meanwhile, in 1944, his two important programs were held in Lahore. About these programs, he himself tells: Before partition [of India], I was invited to Lahore conference. I was paid Rs. 1000 for two programs. People of Panjab became happy in the program."[161]

Pt. Amarnath, a disciple of Ustad Amir Khan heard him directly for the first time at the music conference of Lahore. This conference was organized by Panjab Classical Music Society at YMCA hall. Besides Ustad Amir Khan, the eminent artists who

---

[160] 'Sangeet'-November 1971, P.24, 'Sangeet Sadhakon Se Bhent- Ustad Amir Khan', Interviewer: Shambhunath Mishra.
[161] 'Sangeet'-November 1971, P.24, 'Sangeet Sadhakon Se Bhent- Ustad Amir Khan', Interviewer: Shambhunath Mishra.

participated in it were Bade Ghulam Ali Khan, D.V. Paluskar and Pt. Ravishankar also. There Ustad Amir Khan had presented *raga darbari*.

Ustad Amir Khan said about his progress: "I came to Delhi, then after a year, there were disturbances. I came back to Calcutta. I stayed with a friend. Persons of 'All Bangal' came to know about it. They sent a messenger asking that I should present two items. The same conference where I was made to sing like extra on payment of Rs. 50, now paid me Rs. 1600 for two programs."[162]

During fifties, Ustad Amir Khan was reckoned among the top artists of the country. After Independence, the tradition of public concerts of music established in democratic India; therein increased the opportunity to make progress and gain popularity on the basis of merit. The tradition of organizing music concerts on various occasions took place and Ustad Amir Khan was respectfully invited in them.

Among music conferences organized regularly on non-government basis, Swami Haridas Music Conference of Bombay occupies a special place. This conference is organized every year by Sursingar Sansad. The director of this institution, Mr. Brij Narayan, invited him several times.

The third Swami Haridas music conference was organized at Kawasji Jahangir Hall, Bombay in March 1955 for ten days. On ninth day of this conference, "after presentation of Firoz Dastoor, Latafat Husain Khan, Rasoolan Bai, Bismillah Khan and Ali Akbar Khan, Amir Khan gave his performance in the end. He presented *abhogi kanhada, bhatiyar, tarana lalit* and *asavari of komal rishabh*. His *drut tans* and complex *paltas* are particularly for music community. He is famous for *gayaki* of *chendari* [tranquility], but on that day he also presented an example of *ladant*

---

[162] 'Sangeet'-November 1971, P.24, 'Sangeet Sadhakon Se Bhent- Ustad Amir Khan', Interviewer: Shambhunath Mishra.

[interplay] *gayaki*. But the listeners were actually delighted by *bhatiyar* and *asavari khayals*."[163]

It is to be noted that the *bandish* of *tarana* of *raga lalit* is his own composition; its notation is based on *drut khayal, 'jogiya meray ghar aaye'*, sung by him. Similarly, in the Swami Haridas music conference of 1956, Ustad Amir Khan presented his vocalism. His program was held at the end of the conference on 14th February, wherein he had presented *khayal* in *hem kalyan* and *Chandrakauns* and one *tarana*.

In Swami Haridas Jayanti conference of 1958, held at Bombay, Ustad Amir Khan's vocal program was held in the night of 20th September, 1958. Its information can be obtained from November 1958 issue of 'Sangeet'. In this program, Ustad Amir Khan presented *raga marwa* with detail improvisation, which continued almost for 50 minutes. Besides him, in the said music conference, Imrat Khan [Sitar], Hafiz Ahmad Khan, Abdul Halim Jafar Khan [Sitar] and Ustad Bade Ghulam Ali Khan also presented their art. In Swami Haridas music conference, held from 28th February to 10th March 1956, Ustad Amir Khan was again invited along with Ustad Bade Ghulam Ali Khan. Both these vocalists were friends and they had respect for the art and styles of each other. Both gave their performance in the conference. "Ustad Amir Khan's *chendar gayaki*, clear *tans* and the beauty of his improvisation were appreciated by the audience. Bade Ghulam Ali Khan's melodious vocal activities won the hearts of receptive audience."[164]

Ustad Amir Khan participated in Swami Haridas music conferences organized in 1962, 1964, 1970, 1971 and 1972. In 1964, the eleventh Swami Haridas music conference was held from 1st to 5th October at Birla Matushree Bhavan, Bombay. On the last day of program, Ustad Amir Khan's vocal performance was held. He

---

[163] 'Sangeet'-April 1955, P.47, 'Sangeet Sammelan', Writer: special representative of Sangeet.
[164] 'Sangeet'-March 1959, P.60, 'Saptam Swami Haridas Sangeet Sammelan, Bombay'.

presented *khayal* and *tarana* in *raga shuddha kalyan* and *raga darbari*. Despite some trouble in his throat, his program was successful.

In Swami Haridas music conference of 1972, vocal performance of Ustad Amir Khan was held on 19th April, wherein he presented *khayal* in *raga bageshri kanhada* and *madhukauns* and *tarana* of *malkauns*. this was his last program in the series of Swami Haridas music conference.

Besides Swami Haridas music conferences, Ustad Amir Khan's vocal performance used to be held in music festivals organized by state government and small and big local programs of Bombay, because in the sixties and seventies, he had stayed for a long time in Bombay. Under such programs, Ustad Amir Khan presented his vocal performance in the second conference of Bombay State Music and Dance Festival held in 1957 from 25th October to 4th November. Besides him, the other main artists were- Rahimuddin Khan dagar, Bade Ghulam Ali Khan, Bhimsen Joshi, Hirabai Badodekar, Gangubai Hangal, Moghubai Kurdikar, Omkarnath Thakur, Shivkumar Shukla, Kesarbai Kerkar, Girja Devi, Begum Akhtar etc.

Also in the sixth conference of Maharashtra State Music and Dance Festival held in 1966, Amir Khan Saheb gave his performance. The other artists in this program were- Ustad Bismillah Khan, Kumar Gandharva, Girja Devi, Bhimsen Joshi, Malvika Kanan, Jitendra Abhisheki, Pt. Ramnarayan, Kishori Amonkar, Pt. Jasraj, Pt. Ravishankar etc. In 1971 [which was the last year of his residence in Bombay], Ustad Amir Khan was again invited in Maharashtra State Music Festival along with Hafeez Ahmad Khan, Shobha Gotu, Prabha Atre, Bhimsen Joshi, Lakshmi Shankar, Pt. Jasraj, Parveen Sultana, Nirmala Devi, Jitendra Abhisheki, Kishori Amonkar, Latafat Husain Khan, Hirabai Badodekar, Saraswati Rane, Bismillah Khan, Pt. Ramnarayan, V.G. Jog, Abdul Halim Jafar Khan and Devendra Murdeshwar.[165]

---

[165] The information about these three music festivals of Maharashtra was obtained from the issues of 'Sangeet'-December 1959 [P.55], February 1967 [P.68] and April 1971 [P.64].

Ustad Amir Khan was also used to be invited to perform by the local organizations who organized music programs on small scale. For example, an organization, named 'Sangeet Mehfil', organized a three days music program in November 1970, under the caption 'Aaj ke Kalakar' and held a program of Amir Khan Saheb. Besides Ustad Amir Khan, other main artists were Dagar brothers, Maniprasad, Parveen Sultana etc.

Among cultural activities of Delhi, Sir Shankarlal Music Festival is considered as an important part. This festival was held every year. It was used to be organized by few music lovers of DCM Industrial House since Independence, in some way or the other. Among them, the pioneers were Sir Shankarlal and Lala Shriram. Its expanses were bore by Shankarlal Foundation and on this basis this festival was named. The top artists of the country were used to be invited in this festival. It was but natural for Ustad Amir Khan to being invited on such a unique cultural stage.

The vocal program of Khan Saheb, held in Sir Shankarlal Music Festival of 1965 [from 9th March to 13th March] is worth mentioning. On the second day of the festival [10th March 1965], after presentation of Mrs. Lakshmi Shankar [vocal] and Ustad Mushtaque Ali Khan [Sitar] "the festival ended with fascinating presentation of Ustad Amir Khan. He presented with great tranquility [*chendari*] the *bada khayal* in *swaras* of *raga anandi* set in *jhumra tal* [*ay vare saiyan, tohe sakal ban dhundun*] *chhota khayal* set in *drut ektal [Chahat man ber-ber]*. After *anandi*, *vilambit khayal* of *raga barva [Hamen kaun pehchane]* and *drut khayal [Ayree main kanha]*, one *bandish* of *nayaki [Airee mero piya* and singing '*lagi laganwa*' in *malkauns*, he concluded the program. Mr. Fayyaz Khan, an artist of Akashwani Delhi, was giving accompaniment on Tabla interestingly. The audience could listen to such a good program after a long period."[166]

---

[166] 'Sangeet'-April 1965, P.60, 'Sangeet Jagat- Sir Shankarlal Sangeet Samaroh'.

In the above quote the words of the *Madhya laya bandish* of *raga malkausn* '*lagi laganwa*' is wrong; the actual wordings of what Amir Khan Saheb presented are '*Lagila manwa tum sang, moray mitwa surjanwa*'.

Ustad Amir Khan had been invited to Shri Chankarlal Music Festival, continuously for three years from 1970 to 1972.[167] In the program of 1971, held from 6th to 11th April, Ustad Amir Khan presented *raga vasant mukhari* and *lalit*. According to opinion of the reviewer, "the program of Ustad Amir Khan unfortunately couldn't be successful due to trouble in his throat." The other main artists of that year were- Girja Devi, Gangubai Hangal, Pt. Jasraj, Mrs. Parveen Sultana, Sulochana Yajurvedi, Vilayat Khan, Bismillah Khan, Amjad Ali Khan, Hariprasad Chaurasia, Nikhil Banerjee, Gopal Krishna, Jaya Vishwas etc.

Ustad Amir Khan's program was successful in the Festival of 1972, held from 16th to 19th March at Modern School. Kumar Gandharva, Girja Devi, Amjad Ali Khan, Bismillah Khan, Prabha Atre, Devendra Murdeshwar, Dagar Brothers etc also performed their art that year.

Ustad Amir Khan presented his performance from time to time in other important music conferences and programs of Delhi. As for example, following two of his programs are particularly worth mentioning.

In 1957, a music conference was organized by Sangeet Natak Academy, in which Khan Saheb also participated. The function was held from 1st to 6th April at the ground of Constitution Club. On the third night of the program, that is on third April, after presentations of Miss Masuri [Karnataka vocal], Radhika Mohan Maitra [Sarod], Ustad Mushtaque Husain Khan [vocal] and Altaf Husain [vocal], at the end of the program, "Amir Khan Saheb's *darbari* started. The *meed* of '**d n** s' in the bass moved some what out of the *swara*. At the same time, when '*sa*' of treble octave was

---

[167] Ref: 'Sangeet'-May 1970, P.62, June 1971, P.62 and May 1972, P.45.

applied, it didn't appear to be as accurate s *gandhar*. His *gandhar* had made the *raga* alive. But no sooner on coming to *shadja* of treble octave, its melodiousness was destroyed. It appeared that once *tivra nishad* was also applied. After *darbari*, he also presented *raga lalit*, '*Jogiya meray ghar aaye*'. This *raga* was also some what different, as is heard from other artists. If the *swaras* of his today's *darbari* is analyzed, it can be said that its *gandhar* was very beautiful. But whenever *shadja* was applied, it appeared to be out of *swara*."[168]

Whenever his throat was bad, Ustad Amir Khan could not easily stabilize his voice on the *swaras* of treble octave, though fast *tans* could be performed very easily. It seems that the above mentioned deformity of *shadja* of treble octave might have been due to this reason. Besides it, there was a distinct feature in the presentation of Ustad Amir Khan's *darbari* that he usually kept one of the strings of Tanpura tuned with *shuddha nishad*, whereas in *raga darbari*, only *komal nishad* is included. Along with *shadja* and *pancham*, *shuddha nishad* is heard from the Tanpura, whereas in singing, only *komal nishad* is applied; in such situation, a different kind of atmosphere is created, in which performer, listener or reviewer, anyone can be perplexed.

On the occasion of 25th anniversary of Independence of India, the Education and Social Welfare Ministry of Central Government organized a function of the North Indian Music and Dance on a large scale, from 16th too 18th February 1973. The functions were held at Diwan-e-Aam of historical Red Fort of Delhi, in which top artists like Ustad Bismillah Khan, Ustad Nisar Husain Khan, Sitara Devi, Ustad Amjad Ali Khan, Ustad Sharafat Husain, Miss Uma Sharma, Mrs. Gangubai Hangal, Ustad Abdul Halim Jafar Khan, Dagar Brothers, Pt. Ramnarayan, Pt. Jasraj, Ustad Amir Khan, Pt. Birju Maharaj, Pt. Bhimsen Joshi, Ustad Vilayat Khan, Pt. Samtaprasad, Munir Khan, Karamatullah Khan, Prem Vallabh, Fayyaz Khan, Latif Ahmad Khan etc presented their art in these functions. The function was inaugurated with the address by the then Vice-President, Shri Gopal Swaroop Pathak. "On the

---

[168] 'Sangeet'-May 1957, P.58, 'Dilli Men Sangeet Samaroh'.

same day [18th February 1973] programs of two great vocalists, Ustad Amir Khan and Pt. Bhimsen Joshi were presented at night. The purely aesthetical [*Raswadi*] vocalist of Indore Gharana, Ustad Amir Khan, has given unforgettable contribution to the field of classical music. It is another matter that due to his advancing age, he might not have such stamina. He started his program with *raga priya kalyan* [Southern *raga, ram priya*] of *Marwa that*. Thereafter, he presented various attractive compositions of *raga hansakali*, generated by the mixture of *marwa, bageshri, hansadhwani* and *kalawati*."[169]

Mr. Amique Hanafi also wrote about this function, "on the occasion of 25th anniversary of Independence last year, in the function organized by Ministry of Education, Government of India, held at Red Fort, Amir Khan had performed his *khayal* beautifully, making the first two lines of the *rubayee* of Sufi poet, Sarmad Shaheed, as the refrain of his *khayal*: -
'Sarmad' gham-e-ishque hark as ran a dahem,
Soz-e-dil ay parvana magrasara na dahem.
Sarmad dos not give grief of love to everybody. Does not give the compassion of heart of 'Parvana' [lamp insect] to a fly."[170]

Here it is to be noted that the very *bandish* of *vilambit khayal*, based on above mentioned *rubayee* of Sarmad has been set in *raga priya kalyan*; that is in above mentioned two quotations with regard this function, the presentation of *raga priya kalyan, described in the first* and the presentation of Persian *rubayee* in the form of *khayal* in second, is the same things. Though it is to be noted that the wordings of the *rubayee* actually applied by Ustad Amir Khan, differ from the version given by Mr. Amique Hanafi. The wordings of Sarmad's *rubayee* applied by Ustad Amir Khan are given in chapter-IV/[2]. *Raga rampriya* or *ram manohari of the south*, being adopted

---

[169] 'Sangeet'-March 1973, P.57, 'Sangeet Jagat' the program of classical music and dance on the occasion of 25th anniversary of Independence of India.
[170] Weekly 'Dinman'-3rd March 1974, P.36, 'Ustad Amir Khan-tumharay sharan ab kiyo vishram', Writer: Amique Hanafi.

in Hindustani music, has been named as *'priya kalyan'*. In this *raga* of *sampurna jati* [containing 7 *swaras*], *rishabh* and *nishad* are *komal*, *gandhar* and *dhaivat* are *shuddha* and the *madhyam* is *tivra*.

While living at Calcutta or else-where, he had been participating in important music conferences held at Calcutta. That is why, Ustad Amir Khan's vocal style acquired remarkable popularity in Bengal and even among artists, he had sufficient number of followers and admirers.

While living in Bombay, Ustad Amir Khan participated in 'Sadarang Sangeet Sammelan', held at Calcutta in 1958, along with other top artists of that time. This music conference was organized by Sadarang Sangeet Sansad, which occurred from 27th September to 4th October. Besides Amir Khan Saheb, Pt. Omkarnath Thakur, Ustad Bade Ghulam Ali Khan, Mrs. Manik Verma, Ustad Hafiz Ali Khan, Ishtiyaque Ahmad, Abdul Halim Jafar Khan, Ustad Imrat Khan, Ustad Vilayat Khan, Ustad Karamat Khan, Kanhai Dutta, Prem Vallabh, Samta Prasad etc had come to perform their art. [The detail of this music conference is available in the issue of November 1958 of 'Sangeet'.]

After Independence of India, a music conference in the name of 'Tansen Sangeet Sammelan' was also organized at Calcutta. Ustad Amir Khan's vocal performance was held many times in this Sammelan. Khan Saheb said 'I have been singing in Tansen Sammelan for sixteen years'.[171]

In 22nd 'Tansen Sangeet Sammelan', held in 1970, Ustad Amir Khan participated along with Kashinath Shankar Bodas, Manik Verma, Hafiz Ahmad Khan, Sunanda Patnayak, Prof. M.R. Gotam, Sandhya Mukharjee, Robin Ghose, Vilayat Khan, Nikhil Banerjee, Balram Pathak, Ustad Ali Akbar Khan etc.[172]

---

[171] 'Sangeet'-November 1971, P.13, 'Sangeet Sadhakon Se Bhent-Ustad Amir Khan', Interviewer: Shambhunath Mishra.
[172] 'Sangeet'-February 1970, P.60.

It is a surprising fact that Ustad Amir Khan used to sing at Tansen music conference of Calcutta, but in the government sponsored Tansen Sangeet Samaroh, organized every year at Gwalior, he was usually ignored.

During the last phase of his residence of Calcutta [from 1971 to 1974], Amir Khan Saheb performed in many small and big music conferences and other programs, among them one is worth mentioning, the music conference organized by Surer Maya Sangeet Samaj, held on 31st December 1971. In this function, in addition to Ustad Amir Khan, other national level artists were Kalyani Rai, Shyamal Bose and Samtaprasad. The other artists were local.[173]

Amir Khan Saheb found enough opportunity for demonstration of his art in many music conferences in the country but he was not satisfied about his home town, Indore. In his opinion, he didn't get as much respect in the field of music of Indore, as it should have been. It is possible that this opinion of him might have been formed on account of his more expectations from Indore. Otherwise, his vocal program was held by Abhinav Kala Samaj in All India Music Conference organized at Indore in 1956. In the said program, besides him, the audience had enjoyed art of famous Tabla player, Ustad Jahangir Khan and Shri Pt. Kanthe Maharaj.

In 1963, Pt. Bhatkhande-Paluskar Memorial function was organized at Marwadi Higher Secondary Girls School, Indore, under the president ship of Mr. Pyarelal Shrimal 'Saras Pandit'. Ustad Amir Khan was invited as the chief guest in this function. In his address, Khan Saheb threw light on the wordings of *tarana*.

Abhinav Kala Samaj again invited Ustad Amir Khan in the music conference of 1955. For that music conference, the eminent duet vocalists of Pakistan, Ustad Salamat Ali and Nazakat Ali were invited. But they could not reach Indore due to

---

[173] 'Sangeet'-January 1972, P.58.

tension in the relation between India and Pakistan. Hence, the organizers contingently held vocal programs of Ustad Amir Khan and Kumar Gandharva on that night, which was very successful.

A program was held to felicitate Khan Saheb on the occasion of Maha Shivratri at Bhuteshwar Mahadev Temple on 3rd March 1973, about which Dr. Pyarelal Shrimal mentions in his book as follows: -
"On 3rd March 1973, on the occasion of Maha Shivratri at Bhuteshwar Mahadev Temple, Panchkuiyan, Indore, a musical night was organized for his felicitation. Organized in a well decorated tent, the function was chaired by Deputy Minister of Finance, Govt. of Madhya Pradesh, Mr. Chandra Prabhash Shekhar. The chief guest was the Speaker of the State Assembly, Barrister Gulsher Ahmad. Replying to the welcome, Ustad Amir Khan said, 'whatever I am today is due to blessings of Bhagwan Bhuteshwar'. After receiving of the title, 'Padmabhushan', Bombay Music and Dance Review Club and Sangeet Kala Sandesh of Indore also felicitated him."[174]

Bundelkhand Vikas Pradarshani organized its 3rd All India Music Conference at Jhansi from 2nd to 26th February 1960. Along with Ustad Amir Khan, most of the top musicians of the country participated in it; such as Bade Ghulam Ali Khan, Ustad Nisar Husain Khan, Vinayakrao Patwardhan, Ustad Nazakat Ali-Salamat Ali, Mrs. Girja Devi, Sunanda Patnayak, Bhimsen Joshi, Pt. Ravishankar, Ustad Ali Akbar Khan, Ustad Vilayat Khan, Imrat Khan, Nikhil Banerjee, Shishir Kanadhar Chaudhari, Sitara Devi, Samta Prasad, Kishan Maharaj, Chaturlal, Ramnarayan, Gopal Mishra and Ghulam Sabir.

There is an institution, known as 'Prayag Sangeet Samiti' at Allahabad, which conducts examinations in music and awards diplomas. This Samiti organizes a music concert at Allahabad every year. In this series, 27th music concert was organized from 17th December to 21st December 1969. Along with Pt. Jasraj, Ustad Latafat Husain

---

[174] 'Madhya Pradesh Kay Sangeetagya'-P.20, Author: Dr. Pyarelal Shrimal.

Khan, Girja Devi, Nirmala Arun, Nikhil Banerjee, Hema Malini, Birju Maharaj, Sanyukta Panigrahi, Pt. kishan Maharaj, Ustad Karamatullah Khan etc, Ustad Amir Khan presented his vocal performance in this concert.[175]

In the city of Patna, many music concerts were organized on the occasion of Durga Puja on 17th and 18th October 1972. On this occasion, a music concert was organized at Golghar, where besides other artists, Ustad Amir Khan gave hiss performance. But in this concert, there was no other well known artist except Ustad Amir Khan.[176]

In the 8th music conference, organized by Lions Club of Dhanbad, Ustad Amir Khan was invited on 24th February 1973. The other artists who participated in this concert, the main among them were- Padmashri Siddheshwari Devi, Savita Devi, Pt. V.G. Jog, Sitara Devi, Pt. Samta Prasad 'Gudai Maharaj' etc. The accompanist artists were Ustad Laddan Khan and Bachchalal Mishra for Sarangi and Kelash Mishra and Manakdas for Tabla.[177]

In the memory of Sawai Gandharva, who was a disciple of Ustad Karim Khan, Arya Sangeet Prasarak Mandal has been organizing Sawai Gandharva Music Festival at Pune since 1953. For it, the Mandal has been receiving valuable guidance from Pt. Bhimsen Joshi, a disciple of Sawai Gandharva. On the request of Pt. Bhimsen Joshi, Ustad Amir Khan had also presented his vocal performance in this function.

Prof. Shankar Abhyankar wrote a book on the life of Pt. Bhimsen Joshi in 1983, titled as 'Swara Bhaskar' in Marathi, in which a list of vocalists participating in the Sawai Gandharva music function is given, which confirms the name of Ustad Amir Khan.[178]

---

[175] 'Sangeet'-February 1970, P.70.
[176] 'Sangeet'-November 1972, P.56.
[177] 'Sangeet'-March 1973, P.60.
[178] 'Swara Bhaskar'-P.276, Author: Prof. Shankar Abhyankar.

Ustad Amir Khan was used to be invited in the music conferences organized by 'Pune Art Circle' of Pune. This information is available in the book, 'Swara Bhaskar' as follows:

"About 25 years back, an organization named 'Pune Art Circle' used to organize programs of music. Through this Circle, programs of the well known and budding artists, like Amir Khan, Mallikarjun Mansoor, Bade Ghulam Ali Khan, Omkarnath Thakur, Vilayat Khan etc were used to be presented. The Specialty was that invitation for every program was extended to Dr. Vasant Rao Deshpande and Pt. Bhimsen Joshi. Almost in every program both used to be present together."[179]

[c] Other Vocal Programs in India: Besides participation in big music concerts and functions, other programs of Ustad Amir Khan also used to take place in India. In addition to these small and big public performances, many of his informal and domestic *mehfils* are also remembered by audience and musicians. Hence, on the basis of available references light is being thrown on his programs and domestic *mehfils*

On account of his successful programs at different places and the presentations of play back singing in popular movies, like '*Baiju Bawra*' and '*Jhanak Jhanak Payal Baje*', Ustad Amir Khan's fame had reached to Southern India during the sixth decade and he was used to be invited for his vocal programs there also. For example, the news of a program held at Manglore [Karnataka] published in 'Sangeet': -

"<u>Vocal performance of Ustad Amir Khan-</u> the famous vocalist of music world, Ustad Amir Khan's [who has given play back singing in the film Baiju Bawra and Jhanak Jhanak Payal Baje] program was organized on the night of fourteenth April at 9: 30 P.m. at Kanara High School, Manglore for financial aid to the library of Shri M.K. Natak Sabha. He presented *ragas, yaman kalyan, rageshri, suha kanhada, darbari kanhada, abhogi kanhada* and *bhatiyar*. His program was sent per sent successful.

---

[179] 'Swara Bhaskar'-P.252, Author: Prof. Shankar Abhyankar.

The accompaniment on Tabla was given by Ustad Ahmad Mohammad and on harmonium by Mr. A.K. Billore."[180]

Ustad Amir Khan wanted to encourage small organizations organizing programs of classical music. An example of this can be given about an organization of Pune. There the students of B.J. Medical College had formed an organization for music and art. Some time in the middle of seventh decade, this organization invited Khan Saheb to give his performance in their program. He started the program with the *raga yaman kalyan*. On the demand of the audience, he started singing the song sung by him for the movie, '*Jhanak jhanak payal baje*', which is set in *raga adana*. While singing, he forgot few words of the song, then one of the students told him the wordings and he completed the song. On that day he was not well and by the end of program, he had high fever. Then he was treated in the Medical College by the doctors. Being very pleased, he donated Rs. 1000 to the organization of students for their next program. The same event has been mentioned by Mr. Divakar Bansode in an article written for 'Kalavarta', February-March 1989.

An organization of Bombay, named 'Alankar', organized a vocal program of Ustad Amir Khan on 5th January 1969. There he presented *tarana* in *shuddha kalyan*, *khayal* and *tarana* in *hansadhwani*, *kalawati* and *shahana*. Shripal Nageshwar provided Tabla accompaniment.[181]

After being honored by the President of India with Academy Award Khan Saheb's vocal program was held in the garden of Ravindra Bhawan, New Delhi on 22nd February 1969. There "first he presented *vilambit khayal [jhumra tal]* in *raga marwa* and then a captivating composition of *tarana*. Gradually embellishing the form of *raga* in *vilambit* khayal extensively, Amir Khan presents the real *tans* in the *tarana*. And what a beauty his *tans* have! Whether they are in *akar* or in *sargam*, they are

---

[180] 'Sangeet'-May 1956, P.6, 'Ustad Amir Khan Ka Gayan'.
[181] 'Sangeet'-February 1969, P.67, 'Mumbai Samachar- Ustad Amir Khan Ka Gayan'.

golden, granular [*danedar*] and smooth. All the skillful vocalists use fast ascending *tan* easily but the beauty of Amir Khan's descending *tans* is unique. After *vilambit* and *drut khayal* in *raga yaman*, he sang his two compositions in *raga hansadhwani* on demand. - - - - After the *vilambit* composition, with the help of wordings, '*jai mate, vilamb tajde*', he concluded his singing with *tarana* and Persian couplet in the same *raga*. Fayyaz Khan gave accompaniment to Amir Khan on Tabla."[182]

The two compositions of *hansadhwani* referred in above quotation, only *tarana* is his own composition. The first *vilambit khayal* [*Jai mate vilamb tajde*' is a composition devoted to the goddess Saraswati, composed by Ustad Aman Ali Khan Bhindi Bazarwala.

Various local organizations of Bombay organized music *mehfils* of Ustad Amir Khan.

Dadar Matunga Special Club organized a program on 26th April 1970, in which Khan Saheb presented *khayal* in *multani, shri, marwa* and *jog*, and *tarana* in *shuddha kalyan* and *hansadhwani*. The Tabla accompaniment was given by Madhav Indurkar of Bombay.[183]

Similarly, 'Bal Gandharva Sangeet Sabha' had organized his vocal program on 18th July 1971. The reviewer wrote about the *ragas* presented in this program and the peculiarities of their presentation: "The great voice and the special style of Ustad's vocalism provide a new elegance to the *raga*. This was also revealed in the presentations of *raga komal rishabh asawari, gujari todi, megha* and *ramdasi malhar*."[184]

---

[182] 'Sangeet'-March 1969, P.62, 'Sangeet Jagat: Ustad Amir Khan Ki Shalin Hansadhwani'.
[183] 'Sangeet'-June 1970.
[184] 'Sangeet'-August 1971, P.55, 'Sangeet Jagat- Ustad Amir Khan Ka Gayan'.

A unique program of his singing was held in Bombay, in which the *ragas* presented by him were based on South Indian Music System. The detail description of it has been given in chapter-II, under the description regarding Karnataka Music System.

"once the Press Club of Lucknow organized vocal program of Khan Saheb. On that evening, he had fever, but he didn't cancel the program. He sang for about four hours. In the *mehfil*, Ustad Ahmadjan Thirakawa was also present. He listened silently. When the singing was over, he said 'Amir Khan! You are the only vocalist of your *gayaki*'."[185]

Besides community halls, Ustad Amir Khan's singing programs were used to be held in temples also. One such program was held in the rainy season of 1971 at 'Lakshmi Narayan Temple', situated at Aas Bhairon, Kashi. The description of this program, which was published in 'Sangeet', is given below: -

"The month of Sawan [rainy season]: a crowd of musicians and music loving audience gathered in 'Lakshmi Narayan Temple', situated at Aas Bhairon, Kashi. Among the musicians were Bismillah Khan, Kishan Maharaj, Ishwarlal Mishra, Lachchu Maharaj and some teachers of the music college of Kashi Hindu University, and among the audiences were eminent citizens. Ustad Amir Khan is taking *alap* of *raga megha* in his deep voice. One by one he presents many of his self composed compositions in the *ragas-malhar, kalawati* and *jog*. - - - Being drenched by the rain of *swaras*, the audiences feel that a new meaning of *tarana* is being revealed to them. In the holy silence of the temple, Khan Saheb's deep and tranquil vocalism is creating a strange self-absorption and devotion. For hours, the audiences have been diving into the ocean of *swaras*."[186]

Similarly His vocal programs were held also at Shani Temple, situated in the lane of Juni Indore and at Bhuteshwar Mahadeva Temple of god Shankar, situated near

---

[185] 'Sangeet'-January/February 1980, P.19, 'Meri Gayaki Meri Awaz Hai', Writer: Ravindra Visht.
[186] 'Sangeet'-November 1971, P.72, 'Sangeet Sadhakon Se Bhent- Ustad Amir Khan', Interviewer: Shambhunath Mishra.

Panch Kuiyan cremation ground. Ustad Amir Khan was usually invited to the music concert held every year at Bhuteshwar Mahadeva Temple on the occasion of Mahashivratri. The *mehfil* held there in 1971, is particularly remembered by the audience.

Recollections of the domestic *mehfils* of Ustad Amir Khan, held between his adolescence, are found. In order to understand the qualities of performance of his art, it would be better to throw light on these recollections also.

During the period when Amir Khan was rigorously practicing under the guidance of his father, Shahmir Khan, the famous Sarangi player, Ustad Bundu Khan, who used to live in Delhi, came to the residence of Shahmir Khan for a feast. On that day, Bundu Khan expressed his desire to listen to vocalism of Amir Khan. Then Amir Khan rendered *raga multani*. In this domestic *mehfil*, besides Bundu Khan, other listeners were Tabla player-Dhulji Khan, Sarangi player-Allahdiya Khan, Sarangi player-Sadi Khan [father of Sarangi player-Moinuddin Khan], Bashir Khan etc.[187]

Mr. Moinuddin Khan also mentions about it, because his father, Sadi Khan, was friend of Shahmir Khan and used to accompany him in such sittings.

One such domestic *mehfil* was also held at the residence of Amir Khan Saheb in Indore in 1958, where he performed on desire of Ustad Rajab Ali Khan. A description of this *mehfil* has already been given under the details about influence of Ustad Rajab Ali Khan.

Mr. G.N. Joshi in his English book, 'Down Melody Lane', has mentioned about such an informal sitting of Ustad Amir Khan. At that time Mr. Joshi had specially invited Ustad Amir Khan to the studio of HMV, so that the Maharaja of Jodhpur, Hanumant Singh could listen to him. Mr. Joshi writes: "A little later I met yet another Maharaj.

---

[187] 'Nal'-P.23, Author: Basant Potdar.

This was the late Hanumant Singh of Jodhpur. He was so fond of classical music that at one time he had in employment at his court the now world famous Sarod maestro Ustad Ali Akbar Khan and the Sitar Wizard Pt. Ravi Shankar.

I was introduced to the Maharaja in Bombay at a social function. I extended an invitation to him to visit our studio. He agreed on condition that I provide him with an excellent performance by some classical singer. I was just then arranging a recording of the late Ustad Amir Khan. Therefore I fixed up Amir Khan's recording for one evening and informed the Maharaja. He came accordingly and sat listening to Amir Khan's rehearsals before the recording. Unfortunately the Ustad's voice was not in good enough shape and hence we postponed the recording, but for over an hour he sang an excellent *marwa*. Later, for his long playing disc, I made him sing *marwa*, and his performance on the disc is today considered a model and unparalleled exposition of that *raga*."[188]

Probably, the above event appears to have occurred during the mid sixties, because the LP record of *raga marwa* and *darbari* was made during this period.

Haider Ali, the younger son of Ustad Amir Khan was born on 10th March 1966 at Indore and on that occasion, besides other rituals, a *mehfil* of singing was also held at his residence. About this *mehfil*, Bapurao Agnihotri, a famous accompanist of harmonium, has written: "Once, when he was blessed with a son, he celebrated the occasion at his residence, in which I was also invited. All the acquaintances and musicians of Indore were invited. Along with Khan Saheb, all of us participated in the form of a procession accompanied by a band. Thereafter lavish meals were served. On the happy occasion of his son's birth, he and his son were offered gifts and then the *mehfil* of singing was held. That night I accompanied Ustad Amir Khan on harmonium till 5 A.M. Ustad Saheb encouraged me very much. At that time Tabla accompaniment was provided first by Ustad Dhulji Khan and then by Ustad Daddu

---

[188] 'Down Melody Lane'-P.126, 'Royal Patrons', Author: G.N. Joshi.

Khan. The *mehfil* of that night is still in my memory, because Khan Saheb was very happy on that occasion. And that is why his vocalism was also full of excitement."[189]

One *mehfil* was held on 23rd January 1974; probably it was the last domestic *mehfil*. That time, Govind Bose gave Tabla accompaniment. Arun Chaterjee had tape recorded that *mehfil*. After few days, his untimely demised occurred and The Indian Record Manufacturing Co. LTD [INRECo] wanted to obtain that tape recording from Arun Chatterjee. Arun Chatterjee willingly offered that recording to INRECO for the benefit of students of music and music lovers. Out of it, a *madhya laya bandish* of self composed but untitled *raga* [*Paar karo gun nahin mome*] and *raga chandra madhu* were extracted and LP record [No.2411-0001] was made.

Above information can be obtained from the printed matter on the cover of the record. The photograph of Ustad Amir Khan printed on the cover was also taken while the same *mehfil* was in progress. HMV too issued its own professional edition [No. STC04B7371/74] of four cassettes from private collections of live recordings of the *mehfils* of Ustad Amir Khan.

The detail regarding LP records and cassettes of INRECO and HMV is given in the material relating to the records and cassettes of Ustad Amir Khan.

[d] Vocal Program – Abroad: In foreign countries, Indian classical music was popularized by eminent instrumentalists and due to which classical music was recognized in the form of instrumental music by the musicians and audience of those countries. For them, it was bit difficult to understand and appreciate the *swara* salient vocal form of *khayal gayaki* of Indian classical music. Nevertheless, the vocalists tried to propagate it there and in this field the name of Ustad Amir Khan can be specifically mentioned along with Pt. Omkarnath Thakur and Ustad Bade Ghulam Ali

---

[189] 'Kalavarta'-February/March 1989, P.20, 'Gambhir Vyaktitva Ke Sath Prakriti Ka Gayan', Writer: Bapurao Agnihotri.

Khan. The eminent Sitar maestro, Pt. Ravi Shankar, well known in western countries, has given much cooperation to introduce Indian vocalists in those countries.

Ustad Amir Khan's foreign tours started from a South Asian country, Afghanistan, when in 1964, he first visited Kabul. In 1968, he again went to Kabul. This time, the Government of India sent him under a cultural delegation, on the occasion of their national day, the 14th August. This time, Ismail Daddu Khan went with him as a Tabla accompanist. In the presence of the ruler of Afghanistan, Zaheer Shah, Ustad Amir Khan's vocal program was held at the function of their national day. His vocal program was held also in the Indian Embassy. On these occasions, Frontier Gandhi, Khan Abdul Gaffar Khan was also present. The photograph of Ustad Amir Khan with Frontier Gandhi is preserved with Ismail Daddu Khan.

In 1968, 'New Paltz School of Music', USA, appointed him as Visiting Professor for five months to teach Indian vocal music. 'New Paltz' is situated near New York City and is a branch of New York University. Accepting it he went to New York and stayed there for about a year. Along with him, Sitar player, Umashankar Mishra and as Tabla accompanist, Ismail Daddu Khan, had also gone. Meanwhile, living in New York, he toured to other countries also for music programs. Since he was working as a Visiting Professor for the purpose of teaching music, therefore his public programs, outside the academic field, were rare in America and mostly the presentation of his art was confined to the colleges and universities. His programs were also held at New Jersey and other places which are affiliated to New York University.

While training American students in Indian classical music, he expressed about his experiences: "- - - The boys there learn but they don't have melody in their voice. There is problem of language, still they learn. I adopted my own method. I made them understanding the *swaras*. I taught them short compositions of *khayal* with two or three *tans* – bhupali, malkauns, bilaval, yaman."[190]

In 1969, Mahatma Gandhi's birth century was celebrated. In America, 'Indian Society' also organized a cultural program on this occasion, where Ustad Amir Khan's performance was held. Such a program was also held at the Indian Embassy in Washington, where the then ambassador, Mr. Ali Yavar Jung was also present. In some of such programs, Pt. Ravishankar was also with him, who lived in America in those days.

For few months, Ustad Amir Khan went to Canada from USA. In those days, his elder son, Ikram, an engineer, was working in Montreal, Capital of Canada. His programs were also held in Montreal and the radio station of that place also recorded his performance of an hour for broadcasting. Subsequently that recording was preserved by archive there. In this tour of foreign countries, he also went to Paris and London, where his concerts were held and he satisfied the people having curiosity about Indian music by lecture demonstration. He kept his contact with India while living in foreign countries and he presented himself for some programs in India. His popularity increased in America among the audience of Indian classical music. "His *gayaki* had influenced many contemporaries. In a Gallop poll in America, he got highest number of votes for classical music."[191]

Ustad Amir Khan clearly admitted that Indian vocal music could not attain that much of influence as instrumental music among common people of West. Nevertheless, some groups have emerged there, who can understand the contemplative nature of Indian music.

---

[190] 'Sangeet'-November 1971, P.34, 'Sangeet sadhakon Se Bhent: Ustad Amir Khan', Interviewer: Shambhunath Mishra.
[191] 'Sangeet'-June 1969, P.66, 'Ustad Amir Khan Par Goshthi'.

Khan Saheb was not satisfied with the conduct of the vocalists, instrumentalists and dancers going to the Western countries as the representatives of Indian arts. With regard to them he opines: "While proceeding from here, they suppose to be representatives of Indian arts and culture, and when there pockets are filled with money and their photographs appear on TV and news papers, they forgets every thing else except themselves. Those who have no value here become valuable there and they consider that the treasure of Indian art is in their grasp. Some one asked about the abilities of Pt. Ravishankar, he replied 'he is our true ambassador of music.' And Subbalakshmi? 'I have respect for her.'"[192]

In the same way, commenting on the foreign tours of Indian musicians, Khan Saheb says: "About foreign countries there is a wrong impression among the artists of this country that after returning from a foreign country, there is a great change in the art and the respect gets increased. I would say them that that after return from there, nothing is changed. If a 'khalasi' [a porter on a ship] returns from abroad, he does not become a barrister."[193]

In February or March of 1974, Khan Saheb was to go to America again, but before that unfortunately he died unexpectedly. This time he was appointed as a visiting professor in San Francisco. Pt. Nikhil Banerjee, the eminent Sitar maestro, was to go with him. Though Khan Saheb was unwilling to go to USA again, but he could not resist wish of his elder son, Ikram Ahmad. He was thinking to go to Canada also to meet Ikram. In his last days, he was busy just in making preparations to go to America.

He had told to Shams-uz-zaman, the editor of 'Azad Hind' and working as personal secretary to Khan Saheb in Calcutta: "Dear Shams! Leave the job of 'Azad Hind'. Come with me. On the 14th [14-02-1974], we will go to Indore, after staying for few

---

[192] Maharashtra Times-28 August, 1976, 'Amir Khan', Writer: Vasant Potdar.
[193] 'Sangeet'-November 1971, P.34, 'Sangeet Sadhakon Se Bhent: Ustad Amir Khan', Interviewer: Shambhunath Mishra.

days, we will reach Nagpur on the birth day of Haider. I will show the documentary made on me. From there, we will go to Bombay. After settling you properly in Bombay, I will proceed to California."[194]

Unfortunately, that wish of Amir Khan Saheb could not be fulfilled.

2-Interaction with Eminent Musicians: -

Due to exchange of ideas and experiences, the persons of the same profession come together naturally; similarly despite his reserved nature, Ustad Amir Khan had close relations with other vocalists, instrumentalists, musicologists and critics. He used to meet other top artists in big music concerts. Description of some eminent musicians is given below with whom Ustad Amir Khan had interaction in concerts and programs.

Ustad Rajab Ali Khan:

Ustad Amir Khan respected most Ustad Rajab Ali Khan among the senior artists. As has already been mentioned, there were relations like *guru* and *shishya* [teacher and taught] between these two artists. Contact between Amir Khan and Ustad Rajab Ali Khan was maintained until the last breath of Ustad Rajab Ali Khan. So much so that while residing in different metropolitan cities of the country, he used to visit Rajab Ali Khan Saheb at his residence in Dewas.

Besides having *guru* like respect for Ustad Rajab Ali Khan, also he treated him as confidant and confided to him his personal problems. For example: -
"Amir Khan- Uncle! Persons are trying to degrade my father by calling him a *Sarangiya* [Sarangi player].
Rajab Ali Khan- There is nothing bad in playing Sarangi. And why one should be aggrieved by the truth.

---

[194] Maharashtra Times-28 August, 1976, 'Amir Khan' part I, Writer: Vasant Potdar.

Amir Khan- But, father was also a *binkar* [Bin player].

Rajab Ali Khan- I have no knowledge about it.

Amir Khan- Uncle! You and Allahdiya also had dispute over this because he had said to Chhatrapati that Muglu Khan was disciple of a Sarangiya.

Rajab Ali Khan- Son! That was a different period, and the comment which he made was quite wrong. If there would have been even a grain of truth in it, I would have not taken it ill. That period was quite different. You know, I had proved that it was blame. But, if some one says about me that I have learnt from a Sarangiya, I would not take it ill.

Amir Khan- How?

Rajab Ali Khan- Haider Baksh made me practice for many years. While giving accompaniment, he has added many things in my vocalism. His and mine lessons were same. He had also learnt from my Ustad [teacher]. In addition to it, also he had borrowed many things from Allahdiya Khan, which belonged to my father's Ustad and had returned to me. The treasure on which I had a right, returned to me anyhow.

Amir Khan- But *ganda* was not tied.

Rajab Ali Khan- So, how does it matter? When I have told that he was my Ustad, but he was not lesser than an Ustad. Son! Many of my disciples are Sarangiyas. Just take your maternal uncle."[195]

The extent to which Ustad Rajab Ali Khan had influenced Amir Khan, has already been mentioned in detail in Chapter 2, under the heading 'Influence of Rajab Ali Khan'.

There was a close friendship between Ustad Amir Khan and the nephew and main disciple of Ustad Rajab Ali Khan, Amanat Ali Khan during their youth. Though it did not matter that Amanat Ali Khan was elder than Amir Khan by eleven years in age. Both of them, by their joint efforts, succeeded to agree Ustad Rajab Ali Khan to train them. Living together in Bombay for a long time, they practiced together and both of

---

[195] 'Ustad Rajab Ali Khan'-P.50, 'Baten Jo Bhulayee Nahin Jatee', Author: Amique Hanafi.

them got opportunity at the same time for disc recording of 78RPM from Colombia Company. Amanat Ali died untimely on 3rd January, 1941, at the age of only 40 years, which shocked Amir Khan severely. He had a life long grievance for being separated from his close friend. He often used to applaud virtues of Amanat Ali. Ustad Amir Khan had also friendly relations with one of the main disciples of Ustad Rajab Ali Khan, Mr. Krishnarao Majumdar, also known as Mama Majumdar. Mr. Kishnaroa Majumdar [birth 1907] used to learn singing from Ustad Rajab Ali Khan since his very childhood. He had become his disciple by *ganda bandhan* tradition. He was sent to Bombay to be trained as engineer by the Government of Dewas State [Badi Pati]. He was not a professional singer but he used to present his dynamic vocalism on radio and in various music concerts. For his livelihood, he worked as chief executive engineer in public works department. He retired from there in 1957 and settled permanently in Indore.

Mr. Krishnaroa Majumdar and Ustad Amir Khan often used to visit each other's residence at Indore. They used to discus about vocal styles, various *bandishes* and budding artists of classical music. Whenever Amir Khan Saheb returned to Indore after performing in big music concerts and music tours, he used to tell his experiences to Mr. Majumdar. Mr. Majumdar was main among the contemporary persons of music field in Indore, who understood Ustad Amir Khan intimately. The first Amir Khan memorial function [Amir Khan Smriti Samaroh] was also inaugurated by him on 29th March, 1987. Similarly on the occasion of third Amir Khan memorial function of 1989, he had released the special Issue of 'Kalavarta' based on Ustad Amir Khan. Unfortunately, Mr. Majumdar passed away in May 1991, in Indore, at the age of 84.

Ustad Bade Ghulam Ali Khan:
Ustad Bade Ghulam Ali Khan was born in 1902 at Lahore. He was elder than Amir Khan by ten years. The earlier life of Bade Ghulam Ali Khan passed in Lahore and rest in Bombay. Since 1940, he had been presenting his melodious vocalism in

various music concerts, whereas for Amir Khan, it was a period of struggle. Bade Ghulam Ali Khan became famous as the main representative vocalist of Patiala Gharana.

During the second tenure of Amir Khan's stay at Bombay, both vocalists [Bade Ghulam Ali Khan and Amir Khan] were living near about. Mr. G.N. Joshi writes in this context: "Just beyond the building where Amir Khan lived was the residence of an elderly singer by the name of Gangabai. Ustad Bade Ghulam Ali Khan and Ahmad Jan Thirakwa often stayed with her. This shows that even women of these professions were treated with respect as artists, in artistic circles. As the recording executive of HMV I had to contact artists regardless of time and place."[196]

Both the artists were present together to perform their art in many big concerts. The list of some such concerts is as follows: -
1. The music concert organized by Panjab Classical Music Society at Lahore, in 1944.
2. The music concert organized by Constitution Club, Delhi, from 1st to 6th April 1957.
3. Bombay State Music Festival, 2nd session, from 25th October to 4th November 1957.
4. Swami Haridas Jayanti Samaroh, Bombay on 20th September 1958.
5. Sadarang Music conference, Calcutta, from 27th September to 4th October 1958.
6. 7th Swami Haridas Music conference, Bombay, on 28th February 1959.
7. 3rd All India music conference, Jhansi, from 22nd to 26th February 1960.
8. 11th Swami Haridas Music conference, Bombay, from 1st October to 5th October 1964.

---

[196] 'Down Memory Lane'-P.93, 'Ustad Amir Khan', Author: G.N. Joshi.

Both the vocalists paid utmost respect to the style of each other. In the *mehfil* where both the vocalists were present together, Bade Ghulam Ali Khan mostly centered his singing on *thumri*. Probably he did so to keep respect of the *khayal gayaki* of Ustad Amir Khan. Similarly, Amir Khan too was an admirer of the lofty and flexible voice of Bade Ghulam Ali Khan. He considered him to be an ideal *thumri* singer. When asked about not singing *thumri* in *mehfils*, Amir Khan's reply was, "because, I will not be able to sing like that as Bade Ghulam Ali sings uniquely. So why I should get involved in it?"[197]

Goswami Krishnaraiji Maharaj:

Goswami Krishnaraiji of Govardhannathji temple, situated at Malharganj, Indore was not only a music lover but was a good artist also. He was expert in playing different types of instruments like Jaltarang, Kashthatarang, Nastarang, flute, Sarod, Kachhua etc. He played harmonium with such a skill that his thumb never touched its keys. He was also an excellent *dhrupad* singer.

The music occupies a special consideration in Vallabh sect. Therefore, devotional music named as '*haveli sangeet*', continues in the temple through out the year as per set rules. Local and outside musicians usually visit the temple.

Along with the *Binkar*, Ustad Babu Khan, Ustad Amir Khan used to visit the temple regularly and with the help of Goswami Krishnaraiji, he had the opportunity to understand *haveli sangeet*. Afterward he also lived at Nathadwara for some time.

Nasiruddin Khan Dagar and Rahimuddin Khan Dagar, The *dhrupad* Singers:

Dhrupad singers, Nasiruddin Khan and Rahimuddin Khan were son of the famous *dhrupad* singer, Allahbande Khan of Alwar *Darbar* [court]. These two brothers had been in the court of Tukojirao Holkar of Indore. Ustad Amir Khan's father, Shahmir Khan was also there. Therefore, Ustad Amir Khan had been in contact with these

---

[197] Maharashtra Times-28 August, 1976, 'Amir Khan' part I, Writer: Vasant Potdar.

dhrupad singers since his childhood. Rehimuddin Khan remained in the Holkar court for about seven years. Nasiruddin Khan lived in Indore for a very long period. Nasiruddin Khan used to come to the residence of Shahmir Khan to attend the domestic *mehfils* of music. Also in the sittings of musicians held by Goswami Krishnaraiji Maharaj of Vallabh sect, they often used to meet. Nasiruddin Khan died in 1936, at the early age of 46-47 years. All the four sons of Nasiruddin Khan became good *dhrupad* singers. Their names are: Naeemuddin, Aminuddin [Fakir], Zahiruddin and Fayyazuddin. In them, Muinuddin and Aminuddin used to sing as pair [*jugalbandi* or duet], whereas Zahiruddin and Fayyazuddin as another pair. Fahimuddin, son of Rahimuddin Khan, was also a vocalist of the same generation. Ustad Amir Khan had friendly relations with all these five vocalists of the new generation. "For the first time, the *dhrupad* singer, Rahimuddin Khan added the surname 'Dagar' after his name."[198]

Nasir Muinuddin Khan Dagar, son of Nasiruddin Khan, died on 24th May, 1966. That time, Ustad Amir Khan paid homage to him in very emotional words: "Late Nasir Muinuddin Khan Dagar was the best vocalist of the *dhrupad-dhamar* style. His untimely demise is a loss to the field of music and particularly to *dhrupad gayaki*, which can not be filled. The changes made by him in *alap* and *dhrupad* are praise worthy and show his artistic genius. I had good relations with his elders. I feel deeply grieved by the sudden demise of such a genius and great artist."[199]

Before Independence of India, Nasir Muiddin Khan was in the patronage of Jodhpur court. In Independent India, along with his brother, Nasir Aminuddin Dagar, he had mission to propagate *dhrupad gayaki*. He had been the Head of the department of music at Bharatiya Kala Kendra, Delhi, for many years. Muinuddin Khan initiated the successful tradition of presenting *dhrupad gayaki* in duet. But due to death of Muinuddin Khan, this pair was broken.

---

[198] Nai Duniya -1st July, 1992, P.4, '*Dhrupad* Aur Uski Char Baniyan', Writer: Dr. Pyarelal Shrimal.
[199] 'Sangeet'-July 1966, P.67, 'Swargiya Nasir Muiddin Dagar Ko Ustad Amir Khan Ki Shraddhanjali'.

Babu Khan, The *Binkar*:

Ustad Amir Khan had close contact with Babu Khan, the disciple of famous *binkar*, Murad Khan, since adolescence. Babu Khan was nephew of Ustad Rajab Ali Khan, that is why both were close to each other. With the inspiration of Babu Khan, Ustad Amir Khan started to go to Goswami Krishnaraiji Maharaj of Goverdhannathji temple, situated at Malharganj, Indore. Babu Khan regularly went there and Amir Khan often accompanied him. Ustad Amir Khan also used to get advantage of old *bandishes* collected by Babu Khan. For example, Ustad Amir Khan had taken the *bandish* of *raga miya ki sarang*, '*Pratham pyare aye*' from Babu Khan, which has been mentioned in the material regarding radio programs. Ustad Babu Khan died at the age of 48 years, on 25th November 1941, at Indore.

Ustad Bundu Khan, The Sarangi Player:

Among the important musicians with whom Ustad Amir Khan came into contact in his initial career at Indore itself, one of them was a significant artist, Ustad Bundu Khan, the Sarangi player. Ustad Bundu Khan [born about 1880] received training of Sarangi playing from his maternal grand father, the court singer of Vallabhgarh State, Miya Songi Khan and maternal uncle, Miya mamman Khan. Ustad Bundu Khan lived in Indore for about 25 years of his life and he had been a court artist of Maharaja Tukojirao Holkar. During these years of stay at Indore, he used to visit Shahmir Khan also. One of such domestic *mehfil* of Amir Khan's adolescence has already been mentioned previously, when on demand of Ustad Bundu Khan, Amir Khan had to sing.

Ustad Bundu Khan had the experience of accompaniment with great singers of the country and he was able to secure a permanent job at Akashwani Delhi. During the middle of forties, when Ustad Amir Khan lived in Delhi he used to sing from Akashwani Delhi, in those days also Ustad Bundu Khan had given accompaniment on Sarangi many times. In September 1948, Ustad Bundu Khan went to Pakistan and he died in Karachi on 13th January 1955.

Ustad Allauddin Khan:

Padmavibhushan Ustad Allauddin Khan of Maihar considered Ustad Amir Khan as highly skilled artist among the budding artist of that time. According to his nature, he found touch of spiritualism in Amir Khan's vocalism, which was rare elsewhere. That is why, despite being Amir Khan being much younger in age, Ustad Allauddin Khan addressed him respectfully. In this context, an interview given to the author by Ismail Daddu Khan, is worth quoting: "Once, I and Khan Saheb [Amir Khan Saheb] were going to Calcutta from Bombay by train. After midnight, the train halted at Satna railway station. That time, Khan Saheb was busy in reading, lying on upper birth. At Satna station, some passengers entered the same compartment and they were searching place for sitting. Ustad Allauddin Khan of Maihar was also among them. Seeing him, Amir Khan Saheb got up and wished him. At that time, Ustad Allauddin Khan Introduced him with one of his disciple who was accompanying him and said to him: 'salute him, he is the Tansen of this age."

Among the main disciples of Ustad Allauddin Khan, his son, Ali Akbar Khan, Nikhil Banerjee and Pt. Ravishankar, had very close relations with Amir Khan Saheb. Ustad Amir Khan has sung a *bandish* in a Bangla movie, 'Kshudhit Pashan'; therein Sarod playing of Ustad Ali Akbar Khan has also been included. Thus the movie also became mean of their mutual contact. Another disciple of Allauddin Khan, Nikhil Banerjee, earned fame in Sitar playing. He acquired skill in application of *khandmeru* improvisation and presentation of *raga*, just due to the influence of Ustad Amir Khan and his *gayaki* on him. For the last time, when Ustad Amir Khan planned to go to America, Nikhil Banerjee was to accompany him. But due to death of Ustad Amir Khan, the plan could not be materialized.

Pt. Ravishankar:

Indian classical music was sufficiently propagated in foreign countries due to the efforts of Pt. Ravishankar. In the words of Ustad Amir Khan, Ravishankarji proved to be 'true ambassador of Indian music in foreign countries'.

Pt. Ravishankar has written a book in Bangla, titled as '*Raga Anuraga*', wherein his opinion about the *gayaki* of Ustad Amir Khan can be known and close personal relation between the two artists is also revealed. Pages of this book, No.63-69 and 88-89, are particularly devoted to Ustad Amir Khan. The *gayaki* of Ustad Amir Khan was introduced to Pt. Ravishankar for the first time through the medium of radio in 1938. Thereafter this contact gradually turned into personal relation. Near about 1944, when Ustad Amir Khan had gone to Lahore for his vocal performance, in the same music concert Pt. Ravishankar was to give his Sitar recital. Similarly, both the artists used to meet in many other music concerts.

In his book, Pt. Ravishankar mentions about Amir Khan Saheb with such a sentimental way and addresses him with 'Bhai Amir' [brother Amir]; intimacy between the two can be easily gauged. In this regard following quotations from his book are worth mentioning:

Translation from original Bangla: - "He [Amir Khan] was my ideal as an artist. Why did he pass away untimely in an accident? Why was such a curse of destiny? As a person, he was above than other artists. He was more respectable and his nature was also very good. I don't know, y he had some misunderstanding about me in the beginning, and there was not much friendship also. But from 1968, we began getting closer. Till his last days, he had come so closer to me that he used to be present in my every program and also we used to spend much time together. His passing away is not only a loss to the world of music but also a big shock to my heart. Brother Amir! Your absence is very painful to me, where ever you may be, consider it to be true."[200]

---

[200] 'Raga Anurag'-P.63-69, Writer: Pt. Ravishankar.

Pt. Ravishankar writes further: "I will repeatedly state that Amir Khan was the vocalist who was dear to my heart. Only his vocalism I found confirming to the standard for vocal music fixed by me."[201]

Dattatraya Vishnu Paluskar:

Dattatraya Vishnu Paluskar was born on 18th May 1921. He was son of famous vocalist, Pt. Vishnu Digambar Paluskar. He received training in music from his father and after father's death, he received guidance from his father's disciples, Pt. Vinayakrao Patwardhan and Pt. Narayanrao Vyas. After being well trained in the art of singing, he had gone to Lahore in 1935, with Vinayakrao Patwardhan. He had been as popular among the audience of Panjab as was his father. In the conference in which Ustad Amir Khan had gone to Lahore in about 1944, D.V. Paluskar had also performed in it.

Ustad Amir Khan and D.V. Paluskar had given play back singing in *jugalbandi* in the movie 'Baiju Bawra', for the scene of competition between Tansen and Baiju Bawra. This *bandish* is set in *raga desi*. It was the first time for both to give play back singing for movies.

Telling about the background of that *jugalbandi*, Amir Khan Saheb Said in an interview given to Akashwani indore: -
"He [Noshad Ali] said- there is a *jugalbandi* at one place in 'Baiju Bawra'. That *jugalbandi* is between Baiju Bawra and Tansen. How to accomplish it? I [Amir Khan] replied- brother see! Take a young person, who would obey you. The old vocalists are so conservative that they will not listen to you. Then he [Noshad Ali] asked- who should be taken? I [Amir Khan] said- take D.V. Paluskar, he is a young man and he will understand whatever you will say. D.V. Paluskar was given the songs of Baiju Bawra. D.V. Paluskar had some objections. I said to him [Paluskar], see brother, why have you objection. Tansen is losing, while Baiju Bawra is winning,

---
[201] 'Raga Anurag'-P.88-89, Writer: Pt. Ravishankar.

whose songs you are singing. You should not worry, sing with ease. Incidentally with the blessing of God, it hit so much that Noshad's name was also included among the classical music directors. And since then, interest in classical music was born and increased even in layman."

Khan Saheb's view regarding Pt. D.V. Paluskar is also available in an article written by Mr. Vasant Potdar. When Mr. Potdar asked him that Tansen was defeated, how could you accept that defeat? Khan Saheb replied: -
"Friend! You are asking useless question. Aye! What effect of a defeat or victory in a drama or cinema has on actual life? And then, he was cub of a lion, Pt. Vishnu Digambar. Once I had heard him singing at the residence of Shri Shankarrao vyas, brother of Shri Narayanrao Vyas. Like Amanat, he died at a very early age. If both of them would have been alive today, then you would have wondered."[202]

By these quotations, it is clear that what feelings these two musicians might have for each other. Being much younger in age than him, Ustad Amir Khan proposed the role of Baiju Bawra for Pt. D.V. Paluskar, which was comparatively more respectful. On the other hand, Pt. Paluskar accepted to sing for the movie, giving respect to the advice of Ustad Amir Khan. Pt. D.V. Paluskar passed away at the age of 34 years only, on 26th October 1955. Ustad Amir Khan's lamentable reaction on his untimely death has been mentioned in the quotation.

Ustad Vilayat Khan, The Sitar Player:
Ustad Vilayat Khan was born in 1928 in erstwhile East Bengal. He comes from a famous family of *tantrakars* [players of string instruments]. His father, Inayat Khan, was a famous Sitar Player. He received training in Sitar playing from his father till the age of 10 years. He received training of singing from Bande Hassan, his maternal grand father. He always tried to include all the qualities of *gayaki* in Sitar playing. Hence, it was natural that he had close relations with many vocalists like Fayyaz

---
[202] Maharashtra Times-5th September 1976, 'Amir Khan', Writer: Vasant Potdar.

Khan, Mushtaque Husain Khan, Allahdiya Khan, Amir Khan etc. In the beginning of fifth decade, Ustad Amir Khan lived in the house of Vilayat Khan at Calcutta. At that time his practice of singing also used to be held at his house. They both tried together to get opportunity in the music concerts at Calcutta and Delhi. Maternal grand father of Vilayat Khan, Bande Hassan, was the resident of Delhi. Both of them had performed their art in 'All Bengal' music concert, which has already been mentioned previously. In those days, Vilayat Khan was quite young and his age might have been about 15 or 16 years.

Sister of Vilayat Khan, Sharifan, was married to Amir Khan. Till the end of his life, Ustad Amir Khan used to visit Vilayat Khan's house and meet him. After his death, funeral procession of Ustad Amir Khan was taken out from the residence of Vilayat Khan at Calcutta.

Gyanprakash Ghose, The Harmonium Player:
Besides Vilayat Khan, the famous harmonium player of Calcutta, Mr. Gyanprakash Ghose, had cooperative relations with Amir Khan during his days of struggle. The accompaniment of harmonium has been given by Gyanprakash Ghose in the LP records of Ustad Amir Khan made by HMV.

Begum Akhtar:
Begum Akhtar was born on 14th October 1914. In her initial career, she was known as Akhtaribai Faizabadi. She received basic training of classical music from Ata Mohammad Khan of Patiala Gharana. Later on, she also received training from Ustad Wahid Khan of Kirana Gharana for three years. It should be remembered that it is the same Abdul Wahid Khan, whose comprehensive influence was on Ustad Amir Khan, which has already been mentioned in chapter two. Despite her training in classical music, Begum Akhtar took interest particularly in semi classical vocal style, such as *thumri, dadara* and *ghazal*; and these are the styles which had made her popular. So much so that she was called 'Malika-e-Ghazal' [queen of *ghazal*]. She had

compassion [*dard*] in her voice due to which even the singers like Ustad Amir Khan and Ustad Bade Ghulam Ali Khan were her admirers. In personal relations between Begum Akhtar and Ustad Amir Khan, there was good understanding and familiarity. One such incidence of familiarity is given in the words of Mr. Vasant Potdar: -

"I remember an incidence of Delhi; he [Ustad Amir Khan] had an instant sense of humor. There was a music concert of DCM. Its symbol was a 'Koyal' [cuckoo] sitting on a big Tabla, ready to fly. I and Khan Saheb went Kamani Hall daily. Everybody had seen that symbol on the screen of stage. On the third night, we went into the room near the stage. On that night, Khan Saheb had to give performance. We saw that Akhtaribai was sitting by a cushion. 8 to 10 admirers were also sitting there. Seeing Khan Saheb, Akhtaribai and her companions stood up. Khan Saheb said instantly: 'This time you have taken a very marvelous pose!' She [Begum Akhtar], I and others could not understand anything. Amir Khan said: 'you are sitting directly just on the Tabla'. Laughingly we saw that Begum was Overwhelmed."[203]

Besides above program of DCM, they usually met in many big concerts, where programs of both were held. In Bombay Stage music concert [1957] and Swami Haridas music concert [1972], they both had interacted. During the interaction, they used to discuss about music. This information can be derived from the statements of Ustad Amir Khan's brother, Bashir Khan and Bashir Khan's wife, Munavvar Apa. Begum Akhtar died at Ahmedabad on 30th October, 1974, about eight months after the death of Ustad Amir Khan.

Ustad Bismillah Khan:

Ustad Bismillah Khan was born at Bhojpur [Bihar] in about 1908. He started receiving training of Shehnai playing from his maternal uncle, Ali Baksh, at the age of six years. Ali Baksh was expert in vocalism also. And Bismillah Khan acquired knowledge of singing also from him. In addition to it, he received training particularly in *khayal gayaki*, from Ustad Mohammad Husain of Lucknow. Applying

---

[203] Maharashtra Times-5th September 1976, 'Amir Khan', Part II, Writer: Vasant Potdar.

his whole knowledge of music into Shehnai playing, he made this traditionally auspicious music instrument famous worldwide with his own fame. He was resident of Banaras and was attached to Kashi Vishwanath temple by hereditary. Most of the big music concerts and radio programs used to start with Shenai recital of Ustad Bismillah Khan. So, naturally he used to meet Ustad Amir Khan in these programs. Here it would be relevant to mention one such music concert organized at Indore:

"Abhinav Kala Samaj, the only popular organization of Indore, had organized a program of the famous Shenai player, Padmashri Ustad Bismillah Khan and his party on 5th October 1961 at the ground of local Gandhi Hall. First he played *alap, bada khayal* and *chhota khayal* of *raga yaman* on Shehnai, which were highly captivating. Thereafter he started *chhota khayal* in *raga durga*. After interval, he played tunes of some popular songs of the movie, 'Goonj Uthi Shehnai' on special demand of audience. He played *bhairvi* in the end and finished program at 1 AM. The program was free of charge for general public and people of Indore attended the program in huge number, seeing which Ustad Bismillah Khan was surprised and applauded the people profusely. In the end, Babulalji Malu [secretary of the organization] gave thanks to the people. In the said program, besides all respected citizens and artists of the city, the famous vocalist of India, Ustad Amir Khan, was also present."[204]

Here it is worth noting that as far as some tunes of 'Gunj Uthi Shehnai' are concerned, the playback singing and Shehnai recital for them were performed by Ustad Amir Khan and Ustad Bismillah Khan respectively. In this movie, *raga mala* [chain of *ragas*] and *raga bhatiyar*, have been presented, which have been sung and played in the form of duet [*jugalbandi*]. This application of *jugalbandi* has been unique.

Pandit Bhimsen Joshi:
Pt. Bhimsen Joshi was born in a village, named Gadag of the district Dharwad, Karnataka, on 14th February 1922. Listening to the gramophone records of Ustad

---
[204] 'Sangeet'-November 1961, P.61, 'Bismillah Khan Dwara Shehnaiwadan'.

Abdul Karim Khan's singing, since his childhood, he became crazy for music. After much drifting, he became disciple of the then main vocalist of Kirana Gharana, Rambhau Kundgolkar, alias Sawai Garndharva in 1935, who was a disciple of Ustad Abdul Karim Khan. In his guidance, he practiced vocalism for five years under strict discipline. In 1946, his public programs started in Maharashtra. Ustad Amir Khan, after his generation, was most confident about the progress of Pt. Bhimsen Joshi. On the other hand, Pt. Bhimsen Joshi considered Ustad Amir Khan not only as his senior but also gave respect like a *guru*. The influence of Ustad Amir Khan's *gayaki* on Bhimsen Joshi have been dealt previously [in chapter V]. These two vocalists often used to meet in main music concerts organized all over India.

A biography of Pt. Bhimsen Joshi, 'Swara Bhaskar', written by Prof. Shankar Abhyankar mentions about an event, which throws light on the mutual relations between the two:

"It is a recollection of Bombay. Panditji and Amir Khan were to sing in the same sitting. First Amir khan Saheb was to sing then Panditji. Amir Khan presented '*purva kalyan*'. Amir Khan's *mehfil* had a peculiarity that he never sang anything other than pure classical music. Sub classical vocal styles, like *tappa, thumri, ghazal, bhajan* etc, were certainly excluded at least for *mehfil*. Just after ending one *khayal*, he used to start another *khayal*. He never accepted request of audience. He sang to arouse interest of the audience towards classical music. He never liked to compromise in *mehfil*. So, that was Amir Khan. Amir Khan presented '*purva kalyan*'. Panditji reached the theater a little later. He had not imagined that Amir Khan has already presented '*purva kalyan*'. Coincidently Panditji also selected '*purva kalyan*'. His '*purva kalyan*' was also good. If there would have been other artists, their dispute would have been such that they would not see each other through out their life."[205]

Similarly, an incident in a program at Delhi is worth mentioning: -

---

[205] 'Swara Bhaskar'-P.245, Author: Prof. Shankar Abhyankar.

"Once I [Vasant Potdar] had come from Calcutta for the music concert of Delhi Mill with late Ustad Amir Khan. He wanted to reach the hall on time. I asked, 'your singing is to take place tomorrow, then why today you are in hurry to go there?' Khan Saheb replied, 'Today Bhimsen is going to sing. After me, he is the only singer to continue *khayal gayaki* in India.' When I told Bhimsen Joshi about this proud remark of Khan Saheb, he said 'Khan Saheb has a great affection for me'."[206]

Every year, Pt. Bhimsen Joshi organizes 'Sawai Gandharva Sangeet Mahotsav' at Pune in the memory of his *guru*, Sawai Gandharva, where Ustad Amir Khan had also presented his performance. Similarly Pune Art Circle had also held Ustad Amir Khan's singing programs. In those programs, the chief guests used to be Pt. Bhimsen Joshi and Vasantrao Deshpande. In this way, these two artists used to interact on different occasions, which have been expressed by Pt. Bhimsen Joshi very emotionally.

Ustad Salamat Ali and Nazakat Ali:

Famous vocalist brothers of Pakistan, Salamat Ali-Nazakat Ali, presented their vocal programs also in India along with tours abroad and thus occasions of their interaction with Ustad Amir Khan arose. Once, the famous film actor, Prithviraj Kapoor, had organized a vocal program of Salamat Ali Khan and Nazakat Ali Khan at R.K. Studio, Bombay. There, along with famous personalities of film industry, famous musicians of Bombay were also invited. Salamat Ali and Nazakat Ali started their program with *raga marwa*. Thereafter they presented some other *ragas*. Thus the *mehfil* continued for three-four hours. Though Ustad Amir Khan's singing was not scheduled in this *mehfil*, but the invited guests requested him to give his presentation. Khan Saheb had gone there just to listen to Salamat Ali-Nazakat Ali brothers. So, he said, 'after listening to such a program, what I should sing?' After much insistence he had to sing. He also started his singing with *raga marwa*. Gradually the *swaras* of *raga marwa* started creating their effect and the atmosphere of the *raga* was

---

[206] Daly 'Jansatta'-26 March 1989, 'Ek Raga Ki Kahani', Writer: Vasant Potdar.

accomplished. Then Salamat Ali spoke up 'my God knows; now the singing has just started.' The detail of this incidence was obtained by the author from Ismail Daddu Khan, because he was present in that program.

The popularity of movie, 'Baiju Bawra', earned due to using classical music, was appreciated also by these two vocalists of Pakistan. Most of the presentations of classical singing in this movie are by Ustad Amir Khan. Following part of the interview, written by Mr. Suresh Vrut Rai, makes it clear:
"Question- To what extent is it proper for the musicians to sing in films?
Salamat Ali- If there is an opportunity for classical singing, one should certainly participate in it. By means of films, much progress of the music can be made. In our country, films like 'Baiju Bawra' etc had created very good effect. We should keep pace with the time; we should know the pulse and should not lag behind in using scientific means for progress."[207]

Upcoming artists, Nirmala 'Arun', Sulochana Yajurvedi [Sulochana Brihaspati], Pt. Jasraj, Amjad Ali Khan etc were interested in keeping contact with Ustad Amir Khan and receiving his advice. Ustad Amir Khan was very confident for the progress of Prabha Atre, Nasir Ahmed Khan along with above mentioned artists, looking to their genius, about which he has mentioned in various interviews. In order to encourage these rising artists, generally Khan Saheb attended their programs to listen them. For example, Ghulam Mustafa Khan, a disciple of Ustad Nisar Husain Khan of Rampur-Sahaswan Gharana, gave a demonstration of ancient *jati-gayan* and modern *khayal gayaki*, on sixth June 1959 in Bombay. Amid the eminent personalities, Ustad Amir Khan was also present to listen to the program. Ghulam Mustafa Khan received guidance for practice of singing the ancient *jati-gayan* from Acharya Brihaspati. In the program, Acharya Brihaspati was present and in the beginning, he presented his

---

[207] 'Sangeet'-June 1960, P.52, 'Ustad Salamat Ali Aur Ustad Nazakat Ali Se Bhent', Interviewer: Suresh Vrut Rai.

views about the subject. The description of this program has been published in the monthly 'Sangeet', as follows:

"Bombay 6 June, Today on behalf of a local famous body, 'Alankar', Ghulam Mustafa Khan gave a demonstration of ancient and modern music at Lakshmi Bagh. In this gathering, the names of audience such as Vice Chancellor of Indira University, Mr. Shikrishna Narayan Ratanjankar, President of Gandharva Mahavidyalaya Mandal, Prof. Devdhar, Principal of Bharatiya Vidya Bhawan Music College, Mr. Chidanand Nagarkar, senior singer, Mrs. Anjanibai, Khan Saheb Ustad Amir Khan, founder father of cinema world, Mr. Chandulal, the Music Producer of Akashwani Bombay, Mr. Jog, Mr. K.G. Ginde etc are worth mentioning. Mr. Basantrao Rajopadhye had organized this function. Mr. Rajopadhye is credited for sowing the seed of *jati gayan* in Bombay."[208]

Similarly, in 1969, Ustad Amir Khan was also present to listen a program of Mrs. Sulochana Brihaspati held at Calcutta: "On 3rd October, some experts and music lovers were gathered at 'National Tower' to listen to vocal recital of Mrs. Sulochanaji; among them were Ustad Dabir Khan, Ustad Amir Khan, Ustad Maseet Khan, Mrs. Shishir Kanadhar Chaudhari, Mrs. Uma Dey, Mrs. Kankana Banerjee, Mrs. Som Tiwari, Mr. Viman Ghose, Mr. Parimal Chaudhari, Mr. Manilal Nag, Mr. Santosh Banerjee, Ustad Samir Husain Khan etc."[209]

After listening to vocal performance of Mrs. Sulochana in All India program of Akashwani, Ustad Amir Khan wrote a letter to Acharya Brihaspati, expressing his reaction to encourage her, which is reproduced here: -

---

[208] 'Sangeet'-July 1959, P.61, 'Bombay Mein Jatigan'.
[209] 'Sangeet'-December 1969, P.65, 'Calcutta Mein Sulochana Yajurvedi Ka Sarvajanik Abhinandan', Reviewer: Priti Vardhan.

"Shahmir Manzil
Mohanpura-3, Indore
23-8-70

Dear brother,

Regards!

I am proud to write that yesterday night, the National program of Sulochana was excellent. I pray that she should keep singing like this always and make progress. Yesterday by chance I switched on radio, that time Sulochana was singing. By God, I didn't know that there was a National program of her, I was glad to hear it. For it, I convey many many congratulations to Sulochanaji. May God grant success for your wishes. Just one day back, I had written a letter to you asking for your well being and next day I listened to this program. Tell many blessings to Sulochanaji on my behalf. Blessings to children, convey Salaam to Ghaffar Haider Khan. Casually keep me informed about your well being.

O.K.

Yours humble brother,
Amir Khan"[210]

On 22-03-1990, a program of Mrs. Sulochana Yajurvedi [Brihaspati] was organized at Kalidas Academy, Ujjain. At that time the author had met her. During conversation with her, information about above mentioned letter and some other letters written by Ustad Amir Khan to Brihaspatiji and preserved with Sulochanaji, was obtained.

An incident with Ustad Amjad Ali Khan in a program at Calcutta, is worth mentioning; the information about which was telecast by Doordarshan on 23-12-90. "Once Amjad Ali Khan's Sarod recital was to be held in Tansen Samaroh at Calcutta. When he reached there at about 4 AM in morning, Ustad Amir Khan's vocal program was in progress. After Amir Khan Saheb's program, Amjad Ali Khan met him and

---

[210] 'Sangeet'-March 1974, P.10, 'Ek Darun Aghat, Ek Aur Patra', Writer: Acharya Brihaspati.

sought his blessing for his program. Amjad Ali Khan got opportunity for presentation of his art after much wait. Despite it, Ustad Amir Khan stayed there to listen to Sarod recital of Amjad Ali Khan. Ustad Amir Khan's these feelings for rising artists were applauded by Ustad Amjad Ali Khan."

3-Audio Records of Vocal Presentations: -

Ustad Amir Khan's *gayaki* is available in sufficient number for general public by the means of gramophone records, CDS and cassettes. Before LP came into vogue [before 1960], in the fast rotating [78RPM] records, every *raga* used to be of about three minutes. Such three minutes presentations were given by Ustad Amir Khan also.[211] Afterwards, when production of 33 1/3 RPM long playing record of micro-groove technique started in India, then recording of comparatively longer duration [average 20-20 minutes on both sides] became possible. After 1960, HMV released three LP records of Ustad Amir Khan's vocal presentations for public. After his death, INRICO obtained a collection of recording and released an LP.

Even after death of Khan Saheb, HMV have been issuing LP records and cassettes of Khan Saheb's vocal presentations, obtaining the recordings from archives of Akashwani and private collections. Previously issued *ragas* in the form of LP, were again issued in the form of cassettes. Afterwards these releases were issued in the form of Audio CDs also.

Thus the detail of Khan Saheb's commercially issued audio records, with necessary information, is as follows: -

---

[211] Note: [a] HMV -78RPM Record No.nN-88319-Side 1, *raga shahana-'sundar angana baithi'-trital Madhya laya*, Side 2, *raga chandrakauns-rubayeedar tarana-tal ektal.*
        [b] In another 78RpM record-*raga sugharayee* and *tarana* in *raga todi.*
        [c] Information about gramophone records of film songs of Ustad Amir Khan, presented before 1960, is available in chapter 7.

1) **HMV-EALP-1253**

    Side A, *raga marwa-vilambit khayal-'piya moray anat des'-tal jhumra, drut khayal-'guru bina gyan na pave'-tal trital.*

    Side B, *raga darbari kanhada-vilambit khayal-'airee bir ri'-tal jhumra, drut khayal-'kin bairan kan bharay'-tal trital.*

    It is to be known that in side A, the wordings of the both *bandishes* of *raga marwa* are traditional but their *swara* compositions are composed by Khan Saheb himself.

    The audio recording of above LP was issued again in the form of Cassette No.STC-04B-7339, in 1989.

2) **HMV-EASD-1331, Stereo**

    Side A, *raga megha-vilambit khayal-'barakha ritu aayee'-tal jhumra, rubayeedar tarana-tal ektal.*

    Side B, *raga lalit-vilambit khayal-'kahan jagay rat'-tal jhumra, drut khayal-'jogiya meray ghar aaye'-tal trital.*

    Tabla accompaniment-Afaque Husain, harmonium accompaniment-Gyanprakash Ghose. First release-1968.

3) **HMV-1357, Stereo**

    Side A, *raga hansadhwani-vilambit khayal-'jai mate vilamb tajde'-tal ektal, rubayeedar tarana-tal trital.*

    Side B, *raga malkauns-vilambit khayal-'jinke mana ram biraje'-tal jhumra, drut khayal-'aj moray ghar ayila balama'-tal trital.*

    Tabla accompaniment-Afaque Husain, harmonium accompaniment-Gyanprakash Ghose. First release-1970.

    The audio recording of above LP was issued again in the form of Cassette No.STC-04B-7328, in 1988.

4) **HMV-ECLP-2765**

Side A, *raga bilaskhani todi-vilambit khayal-'bairagi roop dhare'-tal jhumra, drut khayal-'baje niki ghungharia'-tal trital.*

Side B, *raga abhogi-vilambit khayal-'charan ghar aaye'-tal jhaptal.*

First release-1976. Obtained from Akashwani.

The audio recording of above LP was issued again in the form of Cassette No.6TC-02B-2453, in 1983.

5) **HMV-ECLP-41546**

Side A, *raga ahir bhairav-vilambit khayal-'jagare bande'-tal jhumra, drut khayal-'piya parbin'-tal trital.*

Side B, *raga bageshri-vilambit khayal-'bahugun kam na aaye'-tal jhumra, tarana-trital.*

First release-1984.

The audio recording of above LP was issued again in the form of Cassette No.STC-6114, in 1984.

6) **INRICO-LP-2411-0001**

Side A, Untitled *raga*-self composed-*'par karo'-trital Madhya laya.*

Side B, self composed *raga chandramadhu-vilambit khayal-'bairan bhayee rain'-tal jhumra.*

Tabla accompaniment-Govind Bose. First release-1977.

Audio recorded by Arun Chaterjee on 23rd January 1974 and presented to INRICO.

The audio recording of above LP was issued again in the form of Cassette No.2411-001, by INRICO, in 1982.

The *ragas* in above mentioned LP No.EALP-1253, EASD-1331 and EASD-1357, have been again issued with different combinations in cassettes; such as STCS-02B-

5090-*raga lalit, megha, marwa* and *malkauns*, issued in 1981 and STC-04B-7327-*raga lalit, marwa* and *megha*, issued in 1988.

HMV issued an album of three LP records, titled 'Raga Malika', No. EMSE-104, in which presentations of top artists of classical music were included. *Raga darbari kanhada* of Ustad Amir Khan already available in LP No.EALP-1253 was again included by HMV in LP No.104 A part 2 of this album. The other artist included in this album are- Bade Ghulam Ali Khan, Bhimsen Joshi, Manik Verma, Nazakat Ali-Salamat Ali, Abdul Karim Khan, Barkat Ali Khan and Begum Akhtar.

In the set of two cassettes No.STC-02B-6200/6201, issued by HMV, titled 'Festival of India', along with Ustad Amir Khan, Abdul Karim Khan, Fayyaz Khan, Kesarbai Kerkar, Bade Ghulam Ali Khan, Mallikarjun Mansoor, Gangubai Hangal, Pt. Ravishankar, Vilayat Khan, Kishori Amonkar etc's presentations have been included. In the first cassette of this album [No.6200 part 2] Ustad Amir Khan's presentation is available as follows: *Raga ramdasi Malhar-'chhaye badara karay karay'-tal trital madhya laya*. HMV obtained this presentation of Khan Saheb from Akashwani. It was audio recorded by Akashwani Indore in the year 1965. The first edition of the album was issued in 1986.

HMV released five cassettes between 1989 and 1991 by obtaining audio recordings of Ustad Amir Khan's stage performances presented at various places, from private collections, whose detail is as follows:-

1) **STC-04B-7371**

Side A, *raga bairagi-'mana sumarat nis din tumharo nam'-tal trital madhya laya, raga charukeshi-'laj rakho tum mori gusaiyan'-tal trital madhya laya.*
Side B, *raga puriya-'chhin chin bat takat hun tori'-tal trital madhya laya.*

2) **STC-04B-7372**

Side A, *raga shuddha kalyan-vilambit khayal-'karam karo'-tal jhumra, rubayeedar tarana-tal trital.*

Side B, *raga bageshri-vilambit khayal-'bahugun kam na aye'-tal jhumra.*

3) **STC-04B-7373**

Side A, *raga miya malhar-vilambit khayal-'karim nam tero'-tal jhumra.*

Side B, *drut khayal-'barsan lagiray badariya'-tal trital, raga ramdasi malhar-'chhaye badara karay karay'-tal trital madhya laya.*

4) **STC-04B-7374**

Side A, *raga jog-vilambit khayal-'oh balama'-tal rupak, drut khayal-'sajan moray ghar aye'-tal trital.*

Side B, *raga darbari-vilambit khayal-'mori aali ri jabse bhanak pari'-tal jhaptal, drut khayal-'kin bairan kan bhare'-tal trital.*

The first edition of above four cassettes was released in 1989 in the form of an album.

5) **STC-04B-7504**

Raga chandanikedar-vilambit khayal-'airee tu dhan dhan tero bhag'-tal jhumra.

The first edition-1991.

Megna Sound [India] PVT LTD also issued a cassette [No.CHV0636] of Ustad Amir Khan, in which *raga nand* [*vilambit* and *drut*], *bahar* [*drut*] and *darbari* [*vilambit*] are recorded.

Afterward many audio CDs of Ustad Amir Khan also have been released, utilizing some archival recordings and live recordings of private collections. The detail of such released audio CDs is given below:

RPG-Sa Re Ga Ma-CDNF 150641 ADD
A Life in Music

Raga ahir bhairav-vilambit khayal-'jagre bande'-tal jhumra, drut khayal-'piya parbin'-tal trital.

Raga bageshri vilambit-'bahugun kam'-tal jhumra, tarana-tal trital.

Navras-NRCD 0091-ADD
Ananya Disc I

Raga yaman vilambit khayal-tal jhumra, drut khayal-tal trital.

Raga hansadhwani khayal madhya laya ektal, tarana-tal trital.

Harmonium: Pt. Gyan Prakash Ghose, Tabla: Pt. Govinda Bose.

Navras-NRCD 0092-ADD
Ananya Disc II

Raga puriya vilambit khayal-tal jhumra, drut khayal-tal trital.

Raga abhogi khayal-tal jhaptal, tarana-tal trital.

Archival recordings from the collection of Mr. Ain Rashid Khan, Shabaz Khan. [period 1960's]

Ninaad-NCCD 0001 ADD
Taskeen-The Ultimate Bliss Vol. I

Raga komal rishabh asavari vilambit khayal-tal jhumra, madhya laya khayal-tal trital.

Raga jog tarana-tal trital.

Live concert at Bombay.

Ninaad-NCCD 0002 ADD

Taskeen-The Ultimate Bliss Vol. II

Raga todi vilambit khayal-tal jhumra, drut khayal-trital.
Raga megha vilambit khayal-tal jhumra, tarana-tal ektal.

Music Today-CD-A01036-ADD

Pratidhwani-Voices of the Legends-Vol.-I

Raga basantmukhari [40: 38] khayal-'prabhu data vidhata saban ke'-tal madhya laya jhaptal.
Raga nand [25: 31] vilambit khayal-'ae vaare saiyyan'-tal jhumra, drut khayal-'mana bair bair chahat'-tal ektal.

Music Today-CD-A01037-ADD

Pratidhwani-Voices of the Legends-Vol.-II

Raga todi [23: 52] vilambit khayal-'kajo re mohammad shah'-tal jhumra, drut khayal-'mana ke panchhi bhaye bawre'-tal trital.
Raga shahana [10: 10] drut khayal-'sundar angana baithee nikas ke'-tal trital.
Raga yaman [32: 43] vilambit khayal-'shahaje karam barmane'-tal jhumra, drut khayal-'aiso sughar sundarva balamva'-tal trital.

Magnasound D3HV0636 ADD

The Legend Lives On

Raga nand [28: 58] vilambit khayal-tal jhumra, drut khayal-tal ektal.
Raga bahar [15: 03] drut khayal-tal trital.
Raga darbari kanhada [13: 06] vilambit khayal-tal jhumra.

EMI-RPG CD NF 1 5038 AAD

***Khayal* by Ustad Amir Khan**

Raga lalit vilambit khayal-'kahan jage rat'-tal jhumra, drut khayal-'jogiya mere ghar aye'-tal trital.

Raga hansadhwani vilambit khayal-'jai mate vilamb taj de'-tal ektal, tarana-tal trital.

Raga megha vilambit khayal-'barakha ritu ayee'-tal jhumra, tarana-tal ektal.

Accompanists: Afaque Husain-Tabla, Gyan Prakash Ghose-harmonium.

Dhun-Musicurry-CDC0003
Rare & Live-Ustad Amir Khan and Ustad Bade Ghulam Ali Khan

Ustad Amir Khan: *raga adana-'jhanak jhanak payal baje'-tal trital.*

Ustad Bade Ghulam Ali Khan: *raga bihag, thumri.*

Live recording at Bombay in 1956.

Music Today-CD-A 03034
Maestro's Choice

Raga bihag [38: 08].

Raga jansammohini [15: 43].

Raga ramdasi malhar [10: 40].

Vimla Devi Foundation Nyas, Ayodhya, Virgin Records [India] PVT LTD
Surmanjari Vol. I

Raga Abhogi kanhada [26: 55].

Raga shahana kanhada [16: 16].

Raga suha kanhada-tarana [06:42].

Raga Ahir Bhairav [13: 59].

Released in 2004. Provided by Mr. Kunwar Narayan from his private collection of a concert at his residence in Lucknow in 1965.

4-honors and Titles: -

Honors by Sangeet Natak Academy, Government of India and Others:

Ustad Amir Khan was counted among the top musicians of the country during fifties. Ustad Amir Khan provided a new psychological and logical thinking to the development of *khayal* style, looking to which it was natural that governmental and non-governmental bodies of art and the intellectuals of new age would have honored him, for which he deserved. Detail of the honors and the titles which were bestowed on him, is as follows:

Bihar Sangeet Natya Parishad awarded Ustad Amir Khan a fellowship in 1958 for his research done on *tarana*, which has been described in detail in chapter 2. At that time, Dr. Zakir Husain was the Governor of Bihar. In this context, Amir Khan Saheb said: "I continued thinking and searching about *tarana*. I had discussed about *tarana* in the conference of Bihar Sangeet Natak Academy. There Zakir Saheb was the Governor at that time. He invited me, a vocal program was held in Governor's house and I was made 'fellow' of the Academy. Then I started composing *tarana* myself."[212]

In 1966, Khan Saheb was appointed as the member of the Central Board of Audition of Akashwani.

In 1967, Ustad Amir Khan was one of the artists who were selected for the Award and the Honor to be conferred by Central Sangeet Natak Academy. The then Prime Minister, Mrs. Indira Gandhi was President of Sangeet Natak Academy in those days. This Award was conferred on him by the President of India. The copper plate, which was given to him on this occasion, bears the following inscription: -

"This copper plate is awarded to Ustad Amir Khan for being recognized as the main vocalist of Hindustani Music."

3, Falgun	Signature-Indira Gandhi
1889 [Shaka]	President
22 February, 1958"	

---

[212] 'Sangeet'-November 1971, P.70, 'Sangeet Sadhakon Se Bhent: Ustad Amir Khan', Interviewer: Shambhunath Mishra.

Besides Ustad Amir Khan, Ayodhyaprasad [Hindustani Music-Pakhawaj] and K.S. Venkat Ramayya [Karnatak Instrumental Music-violin] were also awarded Academy Awards for the year 1967 and Ustad Bade Ghulam Ali Khan was given fellowship of the Academy.

Thereafter, in August 1968, Government of India sent a cultural delegation to Afghanistan on her National Day and Ustad Amir Khan was included in the same. A detailed description of his tour to Afghanistan has already been given regarding his foreign tours, in this chapter.

Ustad Amir Khan was honored also by non-governmental and local organizations on many occasions in different ways. Some such events can be mentioned as examples: -

In 1969, 'Raga-Ranjan', an organization of Prayag [Allahabad], organized a Seminar on the life and contribution of Ustad Amir Khan. Its information can be obtained from the following quotation from monthly 'Sangeet':
"As 'Raga Ranjan' of Prayag has been organizing seminars and concerts of music since last 6-7 years, in it the seminar organized on life and contribution of Ustad Amir Khan, was good and reflects healthy tradition. - - - During the discussion, *ragas marwa, darbari* and *megha,* sung by Ustad Amir Khan, were played and examples were given from them. The program convener was Keshav Chandra Verma."[213]

In that discussion, Bindu Mukharjee, Shantaram Kushalkar, Ravi Mukharjee and Kanta Khanna expressed their views on the vocal style of Ustad Amir Khan and its influence on modern *khayal gayaki.*

Music and Dance Review Club of Bombay honored Ustad Amir Khan on 13th January 1969 on the occasion of his foreign tour.

---

[213] 'Sangeet'-June 1969, P.66, 'Ustad Amir Khan Par Goshthi'.

The Sursingar Sansad of Bombay started awarding the artists from 1970. Its news was published in the monthly 'Sangeet': "This is the time when the Sursingar Sansad of Bombay awarded the great and eminent vocalists and instrumentalists. In the 17th Swami Haridas Sangeet Conference, before a huge crowd of audience, Acharya Kelash Chandra Brihaspati announced on behalf of the Sansad that the Sansad confers its title of 'Swara Vilas' on the vocalist Ustad Amir Khan, 'Turya Vilas' on the Shehnai player Ustad Bismillah Khan and 'Tantra Vilas' on the Vina player S. Balchandran."[214]

According to the above declaration, at the 18th Swami Haridas Sangeet Conference on 17th April 1971, Ustad Amir Khan was conferred with the title of 'Swara Vilas'. In this conference, welcome address was delivered by the then Central Minister of Education and Cultural Affair, Mr. Siddharth Shankar Rai. The program was presided over by Begum Ali Yawar Jung. Also in the second convocation of Sursingar Sansad Peeth, Ustad Amir Khan was invited.

The climax in the order of Government honors and titles came when on 26th January 1971, Ustad Amir Khan was conferred with the title of 'Padmabhushan'.

Even after his death, many music concerts continued to be organized in his memory on various occasions. Organizing these programs can be placed in the category of honor after death.

"A three day music function was organized on 6th, 7th and 8th March 1980, in Bombay, in the form of 'Surrang Sammelan', in the memory of late Ustad Amir Khan 'Surrang', on behalf of 'Swara Sudha'. In this program, the participants were, Mr. Mukund Goswami [Vina-*shuddha kalyan, gauri* and *adana*], Ustad Salamat Ali Khan [vocal-*nandeshwari* and *chandrakauns*], Pt. Bhimsen Joshi [vocal-*darbari* and *pilu*], Singh brothers [vocal-*abhogi* and *bahar*], Ustad Bismillah Khan [Shehnai-

---

[214] 'Sangeet'-June 1970, P.59, 'Sursingar Sansad Dwara Kalakaron Ka Samman'.

marubihag and *purvi dhun*], Mr. Chandrashekhar Naringrekar [Sitar-*yaman kalyan*], Pt. Jitendra Abhisheki [vocal-*chandrakauns* through *bageshri ang, adana* and *bhajan* of Kabir], Ms. Zarin Daruwala [Sarod-*malkauns, Bhairvi* and *raga-sagar* of nine *ragas*] and Birju Maharaj [*kathak*]. The accompanists were Vishwanath Mishra, Nana Muley, Latif Ahmed, Suresh Talwalkar, Dattoba Atabdekar, Nazir Khan, Rajkumar Naygam [Tabla]."[215]

Ustad Amir Khan used to compose *bandishes* under the pen name, 'Surrang'. In his memory an institution was formed in Delhi in the same name, 'Sirrang', and it used to organize music program every year. In this series, one music program was organized on 20th May 1988, at Kamani Hall, where Ustad Amir Khan's disciple, Dr. Ajeet Singh Pental, presented his vocal recital and Balram Pathak presented his Sitar playing.[216]

Since 1987, Ustad Allauddin Khan Sangeet Academy is organizing a music function every year in the memory of Ustad Amir Khan, in his home town, Indore. In these music functions, from 1987 to 1992, following renown artists had participated: Shri Goswami Gokulotsavji Maharaj, Singh brothers, Mrs. Purbi Mukharjee, Mahendra Sharma, Shrikant Bakare , Mrs. Kankana Banerjee, Uday Bhawalkar, Dinkar Kaikini, Gajendra Bakshi, Ulhas Kashalkar, Ajit Singh Pental, Usha Parkhai, Mashkoor Ali Khan Keranvi, Samresh Rai Chaudhari, Prabhakar Karekar, Milind Chittal, Sarfaraz Husain Khan, Suhasini Koratkar, Sunil Masurkar, Madhu Mudgal, Mujahid Husain Khan etc were vocalists. Munir Khan, Kartik Kumar, Vishwajit Rai Chaudhari, Shamim Ahmed, Keka Mukharjee, Kala Ramnathan, Rajiv Taranath, Abdul Latif Khan, Kain Jukarman and Pt. D.K. Datar were instrumentalists of Sarangi, Sitar, Sarod and violin. And Bahauddin Dagar performed Bin playing and Sangeeta Majumdar performed Tabla playing. These artists had come from different parts of the country.

---

[215] 'Sangeet'-April 1980, P.55, 'Surrang Sangeet Sammelan'.
[216] 'Sangeet'-July 1988, P.54, 'Surrang Banam Amir Khan Ki Yad Mein', Reviewer: Mukesh Garg.

Thus, during these six years, most of the disciples of Ustad Amir Khan and the followers of his style, have participated in the program organized under Ustad Amir Khan memorial music function. Besides them, famous vocalist/instrumentalists of other modes and styles [*gharana*] have also participated. Though the series of Ustad Amir Khan memorial music function is continue, but unfortunately most of the invited artists used to be local and unknown.

A monthly journal published by Madhya Pradesh Kalaparishad, 'Kalavarta', issued a special edition of February/March 1989, in the memory of Ustad Amir Khan, titled 'Indore Gharane Ke Pravartak Gayak Par Vishesh Kendrit' [Specially Centered on Founder Vocalist of Indore Gharana]. It was released by Mr. Krishnarao Majumdar at the third Ustad Amir Khan memorial music function on 14th March 1989. "Recently the Government of Madhya Pradesh has accepted to change the name of 'Bombay Bazar Square' of Indore to 'Amir Khan Square'."[217]

Documentary by Films Division: -
The Ministry of Information and Broadcasting, Government of India has established a cell named as Films Division. This cell prepares documentaries on various subjects along with news-reels. In this category, a series to make documentaries on the life and art of great musicians was started, in which the documentary on Ustad Allauddin Khan of Maihar, is worth mentioning.

"The Films Division made a documentary on the life and *gayaki* of Ustad Amir Khan in 1971. Mohan Wadhawani had made the film and the credit for photography and direction goes to S.N.S. Shastri, who had been touring with Khan Saheb to various places. Its sound editing was done by N.P. Sitaram and R.G. Chandwakar and the editor of film was M.N. Chauble. This documentary was shown all over the country from 5th March 1971. On the occasion of its release and on account of Ustad Amir

---

[217] Nai Duniya-15 January 1996, News-'Nandlal pura Marg Va Bombay Bazar Chauraha Ka Nam Badala'.

Khan being conferred with the title of 'Padmabhushan', Bombay Music and Dance Review Club honored Khan Saheb."[218]

This film continued to be shown for a long time in cinema houses of entire country under the news reel, before the display of the feature films. In this documentary, glimpses of all the aspects of life have been included. Some scenes of his daily routine are worth mentioning, such as- in the morning, having tea at India Tea Hotel, Narsingh Bazar, Indore, buying vegetable from vegetable market of Nandlalpura, Indore, offering Namaz and so on. Some parts of his best vocal performances at Indore, Calcutta and Bombay have also been included in this film, in which some times Ismail Daddu Khan can also be seen as Tabla Accompanist. There is one scene of his flat at Bombay. There he is practicing vocalism and the famous Sarangi player, Sultan Khan is giving accompaniment on Sarangi, who was trained by his father, Shahmir Khan. Thus, in this documentary, different scenes have been shown in brief, after being edited. One copy of this documentary is preserved with the Information and Publication Department of the Government of Madhya Pradesh. Now the digital video of this documentary can be seen on youtube.com.

In another documentary of the Films Division, '*Khayal*', focused on *khayal gayaki*, Ustad Amir Khan is present among other *gharanas* and vocal styles. This film was made at the end of eighties. Its producer, director and script writer is Ms. Usha Deshpande. The famous Tabla player, Zakir Husain is commentator in it, who has presented commentary in English. This film was shown for the firs time at Azad Bhawan, Delhi, and its review was published in the issue of August 1988 of 'Sangeet'. Afterward Doordarshan telecast this documentary in the first week of January 1990.

In this documentary, the origin of music in ancient period, its evolution, the origin of *khayal gayaki* through the fusion of various modes/cultures in the medieval age and

---

[218] 'Sangeet'-April 1971, P.64, 'Ustad Amir Khan Par Vritta Chitra'.

its development in subsequent centuries, have been elaborated. After it, there is description of seven *gharanas* of *khayal gayaki*, namely Gwalior, Jaipur, Kirana, Patiala, Agra, Mewati and Rampur-Sahaswan *gharanas*, their vocal style and the main singers and the parts of available audio recordings of these singers have been included as examples.

Besides the vocal styles of above *gharanas*, Ustad Amir Khan's own distinct style of singing has been recognized, without naming the Indore Gharana. In this context, the words spoken by Ustad Zakir Husain are as follows: -
"Individual creativity, as Ravishankarji pointed out to us, is one of the most important aspects of *khayal gayaki* and this is best expressed in the *gayaki* of Ustad Amir Khan Saheb. He created his own individual style and put a stamp on *khayal gayaki*, which to this day is followed by some of the most talented singers of our time."

After above statement, audio of Ustad Amir Khan's *raga ramdasi malhar* [*chhaye badara karay karay*' was played.

CHAPTER-VII

CONTRIBUTION OF USTAD AMIR KHAN IN THE FIELD OF CINEMA MUSIC

CHAPTER-VII

CONTRIBUTION OF USTAD AMIR KHAN IN THE FIELD OF CINEMA MUSIC

Not adopting the attitude of senior Ustads, Ustad Amir Khan admitted the contribution and significance of cinema, as a medium to bring music to the common man. Among the vocalists of classical music, he was the first who presented *khayal gayaki* in its pure form in Hindi Cinema. Although the lyrics set up in tunes, based on *ragas*, were being presented in films by play back singers; the success of music in the film 'Baiju Bawra', opened the doors for *khayal gayaki* or pure classical music. Going further in this direction, the classical music of Bade Ghulam Ali Khan, Pt. Bhimsen Joshi, Parveen Sultana etc could reach the listeners of cinema music. The information regarding presentation of film music by Ustad Amir Khan is given below in chronological order: -

1- Bangla Film-'Kshudhit Pashan' [hungry stone]: -
This film was produced by Eastern Circuit Pvt. Ltd. in 1942. In the film, music direction was given by the famous Sarod player, Ustad Ali Akbar Khan and lyrics were written by Pt. Bhushan. In those days Ustad Amir Khan lived in Calcutta. Utilizing the classical music, Sarod was played by Ustad Ali Akbar Khan and Sitar by Pt. Nikhil Banerjee in this film. For vocal, Ustad Amir Khan performed three songs in it. In these songs, one is the *bandish* of *raga bageshri*; in which a famous singer of light music and *thumri*, Ms. Pratima Bose has accompanied Khan Saheb. There is a *tarana* in *raga megha* and one *thumri* also. These songs are available in 78RPM records, whose details are given below:

1. N.77010 Side 1- *bageshri* – *'Kaisay katay rajani ab sajani'*, *tal trital*, Ustad Amir Khan and Ms. Pratima Bose. Side 2- *tarana-raga megha – tal ektal*, Ustad Amir Khan.

2. N.77017 Side 1- *thumri khamaj* – *'Piya kay aavan ki may sunat khabariya'*, Ustad Amir Khan.

2- Hindi Film-'Baiju Bawra': -

This film was produced by 'Prakash Pictures', and was first released in 1952. Story of the film is based on the life of a singer of mediaeval age, Baiju Bawra. Hence the whole film is full of music. Mr. Noshad Ali is the music director of this film. Mr. Noshad had taken training in music from Yusuf Ustad, Babban Khan Lucknowwale and Ustad Jhande Khan Patialawale. The lyrics for the film were written by Shakil Badayuni.

In this film, play back singing for the role of Tansen and Baiju Bawra were done by Ustad Amir Khan and Pt. D. V. Paluskar respectively. This is the only example of Ustad Amir Khan performing *jugalbandi* [duet] with any other vocalist.

There are four presentations of Ustad Amir Khan in this film: -
1. Title song – *drut bandish* in *raga puriya dhanashri* – *'Tori jai-jai kartar'*, *tal ektal*.
2. *Sargam* and *swaraalap* in *raga darbari*.
3. *Jugalbandi* in *raga deshi* – *'Tumharay gun gaun'*, *ektal vilambit* and *'Aj gavat mana mero jhumkay'*, *tal trital*.
4. *Bandish* in *raga megha* – *'Ghanan ghanan ghan garjo ray'*, *tal trital*.

Other songs in this film have been performed by Mohammad Rafi and Lata Mangeshkar. The available gramophone records of this film are: -
1. 78 RPM-HMV-FT.17512, Side 1 – *'Tori jai-jai kartar'*, *puriya dhanashri;* Side 2 – *'Ghanan ghanan ghan garjo ray'*, *megha.*
2. *78 RPM-HMV-FT.17513, Side* 1 - *'Tumharay gun gaun'*; Side 2 – *'aj gavat mana mero'*.
3. Columbia 6 E.28044 – *Sargam* – *darbari alap*.

4. LP record of this film-HMV-EA-LP-4069, was issued in 1975.

3- Hindi Film-'Shabab': -

This film was produced by Sadique Productions Pvt. Ltd. in 1954. The director of this film is Sadique, music director Noshad Ali and lyrics are composed by Shakil Badayuni. After the success of 'Baiju Bawra', Noshad Ali included Amir Khan Saheb also in 'Shabab' for singing. A devotional *bandish* set in *raga multani*, '*Daya karo hay girdhar Gopal*' is performed by Amir Khan Saheb, which is in *tal trital*. This *bandish* of *raga multani* is available in LP [M.O.C.E. 4181] of this film, produced by HMV in 1973.

4- Hindi Film-'Jhanak Jhanak Payal Bajay': -

In 1955, this film was produced by Rajkamal Kala Mandir Pvt. Ltd. and was directed by V. Shantaram. This film is mainly centered on music and dance. Vasant Desai has given music direction for it. Some great personalities of classical music have contributed to the film: as the title song is in the voice of Ustad Amir Khan, the Tabla play was of Pt. Samta Prasad, the Sarangi was played by Pt. Gopal Mishra and Pt. Gopi Krishna has played the role of main dancer.

The song performed by Ustad Amir Khan, '*Jhanak-jhanak payal bajay*' is set in *drut khayal* style, in *raga adana*. In it, all the qualities of *tan* style of Ustad Amir Khan have been included in brief. The *bandish* is set in *trital*. Songs of this film were issued also in the form of Stereo LP [HMV-ECSD-5801] in 1982 and above song of Ustad Amir Khan is included there in.

5- Marathi Film-'Yeray Majhya Magalya': -

Produced in 1955, also in this film, music direction was given by Mr. Vasant Desai. The *bandish* of *raga lalit*-'*Jogiya meray ghar*', usually vocalized by Ustad Amir Khan and subsequently recorded for LP, was already included in this film. This *bandish* is set in *trital*. The *bandish* is available in 78 RPM gramophone record [HMV-N.62124] of this film.

6- Hindi Film-'Gunj Uthi Shehnai': -

This film was produced by Prakash Pictures in 1959. Also in this film, the music director was Vasant Desai. The hero of this film is a Shehnai player. His *guru* [teacher] teaches him by singing. For this singing, the voice of Ustad Amir Khan was taken as play back singing and shehnai was played by Ustad Bismillah Khan. For this situation, a *raga mala* [chain of *ragas*] was presented by the vocalism of Ustad Amir Khan and shehnai playing by Ustad Bismillah Khan. Its included *ragas* are: *ramkali, deshi, shuddha sarang, multani, yaman kalyan, surmalhar, bageshri* and *Chandra kauns*. It is a unique example of experiment of combined application of vocalism and instrumental. This *raga mala* is available in 78 RPM record of HMV-N. 53120. IN another presentation, *raga bhatiyar* is taken. In the beginning, Ustad Amir Khan has performed a *bandish* set in *jhaptal*-'*nisa din*'; and the *raga* is concluded with shehnai playing of Ustad Bismillah Khan. This presentation of *raga bhatiyar* is available in 78 RPM record of HMV-No. 53122. A presentation of *jugalbandi* in *raga kedar* by Ustad Bismillah Khan [shehnai] and Ustad Abdul Halim Jafar Khan [Sitar], is also included in this film. LP record [E.A.L.P.-4068] of this film was also issued in 1975, but it is regrettable that above mentioned all the three presentations of classical music were not included in it.

7- Hindi Religious Films: -

In two religious films also Khan Saheb has given play back singing. These films are- 'Jay Shri Krishna' and 'Radha piy Pyari'. Both films were produced by Shri Mukund Goswami. In these two films, Khan Saheb has performed two *bandishes* of Vallabh sect, which are as follows: -

1. 'Jay Shri Krishna' – *raga darbari*, 'Meri palakan son mag jharun', *tal trital*.
2. 'Radha Piy Pyari' – *raga darbari*, 'Ay mori aali', *tal jhaptal*.

In the presentations of Ustad Amir Khan in feature films, there are some *bandishes* which he already used to sing and being impressed by them, music directors adopted them for there films. For example-in Marathi film, 'Yeray Majhya Magalya': *bandish* of *raga lalit*, in Bangla film, 'Kshudhit Pashan': *tarana* of *raga megha*, in Hindi film, 'Gunj Uthi Shehnai': *mukhadas* and *sthayees* of different *bandishes* in the form of *raga mala*, in religious film, 'Radha piy Pyari': *bandish* of *raga darbari* etc.

8- Documentary on Mirza Ghalib: -

One hundred years of death of eminent Urdu poet, Mirza Asadullah Khan Ghalib, were completed in 1969. Hence, on the occasion of death centenary of Ghalib, government of India got a documentary film produced on Mirza Ghalib. In it, Pt. Amarnath, disciple of Ustad Amir Khan, provided music direction and the writer of lyrics was Kaifee Azmi. In this film, the title song was performed by Amir Khan Saheb in the form of a *ghazal* of Ghalib, wordings of which are as follows:

"*Rahiyay ab aisee jagah chal kar, jahan koi na ho.*

Hamsukhan koi na ho, aur hamzuban koi na ho."

Translation: "1) now please let's go and live somewhere, where there would be no one

2) there would be no speech-sharer, and there would be no language-sharer"[219]

It is to be noted that on insistence of Pt. Amarnath, Khan Saheb accepted to sing also a *ghazal,* deviating from his *khayal/tarana* modes. Although, its tune is sufficiently based on *kanhada ang*.

---

[219] http://www.columbia.edu/itc/mealac/pritchett/00ghalib/127/127_01.html

CHAPTER-VIII

LIFE STYLE

CHAPTER-VIII

LIFE STYLE

1- Temperament, Life Style and Philosophy of Life: -

Ustad Amir Khan was blessed with an extraordinary attractive personality. Having a well-built and strong body, his height was more than six feet. Handsome face, broad forehead and grave look produced characteristics of a thoughtful personality. He generally used spectacles of broad frame. One of his disciples, Mr. Prem Prakash Johri writes: "Just thinking about Khan Saheb's *gayaki*, his personality is visualized. Tall and well-built body, grave look and the symbols of being a great thinker of music were the characteristics writ large on his forehead. I had never seen him indulging in trivialities. During conversation, Ustad Saheb spoke only according to necessity and as if in his every sentence, his experience was speaking. Specially, during conversation regarding music, his every sentence was used to be valuable and full of substantial traditional dexterity.[220]

He had stable mind, having philosophical nature. Any person, high or low, could keep contact with him at will. He was always lost in his self made world of music. Whether in the company of friends or alone, his activities remained unaffected. Even today, there is no dearth of people claiming to have close friendship with Khan Saheb, simply to augment their own importance but the fact is that he was engrossed in himself. Awards, titles and popularity could not unbalance his mind.

"Affable, kindly and warm-hearted, humility was native to him, and in conversation, he was more willing to listen than to talk. His sensibility was as refined as his judgment was generous. There was no pretence about him, no callousness. The petty jealousies which afflicted his many confreres were unknown to him. Name and fame

---

[220] 'Sangeet'-May 1974, P.24, 'Aisay Thay Khan Saheb' [Such was Khan Saheb], Writer: Dr. Prem Prakash Johri.

came naturally to him in plenty in the form of national and international honors, awards and titles. But he remained an ardent Sufi till the last."[221]

One more specialty of the personality of Khan Saheb was that in spite of being soft-spoken he was moderate in speech. This is proved by his style of speaking in available recorded interviews of him. There were long intervals between the sentences and many sentences were left incomplete, so that the listener could understand its meaning by his own intelligence. He used to avoid discussing about his own achievements and self appreciation. In this context, late Mr. Krishnarao Majumdar told the author: - "When Khan Saheb returned from any music concert or conference, he used to express his opinion about the program but he never uttered a word about the success of his vocalism."

His behavior towards his disciples is also worth mentioning in the context of his nature. Pt. Amarnath tells about an incidence in this way: - "His nature was very tranquil and serious but moody too. He didn't like questions by the disciples in the presence of other persons. If some thing was asked with humility privately, he explained it. Without understanding this quality of his nature, when a disciple asked for new thing every time, he never lost his temper but told me in despair: 'Amarnath! He has not learnt the first lesson, what new thing should be given?'"[222]

Whenever necessary, Khan Saheb became strict while imparting training of music. The disciples could learn many things during conversations and to make clear some point to understand, he demonstrated by singing himself. Like previous Ustads, he too didn't acclaim his disciples in their presence.

In his routine, Khan Saheb paid special attention to *riyaz* [practice of music]. Generally he got up at 4 a.m., and used to do *riyaz*. During the period allotted for

---

[221] 'At the Centre'-P.18, 'Amir Khan', Author: Mohan Nadkarni.
[222] Maharashtra Times-12th September 1976, 'Amir Khan'-Article 3, Author: Vasant Potdar.

riyaz, he didn't like to think or discuss worldly matters. If some one wanted to listen to his *riyaz*, he had no objection; provided no disturbance would be created. "In many concerts of classical music, he filled the minds of art lovers with divine delight by his sweet voice and enthusiasm. But in this context, it is important that besides music conference, those music lovers who were fortunate enough to listen to music of Ustad during the period of his *riyaz*, actually they enjoyed fully the beauty of *swara* and *rasa*. The very experience of that art consciousness was unique. At the time of practice, his concentration was so deep that he attained *Samadhi*. Like three times worship in a day, he practiced music three times a day. During practice, he became so much indifferent towards his surrounding that he would not like to talk to any one."[223]

In Indore, the residence of Ustad Amir Khan was in the area of Bombay Bazar [Shahmir Manzil, Mohan Pura]. During leisure hours, he used to sit at two places near his residence: 1. India Tea Hotel, Narsingh Bazar Cross Road and 2. Mumtaz Tailor, Bombay Bazar. Here he used to sit for hours. His friends having interest in music and Urdu poetry and other acquaintances used to visit these places to meet him. Even today, on the wall of India Tea Hotel a framed photograph of Ustad Amir Khan is still present in his memory. Also at the time of meal, any one or the other known person used to be present and he used to offer to take meal with him. It was his routine at Indore to go for a walk to India Tea Hotel via Bajaj Khana, Pipli Bazar, Sarafa and Sheetla Mata. During this walk also many people used to meet him on his way and talked freely with him. He was also interested in reading two favorite Urdu Magazines, Huma and Shabistan, published from Delhi. Whenever he returned to Indore from tours, he used to gift shawls and lungies to his relatives and neighbors. In morning, he used to distribute toast and bread to children.

---

[223] 'Sangeet'-March 1985, P.24, 'Sangeet Madhurya Ke Samrat-Ustad Amir Khan', Writer: Chhaya Bhatnagar.

He was not a complete teetotaler. Even then, alcohol was not his necessity before vocal program, nor any of his programs was ever spoiled due to intoxication. "Though, generally Ustad Amir Khan remained calm, he had all the qualities of a kind hearted man. Those who have seen him drinking a glass full of vine, could not remain uninfluenced by his good manners and civility. The vocal art of Ustad Amir Khan was the mirror of vastness, grandeur, greatness, awareness, mysticism and modesty of his personality."[224] At the dusk of life, the requirement of alcohol and cigarette had considerably increased.

On the occasion of Iduddha, Ustad Amir Khan didn't follow tradition of sacrificing a goat. His friend Mr. Ramnath Shail said in an audio recorded program of Akashwani Indore, paying homage to him, that Ustad Amir Khan gave away money in charity equal to the cost of a healthy goat. He had strong spirit of generosity and charity. He willingly used to present his vocalism, free of charge, in the programs organized for public welfare. He considered following couplet of Ghalib, representing his compassionate feelings: -
"*Teray teer neem kash ko koi meray dil say poochhay,*
Voh khalish kahan say hotee, jo jigar kay par hota."
Translation: - "1) let someone ask my heart about your half-drawn arrow
2) where would this pricking/anxiety have come from, if it had [gone through and] been beyond the liver?"[225]

2- His Basic Views and Values: -

In the view of Ustad Amir Khan, for the development of *gayaki*, ideas and thinking have the same importance as that of practice [*riyaz*]. The vocalism which comes out of inner self, will influence the inner self of the audience. He used to say: "I want to know myself. Knowing it, is the real delight. I want to share a part of it with the audience. Why should I sing a cheap thing for the sake of public entertainment?

---
[224] Dinman-weekly, 8th March 1974, P.36 'Ustad Amir Khan- Tumhare Sharan Ab Kiyo Vishram', Writer: Amique Hanafi.
[225] http://www.columbia.edu/itc/mealac/pritchett/00ghalib/020/20_05.html

Music is not the property of Amir Khan inherited from his father. Everybody has equal right in this ocean."[226]

His thinking was such that without abandoning the base of traditions, he used to innovate out of it a new thing. That is why, despite novelties, his music doesn't disregard the basic principle and theory [*shastra*]. In the opinion of Acharya Brihaspati, to become a true follower of his *gayaki*, it is necessary to be a thinker too like him. Khan Saheb had friendship mostly with intellectuals, among whom, besides artists, were men of letters and connoisseurs of music, like Acharya Brihaspati.

Khan Saheb didn't considered *khayal gayaki* simply a means of entertainment; but for him it had a place of devotion, meditation and contemplation. He opined: "*Khayal* meant contemplation, a clear audible contemplation of music, only contemplation. When you are in a state of contemplation, there does not arise any question of entertaining anyone. - - - Actually I sing which is sober and soul satisfying. If you want to listen, listen this only. This is the vocalism of Amir Khan."[227]

How a student of music should be taught, he had his own opinion about it. He believed: "For understanding *swara* and for *riyaz* [practice], repeated exercise of *aroha* [ascending] and *avroha* [descending] is the first step. - - - Along with knowledge of *swara*, the knowledge of *laya* is essential. The voice is prepared well with the flow of *laya*. With the practice of *swara*, habit of *laya* should be cultivated. With *vilambit*, voice gets good exercise; whereas *drut* brings control over *swara* and *laya*. As far as the question of training of *ragas* is concerned, in the training in evening *raga yaman* and in the training in morning *raga bhairav* should be taught."[228]

---

[226] 'Sangeet'-December 1976, P.26, 'Sangeet Jagat Kay 'Amir'-Ustad Amir Khan', Writer: Madanlal Vyas.
[227] Maharashtra Times-12 September 1976, 'Amir Khan'-article 3, Writer: Vasant Potdar.
[228] 'Sangeet'-December 1978, P.28, 'Sangeet Jagat Kay 'Amir': Ustad Amir Khan', Writer: Madanlal Vyas.

He opined that from the very beginning of training, attention should be paid towards the quality of voice of the student and towards application of *swara*. The reason is that once the voice is spoiled, it becomes difficult to make it worth music. Listening to the teacher, taking up only the sequence of *swara* or notation is not sufficient. He also expected from his *shishyas* [students] that they should learn the beauty incorporated in the discharge of every *swara* phrase. He used to tell Pt. Amarnath: "Don't learn what I said [sang]. Learn, as to how I said, how I produced."

For success in music, Ustad Amir Khan considered *riyaz* [practice] very important. He considered three levels of this practice. In this context, his ideas are clarified in his own words in the following quotation: -
"Talking about *sadhana* [practice] and *siddhi* [attainment], Khan Saheb said: 'Jasraj told that despite practice, progress appears to have halted. I said that when a person is child, he grows up rapidly up to the age of eighteen-nineteen. Thereafter his height does increase till the age of twenty-twenty one years but very slowly. The same matter is with singing. In beginning, progress can be felt clearly; thereafter less. But progress continues surely. The *riyaz* must be continued. - - - There are three levels of singing. First, to get command over *swara-tal*. Second, to copy the *gayaki* of *Ustad*. The third level is for one's own new style with the impressions of that *gayaki*. One who reaches this third level; he is an artist in real meaning."[229]

It is necessary to continue hard practice for success in classical music, facing all the difficulties and adverse circumstances. In this respect, the words of Khan Saheb are: "Music is like mercury. On being swallowed, it will get out of the body bursting from any part. One who does not allow mercury of music to burst out but who digest it, is the real musician."[230]

---

[229] 'Sangeet'-January-February 1980, P.19, 'Meri Gayaki Meri Avaz Hay' [My singing is my voice], Writer: Ravindra Visht.
[230] 'Sangeet'-December 1976, P.27, 'Sangeet Jagat Kay 'Amir': Ustad Amir Khan', Writer: Madanlal Vyas.

Looking to the demand of the changing age, Khan Saheb considered it necessary to pay attention to the *rasa* and *bhav*, instead of *tayyari* [speed] and surprising aerobatics. He said: "In the rapidly changing age of today, when the interests are fast changing; and music has no patronage of temples and courts of kingdom, and cinema music has changed the interest of people on its own, so the artists of classical music should also keep their presentation of art melodious and full of *rasa*."[231]

Because of giving importance to *rasa*, Amir Khan Saheb believed it necessary for the vocalists, to give consideration to the meaning and poetic aspect of *bandish*; because with the blending of *swara* and *laya*, the audible aesthetics is created by it, emotional presentation of meaningful lyric in *bandish* and *bol alap*, makes it more elegant. He did not give recognition to poetry less vocalism; more over, he had tendency to find out meaning also in *bols* of *tarana*. In the opinion of Khan Saheb, if a vocalist has poetical imagination also, it helps him in the success of his music.

Many of the *bandishes*, created during the times of kings and nawabs, seemed to him meaningless and defective. He felt the need for amendment in poetical aspect of *bandish*. There is a traditional *bandish* of *vilambit khayal* in *raga ramkali* – "*Darbar dhaun, paun dudh-poot aur anna dhan*". After amending it, he used to sing as: "*darbar dhaun, paun dil ki murad aaj rach-rach kar gaun*".

Ustad Amir Khan did not believe in the narrow mindedness of *Gharanaism*.

Ustad Amir Khan considered it to be improper and unnecessary to mix the *layakaris* of *dhrupad ang* into *khayal gayaki*. According to his opinion: "To sing *khayal* like *dhrupad,* is to say that you wear a dhoti like a pantaloon. *Khayal* and *dhrupad* have their own color; it is not proper to mix both."[232]

---

[231] Weekly Dinman, 3rd March 1974, P.35, 'Ustad Amir Khan-'Tumharay Sharan Ab Kiyo Vishram', Writer: Amique Hanafi.
[232] 'Sangeet'-January-February 1980, P.90, 'Meri Gayaki Meri Avaz Hay', Writer: Ravindra Visht.

In Khan Saheb's personal view, *jugalbandi* [duet] is a show or a thing of deceit. He called it 'julbandi' [duel].

Similarly he wished that the classical music, which is based on spontaneous imagination, should be given a preset form and should be propagated through cinema. While recording of some light songs was in progress for a film in the music direction of Pt. Amarnath; at that time Khan Saheb said: "It would be better, if we present our classical items, set in the same manner."[233]

He liked to hear budding artists of young generation and was also optimistic about their progress. He believed that young artists can make wonderful progress, if given proper guidance and direction. Among his favorite young artists, main were – Mr. Nasir Ahmad Khan, Pt. Amarnath, Mr. Ghulam Mustafa Khan, Pt. Jasraj and Ms Prabha Atre. "Amir Khan had a sense of respect for every artist. Singing was in progress on radio; some one switched it off saying that it was out of tune. Khan Saheb became angry and said: 'What is this? Whether good or bad, listen till the end; why this impatience? Analyze it, where did he make mistake. On not listening to a bad thing, how the sense of self analysis will be inspired? No one can become a real artist if not ready to make amendments every time.'"[234]

He had some expectations from the government for the sake of facilities to the music lovers among poor class. Realizing the financial problems of this class, he opined "The organizers of music conferences want to collect as much money through ticket as much they spend on the program, it is justified too. The programs are held in halls, where number of seats is limited; so rates of ticket will also be high. If the number of seats is for two, four or ten thousand, the rates of ticket may be low. If the government would arrange such programs two or four times a year at different places, where audience could listen free of charge, then musician could be ready to perform

---

[233] 'Kala Varta'-February/March 1989, P.10, 'Aisay Thay Meray Sadguru' [Such was my True Teacher], Writer: Pt. Amarnath.
[234] 'Sangeet'-December 1976, P.26, 'Sangeet Jagat Kay 'Amir': Ustad Amir Khan', Writer: Madanlal Vyas.

on the payment of traveling expanses only. This can not be done by the conference organizers, because the money they spend, must come back. The government spends crores of rupees on projects and plans, so it should spend lacs of rupees to make available music to common man."[235]

About the remuneration of the artists, his suggestion was that the artists themselves should arrive at a consensus for the maximum limit of remuneration; so that the rate of ticket is not increased due to excess remuneration. In his opinion, expressed in 1971, the remuneration of any senior artist should not exceed rupees three thousand.

He believed that the social life of an artist should be full of generosity and charity. According to him, a true artist is above the religious fanatism, linguistic narrowness and separatism of politics; because the language of *swara* is universal. This generosity was found in the behavior of Ustad Amir Khan. He had equal faith in the gods and goddesses of Hindu religion. As Khwaja Saheb of Ajmer and the tomb of Amir Khusro at Delhi were the places of pilgrimage for him; in the same way, he used to visit Kalika temple of Calcutta, Bhuteshwar Mahadev temple and Shani temple of Indore, and Laxmi Narayan temple of Kashi for obeisance. To present his vocalism at the temples willingly was the symbol of this faith.

3- Interesting Reminiscences: -

Those who were fortunate enough to have lived in contact with Ustad Amir Khan, want to preserve these memories and feel proud to express them. Among the recollections related to him, expressed by people from different walks of life, some important reminiscences are reproduced below: -

Ustad Amir Khan had sung a *ghazal* in a documentary on the life and works of Mirza Ghalib, which has already been mentioned in chapter seven. Pt. Amarnath had to face

---

[235] 'Sangeet'-November 1971, P.23, 'Interview with Musicians – Ustad Amir Khan' Interviewer: Shambhunath Mishra.

difficulty in obtaining his permission for this *ghazal* and ultimately he succeeded. The description of the event is given here under:

"He did not like even the idea to sing any thing else besides *khayal gayaki*. Nevertheless I could manage to make him sing a *ghazal*. A documentary film has been made on Mirza Ghalib. I have given music direction in it. The lyric writer, Kaifee Azmi said to me: 'It will be pleasant, if title song is sung by Amir Khan Saheb.' I said: 'He will not sing *ghazal* at any cost.' On this, Kaifee said: 'You prepare a tune for Khan Saheb. I will get his consent.' I composed a tune with hard work and reached Bombay. Kaifee was sitting, putting his hand on forehead in despair. The next day, recording was to be held and Khan Saheb had flatly refused. I reached to Khan Saheb's residence along with Kaifee and the director. He was already angry. He said: 'Why have you put me in this ordeal? Tell me, when I sing *ghazal*?' I requested him with folded hands: 'You sing Persian and Arabic *taranas*, then what wrong Urdu has done? You are just like my father. Whatever change you want to make in the tune, do it, but now don't say no.' He said yes and sang well. But it was only to keep my words. Not only me, he never hurt any one's heart. His nature was child like."[236]

To make the first LP record of his vocalism, the high official of HMV in those days, Mr. G.N. Joshi, had to undergo a great hardship and after a long wait he got the opportunity to record. In this respect, Mr. G.N. Joshi writes: "To obtain Amir Khan's agreement for the recording I had to meet him, and therefore it was incumbent on me to visit his residence. - - - Once in his room I cheered up, and I talked to him for an hour or two. After that I visited him often. He exchanged views on music and *gharanas*, and such visits gave me opportunities to study his likes and dislikes. These visits also gave him confidence in me. After a couple of months and four or five such visits, he agreed to come for recording. Some more time was lost in persuading him to agree to the terms of payment. Finally this hurdle too was crossed. Yet Amir Khan went on canceling dates, giving fresh ones and then again postponing the recording

---

[236] Maharashtra Times-12th September, 1976, 'Amir Khan'-Article 3, Writer: Vasant Potdar.

on some flimsy ground. I got fed up with his dilly-dallying and in spite of my great regard and respect of him, I justifiably felt very annoyed. Ultimately one day I plucked up my courage and said to him 'If I had approached God Almighty as many times as I have come to you, He would have blessed, but all I can get from you is the promise of a future date.' Seeing my exasperation he became thoughtful, smiled a little and replied. 'Please do not disbelieve me. Name any day of this week and I will keep the appointment.' True to his word he came on the day I named, and I got from him his first long-playing disc. His favorite *ragas* were *marwa, darbari kanhada* and *malkauns*. It is indeed rare these days to hear *raga marwa* as it was presented by Bade Ghulam Ali and Amir Khan. His first LP was received with tremendous enthusiasm by the public."[237]

In mutual conversation there was a glimpse of humor in his words. Once Acharya Brihaspati said to Khan Saheb "Khan Saheb! Previously you used to sing like a lion, but now there is no longer that voice." Instantly Khan Saheb replied "Brother! Now it is that I am no longer an animal."[238]

A young poet of Bangla and Urdu and a police officer, Mr. N. Rasheed, was among those who had close contact with Khan Saheb. He writes: "For some days, I was police superintendent at Sivani. Khan Saheb used to come to my place. One night, while in sleep, he started singing *raga vasant mukhari*. I was awaken and started applauding him. Later on I realized that he was in deep sleep."[239]

Dr. Prem Prakash Johri, resident of Meerut and a disciple of Khan Saheb, writes his recollection of his *ganda bandhan* ceremony, when Khan Saheb reached Meerut from Delhi despite some obstacles.

---

[237] 'Down Melody Lane'-P.94, 'Ustad Amir Khan', Author: G.N. Joshi.
[238] 'Sangeet'-December 1976, P.27, 'Sangeet Jagat Kay 'Amir': Ustad Amir Khan', Writer: Madanlal Vyas.
[239] Maharashtra Times-12th September, 1976, 'Amir Khan'-Article 3, Writer: Vasant Potdar.

"Khan Saheb was true to his words. Whatever commitment he made, he tried to fulfill at any cost. In 1970, when I went to Delhi for Akashwani program, Khan Saheb had also come there. I asked him to avail this opportunity. He agreed. The date was fixed. Khan Saheb along with wife, son and Muneer Khan [Sarangi player, Akashwani Delhi] and his disciple, started for Meerut by a taxi. No sooner he crossed Delhi, suddenly his wife fell severely ill, due to which he returned to home with her and after giving primary treatment, he started for Meerut. Just reaching the Yamuna Bridge, a tyre of his taxi burst. So he again went back to Ajmeri Gate to hire another taxi and after hiring another taxi from there, he could reach Meerut three hours late. All the guests gathered at my residence, were very much concerned after a long wait of three hours. When Khan Saheb reached to my home, I felt that such a happy day like today, will never come again in my life. When Khan Saheb was asked for the reason for reaching late, he simply told 'I had said you that I will come, I have come.' Such was he, true to his words. *Ganda bandhan* was solemnized. Khan Saheb sang very well."[240]

Mr. Vasant Potdar narrated a recollection of Calcutta, which is an example that Khan Saheb had tolerance even for those who misbehaved. Mr. Potdar said: "On one night, at about 2:30 AM, I, Sunil Gangopadhyay and Khan Saheb were sitting near Victoria Garden. Khan Saheb began singing *malkauns* suddenly. I and Sunil became nearly unconscious. Meanwhile two persons, fully intoxicated with wine, alighted there from a taxi. And they also started singing in vulgar voice. I was startled an abusing ran towards them. Khan Saheb called me back. He said 'How they know that Amir Khan of all India fame, is singing here. Besides this, they are fully intoxicated. What will you gain by beating them? Look Vasant! I tell you a thoughtful thing; if you like, remember it for ever. Only the artist has an authority on humanity, if there is any one. If an artist fails to become a true human, then how can others imbibe human qualities?'"

---

[240] 'Sangeet'-May, 1974, P.25-26, 'Aisay Thay Khan Saheb', Writer: Dr. Prem Prakash Johri.

The former Secretary of Culture, Govt. of Madhya Pradesh, Mr. Ashok Vajpayee writes his recollection: "My first personal introduction with him was in April 1973, when we had invited him to felicitate him as a top musician of Madhya Pradesh, in Bhopal Utsav-1973. He was with Pt. Krishnarao Shankar Pandit, Kumar Gandharva, Ustad Abdul Halim Jafar Khan and Ustad Amjad Ali khan; Habib Tanveer, Satyadev Dube, Bhavani Prasad Mishra, Naresh Mehta, Hari Shankar Parsai, Shrikant Verma, Shiva Mangal Singh Suman etc were also there. He was looking grand and calm. On the next day of his felicitation, his program was held at Lal Parade Ground, on an open stage. Most of the time, he was singing closing his eyes; almost in the same way when I had seen him singing for the first time, twelve years back. Though there was no sense of inattention in him for the audience, yet there was a calm unawareness, as if he was not singing for others but for himself. In between, whenever he opened his eyes expressing – 'so you are also listening, does not matter.' - - - He was very busy, because many of his relatives had come to meet him, in which many were from Indore. Even while talking with them, he seemed as unattached."[241]

4- Untimely Demise: -

During the last years of his life, Ustad Amir Khan lived in the flat of Mr. Shams-uz-Zaman, situated at Rafi Ahmad Kidwai Road, Calcutta. Mr. Shams-uz-Zaman was a scholar and writer of Urdu and co-editor of Azad Hind. He was also an assistant of Khan Saheb as his personal secretary. In the month of February 1974, some repairing work was to be done in the flat of Shams-uz-Zaman, therefore Khan Saheb stayed for few days in the flat of Mr. Arun Banerjee at 77 A, Lance Down Road.

In the last week of February 1974, Khan Saheb was to go to America and he was busy in making preparation for the same. Before proceeding for America, he was to go to Indore on 14th February 1974, where the Aqeequa [ceremony of shaving of hair of a new born child] of his grand son was to be held. He had dispatched invitation for this function to his relatives and acquaintances from Calcutta.

---

[241] 'Kabhi-Kabhar'-P.54-55, Author: Ashok Vajpayee.

On the evening of 13th February, he went to the residence of Mr. Bobby Sethi at Alipur, on his invitation. There he stayed till 11:00 PM. After about 11 PM, he was returning to residence of Arun Banerjee at Lance Down Road, in the car of Bobby Sethi. In the car, besides himself, MS. Purvi Mukharjee, Shams-uz-Zaman and driver were also there. During this period, at about 12 AM, his car collided with another car coming from opposite direction and met with an accident. This accident took place at the cross roads of Southern Avenue and Sharat Bose Road, in which Khan Saheb was seriously injured. Mr. Shams-uz-Zaman took Khan Saheb to Ramkrishna Seva Pratishthan by another car. There Khan Saheb breathed his last. Thus at the age of 62, his voice became extinct for this world. The Eye witness of this tragedy, Mr. Shams-uz-Zaman, describes the heart rending account of the accident in the following words, which obtained by the author from Mr. Vasant Potdar: -

"The car was going from Alipur to Lance Down Road. Suddenly Khan Saheb put his hand on my shoulder and said: 'Friend Shams, I do not sing the *raga* in a *mehfil* which has been sung by other vocalists; even if those *ragas* which are my favorite, such as *darbari, malkauns, marwa* - - -'. Soon sound of collision was heard. In between conscious and unconsciousness, I felt as if the earth was shaking. It seemed as if the vehicle was falling down from a mountain and I became unconscious. The car collided somewhere and became still and by that push my unconsciousness was gone. As soon as I realized that our car has met an accident, I tried to turn to see behind. I came to know that neither purvi Mukharjee nor Khan Saheb were there. Any how, I came out of the car and saw that Khan Saheb was lying near the meter box, soaked in blood. Breathing had become difficult and appeared to be sounding like 'Allah-Allah'. Then I realized enormity of the accident. I cried for help. A man clad in dhoti-kurta, came near me, staggering. Releasing smell of wine on me, he said: 'my name is Captain K. Singh. Your vehicle has collided with mine. Is there any serious injury? I was shocked. I said almost shouting: 'In our car, there was Amir Khan! Padmabhushan Ustad Amir Khan the great musician'. Instantly his drunkenness had gone. Said: 'Khan, Amir Khan! I am also his fan. I will save him at any cost.' I again started crying for help. A huge man appeared from darkness and came bearing big steps and said: 'I am coming with my car in five minutes. Keep some patience.' He came soon. His name was V.V. Joshi. Keeping Khan Saheb in his car, we reached Ramkrishna Seva Pratishthan. It was midnight. Hearing the name of Amir Khan, staff became active immediately and unconscious body of Khan Saheb was taken to operation theatre. At about 2 or 2:30 AM, a police officer came to us and said: 'He is dead'."

On the other side, close acquaintances of Khan Saheb had reached Indore to celebrate 'Aqeequa'. All of them were waiting for Khan Saheb to reach Indore. But unfortunately, instead of his arrival, they had to bear with ill omen news of his death. The last rites of Khan Saheb were performed at Calcutta. His burial procession started from the residence of Sitar player, Vilayat Khan and he was buried at Gobara cemetery of Calcutta. The cabinet of West Bengal Government offered flowers.

On his death, it was natural to have occurred sorrowful reaction nation wide. Paying homage to Khan Saheb, Ustad Vilayat Khan Said: "With passing away of Amir Khan, vocal music has died in the country. When Ustad Bade Ghulam Ali Khan died we felt bereaved, but nevertheless there was a vocalist of that standard; but with the demise of Amir Khan, the delight of listening *khayal* in this country has come to an end.

On the very day of 14th February 1974, Pt. Shri Krishna Narayan Ratanjankar had also died in Bombay. Paying homage to these two great personalities of music, Acharya Brihaspati wrote an article in issue of 'Sangeet' of March 1974. In it, the homage paid to Amir Khan, his words were: "On the day, Pt. Ratanjankar died, the same night, as a result of an accident, my close friend, Amir Khan, was no more in this world. This tragic shock stunned me. I had close acquaintance with brother Amir Khan. We were related by the discussions of virtue. He was a thinker. He used to innovate new things even from tradition. He loved a thinker. - - - - Amir Khan influenced very much the young artists of this age. One can not become an Amir Khan, without becoming a thinker like him. Demise of Amir Khan is an unimaginable loss to the world of music. May God grant peace to his soul."[242]

Sangeet Natak Academy of Delhi organized a condolence meeting on the death of Ustad Amir Khan. Doordarshan, Akashwani, news papers and magazines etc all the means of communication paid homage to Khan Saheb and reflected on his life and contribution to the music. According to information available in 'Sangeet' monthly, issue of March 1974 [Page 63], following institutions organized condolence meetings – Sur Singar Sansad-Bombay, Rajasthan Sangeet Sansthan-Jaipur, Shankar Gandharva Mahavidyalaya-Gwalior, Ajmer Sangeet Mahavidyalaya-Ajmer, Chatur Sangeet Mahavidyalaya-Nagpur, Bhatkhande Sangeet Mahavidyala-Bilaspur, Rajkiya Sangeet Vidyalaya-Kota, Bihar Sangeet Parishad-Patna, Rajkiya Mahavidyalaya-Nenital, Music College-Rajkot etc.

About three weeks before his death, on 23rd January 1974, Khan Saheb presented his own composition with great fervor, in a domestic *mehfil* of his close acquaintances; whose wordings are – '*Par karo, gun nahin Momen, Ham murakh tum chatur khivayya*'. That presentation was recorded on tape by Mr. Arun Chaterjee and had photographed him during presentation.[243] It was a strange game of fate that as per his wish, expressed in above *bandish*, he passed away from this world suddenly. A sudden accident became the cause of his death. Neither he suffered any pain of Disease nor obtained services of anybody. He remained active till the end of life; continued singing and there were names of *ragas* on his lips, even at the time of death.

---

[242] 'Sangeet'-March 1974, P.9-10, 'Do Shraddhanjaliyan: Ek Patra Vyavhar Tatha Ek Patra' [Two Homages: a Letter Correspondence and a Letter], Writer: Acharya Brihaspati.
[243] Enreco LP No.2411-0001 – The audio recording of this *bandish* and that photograph on its cover is available.

CHAPTER-IX

CONCLUSION

The world of music has been well acquainted with the vocal style of Ustad Amir Khan, but the fact was not clearly known that how this influential and popular style came in existence. After extensive study, the author could clarify that influenced by the qualities of vocalism of Ustad Rajab Ali Khan, Ustad Aman Ali Khan and Ustad Abdul Wahid Khan, this style has been created. Although some experts consider even Ustad Amir Khan of Kirana Gharana, after analysis, the author has humbly opined that this style has obtained such a peculiar form that it can not be placed in any prevalent *gharana*.

It is said that *khandmeru* system reached to Amir Khan from Bhindi Bazar Walas, but the author, for the first time, referring '*khandmeru*' chapter of 'Sangeet Ratnakar', has explained practical aspect of mathematical principle of *khandmeru* in vocal style of Ustad Amir Khan.

Among the musicians, 'Indore Gharana' has been the subject matter of discussion, but what is called 'Indore Gharana' is the special style of Ustad Amir Khan.

Ustad Amir Khan used to sing *rubayeedar taranas*. He considered the words of *tarana* to be meaningful. Explaining in detail his research, views and presentation regarding *tarana*, the author has also presented a comparative study with other contemporary *tarana* singers. Ustad Amir Khan was known as a vocalist of *khayal* and *tarana*, but by this research, the author has brought to knowledge that Amir Khan had sung *thumri* and *ghazal* also. In the same way, about cinema music, all know that he was playback singer in the films 'Baiju Bawra' and 'Jhanak-Jhanak Payal Bajay';

but many people are not aware that he has also performed his singing in Bangla and Marathi film. It has been mentioned in this research.

Published details regarding Ustad Amir Khan on records, cassettes and in different news papers and magazines were lying scattered. It is for the first time that the author collected and studied them all, as far as possible. The information about two *ragas* and *bandishes*, presented in programs on Delhi Doordarshan [TV channel of Govt. of India] was brought to notice for first time by the author. Similarly, for the first time, notations of *bandishes* composed by Ustad Amir Khan, have been prepared and presented by the author. Besides his own compositions, details of *ragas, tals, bandishes* and *taranas*, presented by him, has also been given in this publication.

Along with the works of Ustad Amir Khan, after research, sufficient light has been thrown on his life also. As many unknown aspect have been brought to light, similarly his thought about personal life, self respect, struggle etc have also been explored. There was some confusion regarding place of his birth. ON LP records and in the book, 'Hamaray Sangeet Ratna', place of his birth has been mentioned as Indore, but the author collected information and decided that, although his childhood spent at Indore, the place of his birth was Akola. In order to go ahead towards success, he lived and struggled at Nathadwara, Kankroli, Kishangarh, Bombay, Delhi etc; Its chronological documentation done in this research, shows his ambition. The impact of his Voice culture in development of the form of his vocal style has been made clear by author.

Thus, it is the first, original and authentic attempt by the author to present a thorough and analytical investigation of the works and personality of Ustad Amir Khan.

APPENDIX-I

LIST OF REFERENCE BOOKS

Hindi

S.No.	Title	Author
1.	Hamare Sangeet Ratna	Lakshmi Narayan Garg
2.	Madhyavarti	Mohan Nadkarni
3.	Ustad Rajab Ali Khan	Amique Hanafi
4.	Gharanedar Gayaki	V.H. Deshpande [Translator-Rahul Barpute]
5.	Sangeet Shastra Darpan	Ms. Shanti Govardhan
6.	Tal Prakash	Bhagvatsharan Sharma
7.	Kramik Pustak Malika Vol.2	Pt. Vishnu Narayan Bhatkhande
8.	Sangeetanjali Vol.5	Pt. Omkarnath Thakur
9.	Sangeet Ratnakar Vol.1	Acharya Sharangdev [Translator-Lakshminarayan Garg]
10.	Madhya Pradesh Ke Sangeetagya	Dr. Pyarelal Shrimal
11.	Sangeet Visharad	Prabhulal Garg 'Basant'
12.	Sangeet-Bodh	Dr. Sharadchand Shridhar Paranjape
13.	Kabhi-Kabhar	Ashok Vajpayee

Marathi

1.	Swaramayee	Dr. Prabha Atre
2.	Swaragangechya Tiri	G.N. Joshi
3.	Swara Bhaskar	Prof. Shankar Abhyankar
4.	Nal	Vasant Potdar

English

1. Living Idioms in Hindustani Music: A Dictionary of Terms and Terminology — Pt. Amarnath
2. Listening to Hindustani Music — Chetan Karnani
3. Maharashtra Art Music — Dr. Ashok D. Ranade
4. At the Centre — Mohan Nadkarni
5. Down Melody Lane — G.N. Joshi

Bangla

1. Raga Anurag — Pt. Ravishankar

Journals

Monthly 'Sangeet', Sangeet Karyalaya, Hathras [U.P.], India: -
March 1955, April 1955, May 1955, May 1956, May 1957, March 1959, July 1959, June 1960, November 1961, April 1962, April 1967, December 1967, February 1969, March 1969, June 1969, December 1969, June 1970, April 1971, August 1971, November 1971, March 1973, May 1973, March 1974, May 1974, August 1974, January/February 1976, December 1976, January/February 1980, April 1980, January/February 1982, March 1985, October 1985, April 1986, July 1988.

Monthly 'Sangeet Kala Vihar'-December 1956.
Weekly 'Dinman'-3rd March 1974.
'Kalavarta'-February/March 1989-Ustad Amir Khan Visheshank [Special Issue on Ustad Amir Khan].
'India Today'-15th September 1987.
'Screen'-22nd September 1989.
'The India Magazine'-September 1990.
Monthly 'Ajkal' [Urdu]-August 1956.

News Papers

'Nai Duniya'-29th March 1987, 26th March 1989, 10th October 1990, 1st August 1992.
'Jansatta'-26th March 1989.
'Dainik Bhaskar'-6th May 1989.
'Maharashtra Times' [Marathi]-22nd February 1974, 28th August 1976, 5th September 1976, 12th September 1976.
'Times of India'-15th August 1987.
'Hindustan Times'-30th October 1988.

APPENDIX-II

LIST OF RECORDS AND CASSETTES

[In Addition to Records & Cassettes of Ustad Amir Khan Mentioned in Chapter VI]

Records

S.No.	Company	Record No.	Artist
1.	HMV	EALP-1256	Bade Ghulam Ali Khan
2.	HMV	EALP-1258	Bade Ghulam Ali Khan
3.	HMV	EALP-1516	Bade Ghulam Ali Khan
4.	HMV	IP-7IPI1002	A. Kanan

Cassettes

S.No.	Company	Cassette No.	Artist
1.	HMV	STC-6115	Bade Ghulam Ali Khan
2.	HMV	STC-7368	Bade Ghulam Ali Khan
3.	Rhythm House	240-344 & 240-352	Kankana Banerjee
4.	Magnasound	C.4H	Ustad Allahrakha & Ustad Zakir Husain
5.	HMV	SPHO44465	Hridaynath Mangeshkar-film 'Lekin'
6.	Rhythm House	240-358	Goswami Gokulotsavji Maharaj

Collection of Other Audio Recordings and Radio Broadcast

1. An audio recorded interview of Ustad Amir Khan, in April 1973, at Sangeet Academy, Bhopal [M.P.].
2. An interview of Ustad Amir Khan, at Akashwani Indore.
3. A program paying homage to Ustad Amir Khan, broadcast by Akashwani Indore.
4. A lecture demonstration of Pt. Amarnath at Bharat Bhawan, Bhopal, in 1987.
5. Broadcast of an interview of Nirmala Arun, in the program 'Sangeet Sarita' of Vividh Bharati, on 20th March 1988.

APPENDIX-III

LIST OF HELPMATES

S.N.	Name & Status	Type of Help
1.	Goswami Gokulotsavji Maharaj, Indore, Vocalist	Practical guidance in Gayaki
2.	Mr. Jayant K. Dange, Indore, Owner of collection of classical music's audio recordings	Rare gramophone records & published material
3.	Dr. Ashvin Bhagvat, PhD Music under the guidance of author, Engineer by profession	Advice concerning computer applications and internet
4.	Mr. Sudhir Kumar Solanki, Lecturer in Computer Science	Advice concerning computer applications and tools
5.	Late Mr. Vasant Potdar, Indore, Journalist	Important recollections in interviews
6.	Late Mr. Krishnarao Majumdar, Indore, Vocalist, Disciple of Ustad Rajab Ali Khan	Important recollections in an interview
7.	Ustad Ismail Daddu Khan, Bhopal, Tabla player	Important recollections in an interview
8.	Mr. Amir Karam Ali, Bombay, Director-Rhythm House PVT LTD	Rare recordings of Khan Saheb's stage performances
9.	Mr. Jayant Banerjee, Bhopal, Flute player	Translation of Bangla material
10.	Mr. G.N. Joshi, Bombay, Former Recording Executive of HMV	Important information through correspondence
11.	Mr. Muinuddin Khan, Indore, Former Sarangi player at Akashwani Indore	Important recollections

S.N.	Name & Status	Type of Help
12.	Mrs. Sulochana [Yajurvedi] Brihaspati, Delhi, Vocalist	Important recollections in an interview
13.	Mr. Deepak Garud, Tabla player	Important recollections in interviews
14.	Mr. Ram Meshram, Bhopal, Former Govt. Officer of Archeology Dept.	Rare recordings of Khan Saheb's stage performances
15.	Dr. Pramodchandra, Harvard University, USA, Professor	Information regarding Khan Saheb's abroad tours in an interview
16.	Umakant & Ramakant Gundecha, Bhopal, Dhrupad vocalist	Useful recordings & photographs
17.	Bharat Bhawan, Bhopal	Study of recordings for research
18.	Govt. Music College, Ujjain	Books & journals
19.	Vikram University Library, Ujjain	Books
20.	Govt. Kalidas Girls College, Ujjain	Books, journals & recordings

VDM publishing house ltd.

Scientific Publishing House
offers
free of charge publication

of current academic research papers, Bachelor´s Theses, Master's Theses, Dissertations or Scientific Monographs

If you have written a thesis which satisfies high content as well as formal demands, and you are interested in a remunerated publication of your work, please send an e-mail with some initial information about yourself and your work to *info@vdm-publishing-house.com*.

Our editorial office will get in touch with you shortly.

VDM Publishing House Ltd.
Meldrum Court 17.
Beau Bassin
Mauritius
www.vdm-publishing-house.com

Druck:
Canon Deutschland Business Services GmbH
im Auftrag der KNV-Gruppe
Ferdinand-Jühlke-Str. 7
99095 Erfurt